KING
LUCIUS
OF BRITAIN

KING
LUCIUS
OF BRITAIN

DAVID J. KNIGHT

TEMPUS

In Loving Memory of

My Grandmother Eva Fripp 1906-1993 (Switzerland)

My Uncle Alfred Thomas Knight 1914-1996 (London)

First published 2008

Tempus Publishing
The History Press Ltd.
Cirencester Road, Chalford,
Stroud, Gloucestershire, GL6 8PE
www.thehistorypress.co.uk

Tempus Publishing is an imprint of The History Press Ltd.

© David J. Knight, 2008

The right of David J. Knight to be identified as the Author
of this work has been asserted in accordance with the
Copyrights, Designs and Patents Act 1988.

British Library Cataloguing in Publication Data.
A catalogue record for this book is available from the British Library.

ISBN 978 0 7524 4572 4

Typesetting and origination by The History Press Ltd.
Printed in Great Britain by Ashford Colour Press Ltd., Gosport, Hants.

CONTENTS

ACKNOWLEDGEMENTS

I would like to thank Peter Kemmis Betty, Tom Vivian, Abigail Green and Wendy Logue at Tempus for encouraging me to publish this work and their unfailing assistance in doing so.

My heartfelt appreciation and thanks to my mother, Audrey E., and father, Daniel J. Knight, my sister Dr Kim Knight-Picketts, Al Picketts, Jennifer and Amie. Dr Gary D. Knight for consistent support, encouragement and for lending his talents in enthusiastically reading and making editorial suggestions for 12 years, impossible without the love and support of Sheila Knight and Rachel Harris. My warm thanks to Gianna Giannakopoulou not only for her assistance with Greek translations, Chart C.2 and footnoting, but also for keeping me focused at times when the task seemed impossible.

The generous assistance of several organisations made my research possible and I would like to thank in particular Professor Juerg Simonett and Andrea Holme of the Raetische Museum of Chur, Switzerland, and the resources and facilities I have accessed at St Paul's University Pontifical Library (Jean-Leon Allie), Ottawa, Canada, The Bodleian Library, Oxford, The Greater London Records Office, The Guildhall Library, London, and The British Library, London. The majority of the research for this work took place between 1995 and 2007, and having immersed myself in this material I am grateful to Dr Niall Finneran for suggesting I submit a book proposal to Tempus.

The immense task of preparing this book would have been insurmountable without the generous interest, support and professionalism of several friends and colleagues. I would like to particularly thank Dr Charlotte Tupman for spending some time with the Vita Lucii and sieving out the most important elements from the original Latin, Tehmina Goskar for eagerly translating the Letter of Eleutherius, and Dominic Barker for preparing several maps and plans. Thanks also to Martin Fitzsimons of St Helen's House, Bishopsgate, London, who has been an invaluable friendly contact for allowing me access into the dark corners of St Peter-upon-Cornhill.

Gaining permissions and preparing the images for this book would not have been possible without the genuine interest of The Dean and Chapter of York

Minster, especially Amanda Daw and Vicky Harrison, and the Dean and Chapter of Gloucester Cathedral, especially Mark Beckett (Chapter Steward), Robin Lunn and Richard Cann. Thanks are also due to Gareth Beale, Nick Schiavottiello and Mary Stubbington for their assistance.

The support of friends so often goes unsaid, therefore I would like to thank Mark and Jill, Daisy and Ben Houliston, Tom and Tehmina Goskar, Nick and Carol Ford, Francis P.D. Crosby, John R. Dowling, Jackie Laing, Greg Robertson, Sylvia Galletta, Jennifer Liefeld-O'Brien, Saleh Al Hassy, Joe Viall, Kevin and Pauline Hogg, Catherine Taylor and Patty Murrieta.

FOREWORD

When we try and explore the extent of Christianity in Roman Britain we look through a glass darkly. The evidence for early Christianity in Britain is often intractable, whether using the documentary sources or the archaeological material. The textual evidence of all aspects of late Roman and early medieval society is sparse, and was often re-worked and embroidered for a range of political and theological purposes. Equally, the material culture evidence can be difficult to interpret, with particular problems in understanding the chronology of the spread of Christianity in the diocese and recognizing diagnostically distinctive artefacts.

As David Knight shows, the material relating to the establishment of Christianity in Britain was particularly vulnerable to emendation, editorialising and fabrication, as individuals and factions of all periods from the fourth century to the nineteenth century used the meagre documentary record to sketch out the earliest origins of the faith in this country. Beyond the brief references in the work of some of the church fathers and the *Confessio* and *Epistola* of Patrick there is relatively little contemporary documentary evidence for Christianity in Roman Britain. Most historical accounts instead rely on the versions of the introduction of the religion in the *De Excidio* of Gildas and Bede's *Ecclesiastical History*. Whilst both these works have their strengths they are difficult texts and cannot be read as simple historical expositions, rather they are ideologically charged manifestos linking the development of Christianity in Britain to the unfolding of the perceived manifest dynasty of the Church. As such, it is often assumed that much that is set out in these documents, which does not seemingly chime with our understanding of events are simply misunderstandings, legends or myths.

It is easy to overlook or ignore facts or ideas that do not fit into our pre-existing mental frameworks. In this book the author performs a signal service in returning to the story of Lucius and Eleutherius with an open mind. Much of the book consists of a detailed unpicking of the treatment of King Lucius in traditional history and modern scholarship. He traces the creation and growth of the figure of Lucius from his first appearance in the *Liber Pontificalis,* following the slow accretion of myth and legend around him to the complete dismissal of his story as one of mistaken identity in the early twentieth century. The author tries to re-claim Lucius from this charge and repatriate him from Edessa to Britain. Knight's attempt to re-construct a brief biography of Lucius is bound to stimulate debate, but if in the process we rethink the ways in which we understand some of the earliest evidence for Christianity in Britain, this can be no bad thing.

David Petts
March 2008

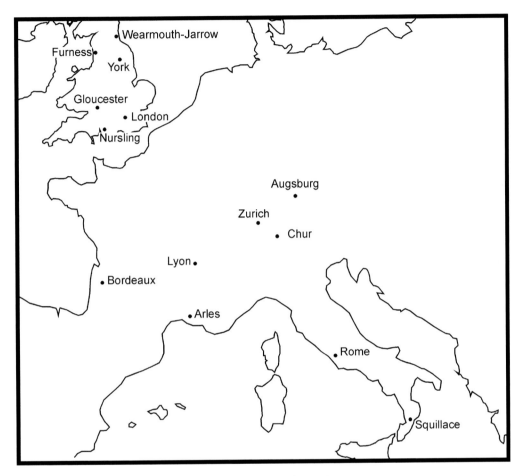

Location map of places mentioned in the text (*Dominic Barker 2007*)

INTRODUCTION

Why write about a legend in the context of history and archaeology? Geoffrey Ashe gave one incisive answer:

> Legends must be looked at critically. True, and that applies to twentieth-century academic legends as well as twelfth-century monastic ones.[1]

With this encouragement in mind the figure of King Lucius, a second-century king in Britannia who from 1904 was written out of history, can recover lost intrigue. Late nineteenth- and early twentieth-century historical support had been adduced for equating Lucius with an ancient king of Edessa in Mesopotamia's northern deserts; Abgar VIII, thus removing him from Britain. However, in the light of more recent academic scholarship, this support began to crumble. Historical scholarship has perhaps unwittingly provided for a reassessment of Lucius, whereas archaeology was in its infancy when the Abgar hypothesis was formulated. Not only has the methodology advanced rapidly since even the early 1980s, but the number of challenging discoveries and interpretations seems to exponentially increase each year. Some of these recent discoveries shed invaluable new light on what had been deemed fanciful and fabulous.

Lucius had original gravitas not least because he was included in the historical writings of the Venerable Bede. He was subsequently employed for ancient precedence and authority in the territorial claims of twelfth-century monastic foundations, baronial disputes with King John, and the Tudor legitimation of an unmediated divine right of kingship. However, Lucius suffered as a prisoner of woven words and mangled oral traditions, falling foul at last to nineteenth-century criticism based on contemporary concepts of empire applied to the Roman past, and to some extent by renewed internecine dispute. To free him and assess the extent of his provenance requires picking through the literary threads in which he has been entangled. The present work is therefore both an exegesis and synthesis, gathering over 160 literary references to King Lucius of Britain ranging from the mid sixth century to 1904. What we unearth is as enthralling as a stray gold skein amid mounds of mouldering straw.

As such, this study reopens the once vital debate over the historical reality of a second-century British king, arguably one of the most important monarchs in the history of Britain, who reigned for 77 years – longer even than Victoria at the height of the British Empire. Surprisingly, the content of his curious story has not yet benefited from a dedicated and scholarly treatment: not a single substantive work over the course of 14 centuries has been devoted to this subject.[2] In most sources 'King Lucius of Britain' lay hidden away in short chapters, footnotes, marginal comments, asides and personal correspondence.

Following a short article[3] in 1904 by the theological scholar Adolph von Harnack, the discursive argument of many centuries over dates and the historical veracity of King Lucius was presumed concluded. Since Harnack, all reference to Lucius is qualified with his definitive statement on the matter, with the consequence that King Lucius of Britain has been relegated to fable, or mythic legend emerging from mistaken identity. However, the present book begins by unearthing the shaky ground of such a mythologising presupposition. With its riddled foundations exposed, Harnack's construction is shown to be its own instance of the 'twentieth-century academic legend'. This critique of it (following Ashe's advice) will open the door for genuine study, where distinct possibilities become clear for a fuller interpretation based on modern archaeological investigation and scholarship.

Archaeological investigation in Britain was in its infancy in 1904. Historians have long decided that the date AD 314 is the reliable *post ante quem* for the presence of Christianity in these islands. In that year three British Bishops attended the Council of Arles in southern Gaul: Eborius of York, Restitutus of London and Adelfius of Caerleon. Developed bishoprics are not known to suddenly arise without years of development, yet the bulk of archaeological interpretation of Christianity in Roman Britannia has tended to focus on this date as a beginning, rather than astride broader processes in the emergence of Christianity and development of a culture.

The error has been to use the Council of Arles as the datum by which material evidence of Christianity is supposed to take its origin. Awareness of this trend elucidates one important reason (apart from destructive events such as the Dissolution and the Great Fire) there is little material evidence attributed to Christian practice in third-century Britain, let alone the second century. Evidence of Christianity in Britain prior to 314 has comprised mere ephemeral traces, such as portable objects bearing the Chi-Rho insignia. Accordingly, late second- and third-century evidence remains quite open to further interpretation.

For these several reasons, Lucius has remained 'an invisible king' relatively unknown to archaeology in the UK and buried in a thorny lineage of twentieth-century footnotes. He is referred to as one colourful and eccentric instance of the myriad 'origin myths' of how Christianity was introduced into Britannia, and thus relegated to fabled obscurity in company with Joseph of Arimathea and King Arthur. Yet after all, from at least 725 to 1904 the vast majority of people in the British Isles had no doubt of his existence and we remain very much impoverished if we do not at least revisit and re-evaluate the facts behind King Lucius of Britain.

This book, as a contribution to the much-needed scholarship, traces 14 centuries of tradition through primary and secondary sources and dissects various debates over King Lucius' identity and personhood. It offers some good support for feasible reconstructions of the first Christian king of Britain. It is also, it may be hoped, a popular read because the vast majority of the United Kingdom's population has not heard of Lucius; at most he is encountered as the stuff of legend.

Chapter 1 reassesses Harnack's thesis for identifying Lucius of Britannia with Abgar of Edessa. Moving chronologically through literary material, Chapter 2 explores the earliest written sources of the king from the *Liber Pontificalis* to the early twelfth century while Chapter 3 treats the legend-making 'embroidery' woven by Geoffrey of Monmouth and his followers. Chapter 4 then discusses how Lucius became central to some of the disputes and machinations of the Tudors and Elizabethans, eventually reshaped into a dramatically mangled figure for the eighteenth-century stage amidst growing academic discontent over his supposed station and dates. It discusses how, in the nineteenth century, the nascent discipline of archaeology was brought to bear on what little evidence there remained of him. Chapter 5 reassesses the archaeological traces of Lucius from the vantage of recent information in London and Chapter 6 explores the Raetian tradition of Luzius von Chur and his possible connection to Britannia, suggesting ways the story of Lucius might have been transported from or to the continent. Chapter 7 brings all of the former details and arguments together in feasible reconstructions of the second-century king, as a way of inviting further archaeological and historical investigation.

Lucius has been obscured by century-old encrustations of positive, negative and opportunistic discourse. The present study may initiate serious reconsideration of artefacts, sites and historical periods in light of Lucius' probable existence. It can be hoped, thereby, that these pages will awaken great interest and lively investigations into one of the earliest phases of cultural heritage in the United Kingdom.

CHAPTER 1

KING LUCIUS OF BRITIO?

However learned men differ in the date, they agree in the deed[1]

The primary source for the story of King Lucius of Britannia is the *Liber Pontificalis* (the Book of Popes) whose development is necessary to understand before assessing the historical veracity of King Lucius (see Table 1.1 below). In the early second century Hippolytus of Portus, near Rome, compiled a list of Bishops of Rome, which he entitled *Liber generationis*. He was a contemporary and likely disciple of Bishop Irenaeus of Lugdunum (Lyon) whom we will encounter again in Chapter 7. Hippolytus created a decade-long ecclesial schism and was exiled to the island of Sardinia but he appears to have recanted shortly before his martyrdom in AD 235. Known as St Ippolito in Middle English, he apparently based his *Liber generationis* upon a still earlier catalogue that included short historical notices on each of the Popes.

Hippolytus' work would have been a primary source for the Chronography or Calendar of the year 354, as compiled and edited by Furius Dionysius Philocalus for one Valentius, a wealthy Christian. According to Mommsen,[2] Part XIII of Philocalus' Chronography is the earliest extant list of Bishops of Rome, the oldest section running up to the pontificate of Pope Urban (AD 230). This and the extension to the life of Pope Liberius (352-366) are accordingly known as the *Catalogus Liberianus*. The *Catalogus* offers short historical notices for the pontificates of Peter, Pius, Pontianus, Fabianus, Cornelius, Lucius I, Xystus, Marcellinus and Iulius, but if there had been such a notice for Eleutherius it is not preserved fully intact. The incomplete, possibly damaged or ill-preserved entry reads:

> … m. III d. II. fuit temporibus Antonini et Commodi, a cons. Veri et Hereniani usque Paterno et Bradua.[3]

> … 3 months, 2 days. He was in the time of Antoninus and Commodus, from the consulate of Verus and Herenianus to that of Paternus and Bradua.[4]

These early entries were expanded in the lifetimes of Popes Anastasius II (496-8) and Symmachus (498-514) as Duchesne demonstrated.[5] Boniface II (530-532) compiled the existing list that extended as far as Pope Felix IV who died in 530 and hence this document is accordingly known as the *Catalogus Felicianus*, the immediate precursor of the *Liber Pontificalis*. In the earliest known codex of the *Catalogus Felicianus*, existing in the Vatican and dating to the ninth century, occurs the following disputed statement in the entry for Pope Eleutherius:

> Hic accepit epistolam a Lucio Brittaniorum rege ut Xrianus efficeretur per ejus mandatum.

In 1965, Loomis translated the full entry (the above excerpt is in bold):

> Eleuther, by nationality a Greek, son of Habundius, from the town of Nicopolis, occupied the see 15 years, 3 months and 2 days. He was bishop in the time of Antoninus and Commodus until the year when Paternus and Bradua were consuls.
>
> **He received a letter from Lucius, King of Britain, asking him to appoint a way by which Lucius might become a Christian.**
>
> He also decreed (He also confirmed again the decree that no kind of food in common use) should be rejected especially by the Christian faithful, inasmuch as God created it; provided, however, it were rational food and fit for human kind.
>
> He held 3 ordinations in the month of December, 12 priests, 8 deacons, 15 bishops in divers places.
>
> He also was buried near the body of the blessed Peter in the Batican, May 24.
>
> And the bishopric was empty 15 days.[6]

(The words in brackets indicate Loomis' use of an alternate manuscript). The statement in bold has been central to all discussion of King Lucius of Britain. Since this sentence is absent from the fragmentary entry of the earlier *Catalogus Liberianus* (*c*.354) it has been argued that it could have been a sixth-century addition made for example by Boniface II, in compiling the later *Catalogus Felicianus* (530-532) or the *Liber Pontificalis* (*c*.535). However, the controverted record could just as well have been in the original *Catalogus Liberianus* and as such it would derive from an older source no longer extant. Moreover, even if it *were* a sixth-century addition, it does not follow that it must be a fabrication, invention or mistake of facts, notwithstanding the view of Harnack as we shall see.

The *Liber Pontificalis* was part of an ambitious project initiated by Pope Agapetus I (535-536) to found a *scriptorium* (library) at Rome collecting together the major ecclesiastical authors in both Greek and Latin. He was assisted in this immense task by the statesman Flavius Magnus Aurelius Cassiodorus Senator (*c*.485-*c*.585), better known as Cassiodorus, who was nearing the end of his civic career at Ravenna and about to embark upon his own monastic establishment of Vivarium in Calabria (Squillace). Cassiodorus is perhaps best known for his *Variae epistolae*, the state correspondence of King Theoderic, but at Vivarium he established another library to preserve for posterity texts both sacred and profane. He retired from Ravenna and public office in *c.*540 and devoted the remainder of a long life to writing prolifically until he died in 585. Figuring among his influential works is *Institutiones Divinarum et Saecularium Litterarum* (543-555). Shortly after *c.*630 the library at Vivarium was unfortunately dispersed and lost, but the pontifical *scriptorium* in Rome remained a long-standing foundation.

For centuries it has proved difficult to determine the exact dates of the early Popes. For instance, the pontificate of Eleutherius is variously given as 171-185, *c.*174-189[7] and 177-193. As mentioned in the entry of the *Liber Pontificalis*, Eleutherius apparently survived until the consulship of Paternus and Bradua. This pairing does not appear in the consular lists and may be a compression of the known consulships of Maternus and Bradua in 185, and Apronianus and Bradua in 191.[8]

If, as stated, Eleutherius was Pope for '15 years, 3 months and 2 days' and we note his feast-day, marking his death, is May 26, this places the recorded period of his pontificate between 24 February 177 (a Sunday) and 26 May 192 (a Friday). If we infer he died as late as the last year of Commodus (AD 192), then by counting backwards from a day in 192, Eleutherius would have become Bishop of Rome not later than a day between 30 October 176 and 29 September 177. Although the consul Paternus mentioned in the *Liber* is otherwise unknown, the communication

Table 1.1: Manuscript history of the *Liber Pontificalis*

Date	Title	Author	Description
*c.*230	?	?	Terminates with Pope Urban (-230)
*c.*235	*Liber generationis*	Hippolytus of Rome (?-235)	A Papal catalogue
*c.*354	*Catalogus Liberianus*	Edited by Furius Dionysius Philocalus (*Chronography*)	Terminates with Pope Liberius (352-366)
*c.*496-514	?	A contemporary of Anastasius II and Symmachus	Terminates with Pope Symmachus (498-514)
530-532	*Catalogus Felicianus*	Compiled and extended by Boniface II (530-532)	Terminates with Pope Felix IV (d.530)
*c.*535-	*Liber Pontificalis*	Initially compiled by Pope Agapetus (535-536)	Extending throughout the ages

Table 1.2: Variant forms of the name 'Britannia' in the MSS of the *Liber Pontificalis*

Neapolitanus IVA 8 (7th c.)	Britanio
Lucensis 490 (8th c.)	Brittanio
Vossianus 60 (8-9th c.)	Brettanio
Parisinus 13729 (9th c.)	Brittannio
Coloniensis 164 (9th c.)	Brittanio
Vossianus 41 (9th c.)	Brittannio
Vindobonensis 473 (9th c.)	Brittanio
Ambrosianus M77 (9th c.)	Brittanio
Guelferbytanus 10, 11 (9th c.)	Bretanie
Bernensis 408 (9th c.)	Brintanniae
Parisinus 5516 (9th c.)	Brittannii
Laurentianus S. Marci 604 (12th c.)	Brittanio
Vindobonensis 632 (12th c.)	Britanio
Vaticanus 5269 (13th c.)	Britannio

the *Liber Pontificalis* relates between King Lucius and Pope Eleutherius can with reasonable confidence be located within this time-span (177-192).

The intention here is not to validate specific biographical entries in the *Liber Pontificalis* but rather to follow the transmission of the story of King Lucius and compare its internal implications with our current historical and archaeological knowledge of the second and later centuries in order to explore its veracity. Questions of indeterminacy in the period of Eleutherius' primacy and Lucius' reign will prove germane to this study.

The intriguing statement that King Lucius of Britain requested of Pope Eleutherius to become a Christian was very often quoted and sometimes embellished for centuries until 1904. In that year Adolph von Harnack uttered what has been widely taken as the final word on the matter.

CARL GUSTAV ADOLPH VON HARNACK

Carl Gustav Adolph von Harnack (1851-1930), in his capacity as an eminent German theologian and church historian, has the distinction of terminating, in a short but influential article published in 1904,[9] nearly 12 centuries of debate over the identity

1.1 Adolph von Harnack (*Project Gutenberg eText 13635*)

of King Lucius of Britain. Immediately prior to this, in the first volume of Harnack's 1902 major work, *The Mission and Expansion of Christianity in the First Three Centuries*, he had already begun to cast Lucius as fabulous, stating:

> All the stories about Peter founding churches in Western and Northern Europe (by means of delegates and subordinates) are pure fables. Equally fabulous is the mass of similar legends about the early Roman bishops, e.g., the legend of Eleutherus and Britain. The sole residuum of truth is the tradition, underlying the above-mentioned legend [of the correspondence between King Abgar the Black and Jesus] that Rome and Edessa were in touch about 200 A.D. This fragment of information is isolated, but, so far as I can see, it is trustworthy. We must not infer from it, however, that any deliberate missionary movement had been undertaken by Rome. The Christianizing of Edessa was a spontaneous result. Abgar the king may indeed have spoken to the local bishop when he was at Rome, and a letter which purports to be from Eleutherus to Abgar might also be historical. The Roman bishop may perhaps have had some

influence in the catholicizing of Edessa and the bishops of Osrhoene. But a missionary movement in any sense of the term is out of the question.[10]

There had been considerable debate in the nineteenth century, as we shall see in Chapter 4, about whether there could have been a king who wielded political power over all Britannia at such an early date and if so how he could have appealed to the Roman pontiff, implicitly bypassing the administrative authority of the Empire. The question of Britons accepting Christianity and establishing churches, in the midst of Roman provincial administration in the hearts of major cities, fuelled these doubts. However, there were also those who followed Thomas Fuller's suggestion in 1661 that 'however learned men differ in the date, they agree in the deed'.[11] Thus scholars remained willing to entertain the likelihood of a kernel of truth to the story, even if the dating is uncertain. However, with Harnack's 1904 article nearly any subsequent mention of Lucius, as for example in modern editions of the Venerable Bede, is qualified by redirecting the reader's attention to Harnack. The result is that this King of Britain is either generally unknown or is consistently deemed a mythical and legendary invention fostered by a sixth-century clerical error. All such attitudes are founded on the strength of one singular authority: Harnack. It is therefore important to reassess Harnack's argument and conclusions in the light of more recent discoveries and scholarship.

The central thrust of Harnack's 1904 argument, in his *Der Brief des britischen Königs Lucius an den Papst Eleutherus*,[12] was that the entry in the *Liber Pontificalis* was a scribal error and the word 'Britannio' should more correctly have been written 'Britio', apparently the citadel of Edessa in the Roman province of Osrhoene. Harnack claimed the cited King Lucius was actually King Lucius Aelius Septimius Megas Abgarus VIII of Edessa who reigned from AD 177 to 212, basing this transfer of identity on Britio appearing in a previous work by Theodor von Zahn (1838-1933).[13]

In 1884 Zahn, Professor of Theology at Erlangen in Bavaria, discussed a rediscovered Latin version of Clement of Alexandria's (*c.*160-215) *Hypotyposis*.[14] The original work in Greek (*hypotyposis* means 'to outline events') is unfortunately lost, but this Latin version states that '*Thaddaeus et Iudas in Britio Edessenorum*' – the saints Thaddaeus and Judas were buried at Edessa.

Zahn suggested this detail was added by the Latin translator who was probably Cassiodorus, whose *Adumbrationes Clementis Alexandrini in epistolas canonicas* included a partial, edited Latin translation of Clement's *Hypotyposis*. Previously Denis-Nicolas Le Nourry (assisting John Garret in publishing Cassiodorus in 1679) had not agreed that Cassiodorus' *Adumbrationes* were sections of the *Hypotyposis* but John Kaye, the Bishop of Lincoln (1783-1853), comprehensively disputed Le Nourry's conclusion. Zahn consequently developed this position, with support from Bishop Wescott.[15]

A later story which the Gallic pilgrim Egeria received first-hand at Edessa,[16] in 384, says that it was St Thomas, not Thaddaeus, who was buried with St Judas. The Latin translation of the original Greek *Hypotyposis* has replaced Thomas with

1.2 Remains of the citadel (*birtha*) of Edessa (*Photograph by J.B. Segal, 1959; Reproduced by kind permission from the J.B. Segal Collection*)

Thaddeus, suggesting that it is based upon an older source than the version related to Egeria. Thomas' body may have been returned from India to Edessa as late as AD 371[17] and reburied there in AD 394, but since Clement died in 215, it is feasible that the original *Hypotyposis* did not contain a notice of Thomas' body at Edessa but rather contained one of Thaddeus. When the work was translated into Latin in the sixth century, Cassiodorus or someone under his guidance followed Clement accurately, though apparently adding a Latinised version of the place-name. This is significant because Clement in Latin translation offers a historically unique and solitary reference to the *Britio Edessenorum*. By Harnack's own admission the more usual and correct expression is Birtha Edessenorum or 'the citadel of Edessa'.

It is important to be clear about what Harnack proposed; firstly, that a translator of Clement introduced a unique and distinctive term: *Birtha Edessenorum*, a compound expression, the first element meaning 'citadel', and secondly, that separately a scribe at Rome working from trusted sources copied, for the realm of one Lucius, a word, *Brittaniorum* that should have been rendered *Britio*, the unprecedented name of a mere edifice. This construction Harnack erected on the strength that the place happened to have a client-king who took on the Latin *praenomen* Lucius, an

Edessan king reigning about the same time as the purported British king whose Brythonic name was similar when Latinised. That this Edessan king wrote to Pope Eleutherius is posited, for after all, only one from a Lucius is mentioned. It is set aside by Harnack and subsequent academics because King Abgar was probably already Christian, needing no special pontifical permissions.[18] Harnack's academic problem boils down to whether a biographer of Eleutherius would mention a letter from Britannia and not one from Edessa. His solution of removing the one and inserting the other by means of something that could obviously *not* be a mere copy error, is certainly ingenious if not ingenuous.

Indeed Cassiodorus may have Latinised the location of the tombs of the Apostles at Edessa, but his work was contemporary with Pope Agapetus I and the *scriptorium* project at Rome: the same project that produced the *Liber Pontificalis*. In this project, which involved Cassiodorus' close involvement, he would also very likely have overseen the copy or addition from original sources of the notice about King Lucius in the *Liber Pontificalis*. If so, one is confronted with having to believe Cassiodorus would allow so glaring a confusion, which would certainly have come to his notice, between Britio and Britannio in the *Catalogus* while putting it 'correctly' or at least distinctively in Clement's *Hypotyposis*. The scribes of the *Liber Pontificalis* were working under the close guidance of Cassiodorus, and he even wrote useful instructions to his monks on methods of copying texts accurately. It is therefore untenable to assume that while under his guidance whoever copied the *Catalogus Felicianus* entry could have confused Birtha Edessenorum or even Brittio Edessenorum for Britannia.

Since Cassiodorus did not retire from his public post at Ravenna until shortly after 540, it is just possible he was not responsible for the appearance of the sentence about Lucius in the *Catalogus Felicianus*. The entry in the *Catalogus Felicianus* could predate him and, therefore, also predate his Latin version of Clement's *Hypotyposis* and the entry regarding Britium Edessenorum. Yet if so, the invention 'Britio' for 'Birtha' could hardly be seen as any attempt to link it with Britannia, rather its uniqueness makes it separate and quite distinct. Moreover, coming later could not then have influenced the original scribe of the *Catalogus*. One could perhaps envisage a clerical error in the *Liber Pontificalis* if the original word was 'Britannio' and the cleric wrote 'Britio'. A contraction could be a conceivable error, but to imagine mistakenly expanding the word 'Britio' into 'Britannio' is very far-fetched.

Were Harnack correct, one would have to suppose further that the cleric reading 'Britio' was ignorant of letters from a Lucius of Britium or Birtha Edessenorum and identified it with a name he did know: Britannia. However, this convolution doesn't work either, since it is impossible that a cleric writing in Rome in the sixth century was ignorant of the fame of Edessa, as the celebrated works of Sextus Africanus and Eusebius both mention the famous 'holy man' King Abgar the Great. Even more famous was King Abgar the Black, the first-century ruler of Edessa who was renowned in antiquity for corresponding with Christ. It is because of, and certainly since the time of, Abgar the Great in the second century

1.3 Coin of Abgar VIII [ABGAROC]
(*Reproduced by kind permission of the*
J.B. Segal Collection)

that Edessa was claimed throughout Christendom as the first city to 'officially' accept the new religion. In this broader context it would be more than curious that Abgar the Great should be celebrated for asking Eleutherius to be converted to Christianity.

There is no evidence that King Lucius Aelius Septimius Megas Abgar VIII was ever simply known as 'King Lucius'. Rather, he was consistently known as King Abgar, *Abgaros* on his coinage and by his appellation *Megas* (the Great). Nowhere on record is he referred to merely as King Lucius. It is also known that King Abgar the Great did not receive the names *Lucius Aelius Septimius* until the reign of Lucius Septimius Severus (193-211), clearly after the rule of Marcus Aurelius and Commodus.

Finally, King Abgar of Edessa could not have been in communication with Pope Eleutherius because the dates do not allow for it. While Abgar the Great ruled from 177 to 212 and the pontificate of Eleutherius is within that period (177-192), it is known that King Abgar the Great built his *birtha* or citadel/palace/fort at Edessa, the Britio Edessenorum, in AD 205 after the flood of Edessa in 201, in which a Christian church was ruined. The additional fact that he did not receive the names Lucius Aelius Septimius until the time of Septimius Severus again demonstrates that these events were after the life of Eleutherius.

Harnack's thesis or construction therefore stands on shaky ground. His argument nearly demolished, one may yet ask, aside from the apparent problems in interpreting the name of King Lucius as King Abgar, had Harnack without a sound basis of inference somehow guessed right? Should we indeed read Britio for Britannio, and did Abgar of Edessa solicit Christianity from a Pope, and is this the communication intended to be recorded in the *Catalogus Felicianus* albeit under the wrong pontificate?

THE PROBLEM OF BIRTHA

As stated, it is known that Abgar VIII built the *Birta* in his capital city of Edessa in the year AD 205. Naturally his realm would include a *Birta*, as it would the city walls and palaces, but it is unnatural to think of the King of Edessa being remembered in history as king of one part of his city rather than of the whole, if not the entire territory of Osrhoene. Sextus Julianus Africanus, Eusebius and Bede all know of Abgar as King Abgar, the holy man of Edessa, not 'King Lucius of *Birta*'.

It is reasonable to identify Harnack's reconstructed Britio/Britium with the more common word 'Birtha' which means 'fort' in both Armenian (*birtha*) and Arabic (*bira*), Byrt being a known place-name in the region, and there are examples from the middle Euphrates such as Birtha/Beirtha Okbanon and Birtha Asporakou.[19] If Birtha is the citadel of Edessa, it would be anachronistic for the territorial ruler to be remembered as 'king of the castle'. To rescue Harnack from this unhistorical sort of error, perhaps another Birtha is meant. Let us consider which places under the rule of the Edessan King are the most likely possibilities.

Birtha Achuran (modern Deir ez Zor) is in north-east Syria on the River Euphrates and when the Palmyrene Queen Iulia Aurelia Zenobia, who ruled Palmyra from AD 266/7 to 272/3, conquered this city it became part of her kingdom of Palmyra. North-east of Birtha Achuran is Birtha Asporaku/Asporakou (Fort of Asporaces), originally called Zanqi under the Assyrians in the ninth century BC and later renamed Zenobia. This city is now believed to be the present city of Halabiya.[20] Twelve kilometres upstream of Birtha Achuran is the Roman fort of Birtha Arupan. It is only mentioned in the Parthian version of the trilingual *res gestae* of the Sassanian ruler Shapur I as conquered in the spring of AD 253. In the 1930s Poidebard[21] made systematic reconnaissance flights over the Syrian Steppe and located Birtha Arupan at Qreiye/Ayyash, recent excavations have confirmed that the fort is 220m x 220m and the associated civilian settlement and necropolis may be situated under the nearby modern village of Ayyash. Britio may even refer to the Roman veteran colonia of Berytus (modern Beirut), as Lipsius argued in 1884,[22] but none of these forts/cities were within the province of Osrhoene or under the rule of the King of Edessa.

J.B. Segal (*colour plate 1*) commented[23] that the literature is somewhat unclear whether the Birtha of Edessa is in fact Birtha (modern Bireçik), situated 85km west of Edessa and straddling the River Euphrates (modern Firat) at 37° 03' North, 37° 59' East. Bireçek was formerly known as Apamea-Zeugma, the fortified city overlooking the bridge of boats (Zeugma) across the Euphrates. The city's pre-Seleucid name was Birtha and that name was revived under Roman rule. Since 2000, it finds itself 8km downstream of the controversial Bireçek Dam that has, with the other 20 dams of the South Eastern Anatolia Project of Turkey, flooded parts of Zeugma and many

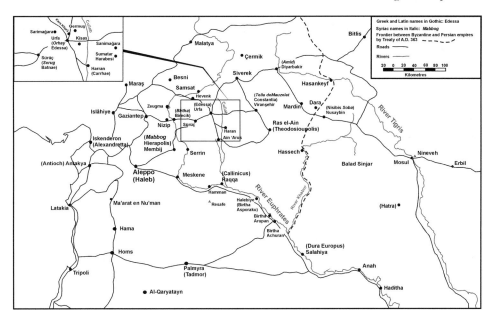

1.4 Location map of Edessa and Birtha place-names (*From J.B. Segal 1970:261, Map; Dominic Barker 2007*)

other important archaeological sites. It has also recently been demonstrated that this was the city named Macedonopolis by the Greeks, and if Clement did describe the resting place of Thaddaeus and Iudas one might reasonably expect him to have recorded Macedonopolis rather than Birtha.

Zosimus, in his unfinished *Historia Nova* (iii. 19), written between AD 498 and 518, mentions that the Emperor Julian (the Apostate) rested at a town called Bithra (Greek Βιθρα), meaning 'seed' in Arabic, in the year 363 during his march into Mesopotamia. Despite the fact that this city is not mentioned by Ammianus Marcellinus in his account of Julian's Persian expansion, it has been consistently identified as Birtha/Bireçek. Nonetheless, whether Bithra be Birtha, there is no evidence of a King Lucius of Birtha/Bireçek.

J.B. Segal noted that a Syriac inscription of Birtha/Bireçek records a burial place constructed by its ruler (*shallita*) in AD 6. This ruler of Birtha was, we are told, tutor to the son of a certain Ma'nu bar Ma'nu. This, the oldest Syriac inscription, reads:

> In the month of Adar of the year 317, I, ZRBYN bar Ab[gar] ruler of Birtha, tutor of 'WYDNT' bar Ma'nu bar Ma'nu, made [this bu]rial place [for my]self and for HLWY', mistress of my house and for [my] children [...]. Whoever will enter this b[urial place] and shall show respect [lit., see] and shall give praise – all the [gods shall bless him].

Ma'nu, however, has no title, and hence would not reasonably be known as King of Edessa.[24] It is untenable to think that King Abgar who resided at the city of Edessa, his capital, could have been referred to as King of Birtha, an outpost city

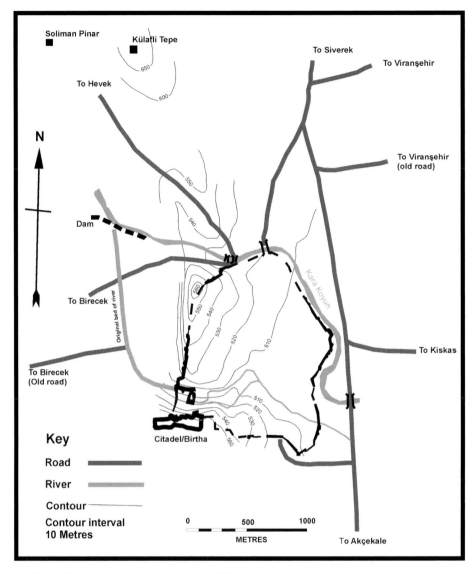

1.5 Plan of Edessa (*After Segal 1970:264, Plan II; Dominic Barker 2007*)

62 miles/85km distant from the capital. There is in any case no evidence for this method of referring to the King of Edessa.

JUDAH BEN ZION SEGAL AND THE PROBLEM OF DATES

In 1970, J.B. Segal, the renowned scholar of the epigraphy, archaeology and history of Edessa, had occasion to include a footnote in his book *Edessa; The Blessed City*,

1.6 J.B. Segal at the School of Oriental and African Studies, London (*Reproduced by kind permission by Mrs Leah Segal and Dr Naomi Segal*)

a footnote of such importance that he deserves the credit of being the first to challenge Harnack's identification of King Lucius with King Abgar. Speaking of King Abgar VIII (The Great), Segal wrote:

> The coins of Edessa carry the portrait of this Abgar [the Great] – a bearded head, wearing with assurance and dignity the great tiara and diadem of his office. He was, we are told, friendly with Bardaisan, the philosopher-poet of Edessa, and he must have been a man of culture. He was a wise administrator, concerned with the welfare of his subjects. It was he who outlawed the practice of castration at Edessa – but this need not have been, as our source suggests, under the influence of Christianity. For Abgar was also a man of the world. He had, no doubt, like Bardaisan, met ambassadors from India, and he visited Rome towards the end of his life.

In the footnote Segal states that:

> There is no foundation for the hypothesis of Harnack that Abgar was in direct touch with Eleutherius, Bishop of Rome from 174 to 189.[25]

As mentioned earlier, King Abgar of Edessa could not have been in communication with Pope Eleutherius because the dates do not allow for it.

CONCLUSION/A POST-HARNACK REINVESTIGATION

There are now compelling reasons why Harnack's thesis cannot be maintained. We have seen that it is strained in the extreme to explain away the entry in the *Liber Pontificalis* as a clerical blunder. King Abgar of Edessa was not referred to as King Lucius of Birtha and the dates when he did take on the *praenomen* Lucius, let alone his construction of a *birtha*/citadel at Edessa, came years after the pontificate of Eleutherius.

In this connection there is one further point of interest. Harnack drew his conclusions by comparing Zahn's 1884 work on the Latin version of Clement of Alexandria and the early version of the *Liber Pontificalis*, the *Catalogus Felicianus*. He would likely have also consulted Bede's *Ecclesiastical History* written in 731, but it seems unlikely that he compared that work with Bede's earlier *Chronica maiora* of 725, which has an entry regarding King Abgar of Edessa in the time of Septimius Severus (193-211). Bede's various contributions will be studied in detail in the following chapter, but it is worth noting here that in the eighth-century Bede knew that King Lucius of Britannia and King Abgar of Edessa were two distinct rulers. Bede, or rather Benedict Biscop or Nothelm, his faithful and intrepid researcher, would not have learned of their difference from the *Liber Pontificalis* alone, as that book does not make mention of King Abgar. Bede explicitly mentions his source as (Sextus Julianus) Africanus (*c*.160-*c*.240) and, whether Bede consulted a now lost copy of Africanus or was simply getting his information from Eusebius, the fact remains that he knew the two kings were not the same.

In conclusion, the overwhelming weight of evidence is contrary to the construct proposed by Harnack in 1904. The construct proves so untenable that it cannot even be called a hypothesis. This leaves us now, after a century, in a position to reconsider the entry in the *Liber Pontificalis* and consider whether it refers to genuine events surrounding a genuine person, King Lucius of Britannia. All of the evidence, and many references to Lucius need to be gathered and restudied. As a contribution to that end, the next three chapters follow the citations, embroidered embellishments, debates and potential forgeries to a story that was an integral though contested part of Britain's historical tradition for at least 13 centuries.

CHAPTER 2

LUCIO BRITTANIORUM REGE (KING LUCIUS OF BRITAIN)

We can now rationally survey the provenance of the story of King Lucius of Britain with attention to works that predate Geoffrey of Monmouth's *Historia Regum Britanniae* (*History of the Kings of Britain*). This work, completed sometime between 1134 and 1138, likely 1136, is unfortunately overflowing with the fabulous, including a chapter on the Prophecies of Merlin.[1] Geoffrey's *History* therefore marks a division between what we can consider reliable primary and less reliable secondary source material on Lucius, allowing that primary material is often referenced in later writings. Geoffrey's *History* is revisited in the following chapter, since many later works either elaborate his version of events or conflate his details with those of the Venerable Bede.

King Lucius is referred to by all 14 works listed in Table 2.1, between the *Catalogus Felicianus* and the completion of Ordericus Vitalis' *Ecclesiastical History* in *c*.1135. Those detailed below belong to what we might call the 'British tradition' notwithstanding the eighth-century *Vita Lucii*, along with the petition of Bishop Victor III to the Emperor Louis the Pious, and Notker's *Martyrology*. These works will be discussed in Chapter 6 as part of the 'Raetian tradition'.

The most relevant 'British tradition' entries include the *Liber Pontificalis* (*Catalogus Felicianus*: *c*.530), The Venerable Bede (*Chronica maiora*: 725, *An Ecclesiastical History of the English People*: 731), 'Nennius' (*Historia Brittonum*: *c*.796), *The Welsh Triads*, Aethelweard (*Chronicle*: *c*.988), Ordericus Vitalis (*The Ecclesiastical History of England and Normandy*: completed *c*.1135) and Henry of Huntingdon (*Historia Anglorum*, composed between 1129 and 1154). Before examining these sources it is noteworthy that several of the earliest entries are often used to support the argument for early Christianity in Britain. Aside from the many nineteenth-century opinions on when Christianity arrived,[2] the subject has received recent archaeological interest from authors such as David Petts and Dorothy Watts who suggested: 'Christianity reached Britain, perhaps some time towards the close of the second century',[3] and went on to observe that 'while the value of these sources as evidence has been questioned in recent times by Thomas, … even he accepts a Christian presence in Britain by

Table 2.1: Pre-Geoffrey of Monmouth selection of works referring to King Lucius

Date	Author	Title
*c.*498-*c.*530		*Liber Pontificalis: Catalogus Felicianus*
725	The Venerable Bede (*c.*672/3-735)	*Chronica Maiora*
731	The Venerable Bede (*c.*672/3-735)	*Historia Ecclesiastica gentis Anglorum*
8th c.		*Vita Lucii confessoris Curiensis* (Codex Sangallensis 567)
*c.*796	*Nennius*	*Historia Brittonum*
821	Bishop Victor III of Chur (820-833)	Petition to Emperor Louis the Pious
After *c.*850		Bern Codex 178
896	Notker Balbulus (*c.*840-912)	*Martyrology*
*c.*988	Aethelweard (flourished 973-998)	*Chronicle*
*c.*1082	Marianus Scotus (1028-1082/3)	*Chronicle* (printed in 1559, Basel)
*c.*1125		*The Book of Llandaff (De Primo Statu Landauensis Ecclesiae)*
*c.*1125	Community of St David's, Wales	Letter from St Davids to Pope Honorius II 1124-1130
*c.*1135, 1148, 1154	Henry of Huntingdon (?-after 1154)	*Historiae Anglorum*
Completed *c.*1135	Ordericus Vitalis (1075-*c.*1142)	*The Ecclesiastical History of England and Normandy*

the last quarter of the second century'.[4] The sources to which she refers begin with Tertullian (*c.*155-222), a Montanist who is our earliest source and who wrote in *Adversus Iudaeos* (*c.*208):

Britannorum inaccessa Romanis loca, Christo vero subdita.

... the regions of Britain which have never been penetrated by Roman arms have received the religion of Christ.[5]

Origen Adamantius (*c*.185–*c*.254) was a scholar and teacher at Alexandria who revived Clement's Catechetical School and eventually retired to Caesarea Maritima. His theological views on a hierarchical concept of the Trinity were later pronounced *anathema*, but of interest here is that he noted in *c*.240 in his *Homily IV* on Ezekial, that Christianity was a universal force extending beyond the reaches of the Roman Empire in Britain:[6]

Virtus Domini Salvatoris et cum his est, qui ab orbe nostro in Britannia dividuntur.

The power of God our Saviour is even with them which in Britain are [apart] from our world.[7]

In the Diocletian Persecution (*c*.300) Christian martyrs were reported from Britain including Stephen and Argulius (both apparently Bishops of London), Socrates (Bishop of York), Amphibalus (Bishop of Llandaff), Nicholas (Bishop of Penryn, Glasgow), Melior (Bishop of Carlisle), Julius and Aaron (of Caerleon), and of course the most famous among them, St Alban of Verulamion.[8] In 303 Dorotheus, the Bishop of Tyre (*c*.255–362), indeed 107 years old when he died, declared that 'Aristobulus, whom Paul saluted[9] was Bishop of Britain'. He also claimed that Simon the Canaanite, surnamed Zelotes (Simon the Zealot) preached Christianity and was crucified, slain and buried in Britannia. Mythical legends like the latter are obviously baseless; perhaps old Dorotheus was losing his memory in senility. They regrettably offset histories that can be verified.

Much more certain and useful are the three British bishops who attended and signed the documents of the Council of Arles in AD 314: Eborius, Restitutus and Adelfius, who will be discussed in more depth in Chapter 6. Eusebius of Caesaria (*c*.260/75–340) in his *Demonstratio Evangelica* (Book 3) completed in *c*.311, wrote 'The Apostles passed beyond the ocean to the isles called the Britannic Isles'. For there to have been bishops in Britannia important enough to attend a major ecumenical council, a lineage of belief and praxis in their sees would have to have been considerable and long-standing. St Hilarius (Hilary) of Poitiers (300–367) reiterated a record of early apostolic missions reaching Britannia.[10] John Chrysostom, the renowned Patriarch of Constantinople from 347 to 407 gave one of his sermons the title 'Logos kata Ioudaion[11] kai Ethnikon peri tis Theotitos tou Xristou'.[12] It read:

… also the British Isles that are beyond the [Mediterranean] sea in the Ocean, learned about the power of Christ's speech, because churches and altars have been founded there. His prophecy, which was spoken then, has now been planted in everyone's souls and is said by everyone.[13]

This is the earliest surviving direct reference to Christian altars and churches built in Britannia (Brettanikai).

Theodoret the Blessed (387–458) as Bishop of Cyrus, Syria, included in his continuation of Eusebius' *Historia Ecclesiastica* (Church History) the following statement (435):

Paul, liberated from his first captivity at Rome, preached the gospel to the Britons and others in the west. Our fishermen and publicans not only persuaded some Romans and their tributaries to acknowledge the Crucified and His laws, but the Britons also and the Cymry [the Britons of Wales].

From Britain itself Gildas Sapiens, the Wise (flourished *c*.520s-540) wrote in his sermon *De Excidio Britanniae* (On the Ruin of Britain) of *c*.520s:

Christ the True Sun afforded his light, the knowledge of his precepts, to our Island in the last year of Tiberius Caesar.

The last year of the Emperor Tiberius Caesar Augustus's 23-year reign was AD 37. Much has been made of the fact that Gildas does not mention King Lucius in *De Excidio* while naming several other British kings (Constantine of Dumnonia, Aurelius Caninus, Vortiporius of the Demetae, Cuneglasus and Maglocunus/Maelgwn) and this has been taken as a reason to doubt the authenticity of later reports about Lucius. Why would a British writer living two centuries before Bede not mention this ancient King who did so much in establishing Christianity in Britannia? The answer to this often-posed question rests in part[14] on the incorrect treatment of *Excidio* as a history, rather than as the polemical sermon it was originally intended as. The kings Gildas did mention support his central thesis that Britain was invaded by the Saxons as a divine punishment for the sinful corruption of its early sixth-century rulers. There is no compelling reason why he should have mentioned or illustrated the life of King Lucius as he was both too early and presumably more upstanding than the examples given. In short, King Lucius was a good king,[15] so Gildas did not need to mention or complain about him. There is another little-known work by Gildas apparently on the Victories of Aurelius Ambrosius mentioned by Geoffrey of Monmouth, but this shall be considered in the next chapter.

In summation there is a general consensus from third- to sixth-century textual sources that Christians were well established in Britannia as early as 208 or before on Tertullian's reckoning. As that author stated, Christianity may have bloomed in Britannia in areas outside the reach of Roman administrative rule. This idea is revisited in Chapter 7, when dealing with the tribal kingdom of the Brigantes in northern Britain.

Many of these ancient sources may well have been written in a context of disputation between rival interpretations of Christianity or Christian history. Nonetheless the authors, even if utilising embellishment or colourful hagiographic didactics, would not have been taken seriously, as they evidently were, had a general consensus over the underlying facts not already arisen. One should hardly figure these diverse writers as tapping a consistent but false idea of Christianity arriving early in Britain, when the idea could easily have exposed them to disproof especially when they were in dispute over theological matters. There are numerous authoritative and scholarly books devoted to the missionary expansion and reach of early Christianity.

The cultural topic of Christian settlement in Britain is associated with stories either historical or legendary corresponding to figures like St Alban and Joseph of Arimethea. In a substantive sense these histories, historical legends and legendary myths have imparted profound cultural importance to real places such as Glastonbury and the Roman amphitheatre of St Alban's. As distinct from these examples of the credible and the conjectural, the legendary history of King Lucius, possibly for the simple reason of an undiscovered site[16] and for reasons to be addressed more fully in Chapter 7, is hardly present in modern British culture. The cover image for the cover of this book (also *colour plate 2*) is a detail of an early fifteenfth-century stained glass window in the south side of the Choir Clerestory in York Minster, beside another depicting Pope Eleutherius.[17] Together with one other – the nineteenth-century stained-glass window in the north aisle of Gloucester Cathedral[18] (discussed in Chapter 6) – such vivid depictions are rare in the United Kingdom. While a search for early representations of King Lucius in Britain is an ongoing endeavour, at present the York Minster windows appear to be the earliest instances extant. Certainly Pope Eleutherius' window there seems to be unique in Britain.

We have already discussed the entry in the *Liber Pontificalis* and it is worth reiterating that this is the earliest extant reference to King Lucius. After Lucius' death or emigration it eventually settled into British awareness via Nothelm's research and Bede's writing. The way it did this is as much a story of how cultural history was transmitted and transformed through the ages as it is an example of how an important figure from the distant past became central to religious and political debates.

A typical example of how King Lucius was lately relegated beyond the pale even of historical myth, to fable and fallacy, can be found in Rositze's footnote in the *Peterborough Chronicle (Anglo-Saxon Chronicle)*[19] under the entry for the year AD 167:

> A curious and impossible story first found in the *Liber Pontificalis* I. 136, translated by L. R. Loomis, *The Book of Popes* [New York, 1916], page 17. It is very likely based upon a false identification of Lucius Abgar, king of Edessa in Mesopotamia, whose fortress was called *Birtha* [found written *Britium*]: Adolf Harnack, "Der Brief des britischen Konigs Lucius an den Papst Eleutherus," Sitzungsberichte der koniglich preussischen Akademie der Wissenschaften, 1904, pp. 909-916.

As we have already seen, Adolph von Harnack had uttered what is widely and mistakenly accepted as the final word upon 17 centuries of tradition and debate regarding this late second-century British king. Harnack wrote his remarks regarding the entry in the *Liber Pontificalis* to explain the notice made by Bede in his *Ecclesiastical History*, written in 731. As mentioned in the previous chapter, amidst more egregious faults he failed to consider Bede's *Chronica maiora* written six years earlier. Harnack's conclusion, that King Lucius of Britain must refer to King Abgar VIII of Edessa, is groundless.

Besides the faults or oversights already detailed, Bede mentions this Abgar in his *Chronica maiora* in a subsequent entry to that of King Lucius, and under a later date.

THE VENERABLE BEDE (C.672–735)

Bede's entry in his *Chronica maiora* dating to 725 is a compilation of several sources including the late Roman *Scriptores Historiae Augustae* (*Augustan History*), Eusebius of Caesarea (*c.*275-339), Sextus Iulius Africanus (170-243), and the *Liber Pontificalis*. The relevant entries read:

> Marcus Antoninus Verus [ruled] with his brother Lucius Aurelius Commodus for nineteen years and one month.[20] From the first they administered the empire with equal authority, although until that time there had only ever been single emperors.[21] They carried on war against the Parthians with great skill and success.[22] Persecution having broken out in Asia, Polycarp and Pionius were martyred; in Gaul too, many also gloriously shed their blood for Christ.[23] Not long after a plague, the avenger of evil deeds, devastated many provinces, especially Italy and the city of Rome. His brother Commodus having died, Antoninus made his own son [also called] Commodus his colleague as emperor.
>
> Melitus of Asia, the bishop of Sardis, gave the emperor Antoninus his 'Apology for the Christians'.[24] Lucius the king of Britain sent a letter to bishop Eleutherius of Rome, seeking to be made a Christian.[25] At this time there lived Apollinaris of Asia the bishop of Hierapolis, and Dionysius bishop of Corinth.[26]
>
> (4131)

Further, there is the entry:

> Macrinus [reigned for] one year.
> Abgar the holy man ruled at Edessa, as Africanus wanted …
>
> (4170)

In Bede's chronological scheme, 4131 represents the year AD 179, and 4170 is AD 218. Sextus Julius Africanus was in Edessa in the year 195, while King Abgar VIII (177–212) was on the throne and is mentioned as the famed 'holy man' in this *Chronicle*.

A comparison between Bede's entry in the *Chronica maiora* (725) and his later more popular *Historia ecclesiastica gentis Anglorum* (731) is illuminating. Lucius, a British king, writes to Pope Eleutherus and asks to be made a Christian:

> Anno ab incarnatione Domini centesimo quinqua gesimo sexto Marcus Antoninus Uerus quartus decimus ab Augusto regnum cum Aurelio Commodo fratre suscepit. Quorum temporibus cum Eleuther uir sanctus pontificatui Romanae ecclesiae prae

esset, misit ad eum Lucius Brittaniarum rex epistolam, obsecrans ut per eius mandatum Christianus efficeretur et mox effectum piae postulationis consecutus est, susceptamque fidem Brittani usque in tempora Diocletiani principis inuiolatam integramque quieta in pace seruabant.

In the year of our Lord's Incarnation 156, Marcus Antoninus Verus, fourteenth from Augustus, became Emperor jointly with his brother Aurelius Commodus. During their reign, and while the holy Eleutherus ruled the Roman Church, Lucius, a British king, sent him a letter, asking to be made a Christian by his direction. This pious request was quickly granted, and the Britons received the Faith and held it peacefully in all its purity and fullness until the time of the Emperor Diocletian.

Book I, Chapter IV

In Book V, Chapter XXIV:

In the year of our Lord 167, Eleutherus became Bishop of Rome, and ruled the Church most gloriously for fifteen years. Lucius, a king of Britain, sent him a letter asking to be made a Christian, and obtained his request.

There is no entry regarding the holy man Abgar, ruler of Edessa in the *Ecclesiastical History*, as this work is concerned with matters directly affecting British history whereas the scope and scheme of the *Chronica maiora* encompasses the six ages of the world. The version of King Lucius given in Bede's *Ecclesiastical History* is relatively imprecise, compared with his earlier *Chronica maiora*. In the *History* Bede states that 'Marcus Antoninus Verus … became Emperor jointly with his brother Aurelius Commodus' and moves immediately to King Lucius and Pope Eleutherius, implying to the unwary that their correspondence might be dated to the same period as Marcus' joint rule with his brother Lucius Verus (Lucius Ceionius Commodus Verus Armeniacus, 161-169). Yet in the earlier *Chronica* Bede had expressed this in a much clearer and more accurate way: 'Marcus Antoninus Verus [ruled] with his brother Lucius Aurelius Commodus for nineteen years and one month' and then, Bede explains, 'His brother Commodus having died, Antoninus made his own son [also called] Commodus his colleague as emperor', after which Lucius and Eleutherius made contact. This moves the date of correspondence to between AD 177 and 180, when Marcus ruled jointly with his son Commodus (Lucius Aurelius Commodus Antoninus). Despite the dangers of an uninformed reading of the *Ecclesiastical History* most students of Bede refer to his later work rather than the *Chronica*. To be fair to Harnack, no critical analysis of the two versions appears even in the sixteenth and seventeenth centuries, when discussion about King Lucius reached its peak (as outlined in Chapter 4).

Bede's statement regarding King Lucius has long been agreed to derive from the entry in the *Liber Pontificalis*. Bede received the aid of Nothelm who traveled to Rome and made notes from the Vatican library of the late sixth-century correspondence between Gregory the Great and St Augustine of Canterbury. While at Rome sometime between 715 and 725, Nothelm apparently also made note of the sentence concerning King Lucius in the *Liber Pontificalis*. This visit to Rome was under Gregory II (715/6 to 11 February 731) whose papacy laid an emphasis on missionary efforts in Germany and strengthening papal authority in England and Ireland, perhaps to emulate the famed missionary achievements of his namesake Gregory the Great. Bede acknowledged Gregory II in his *Ecclesiastical History* and it seems reasonable and natural to agree that it was Nothelm who 'discovered' mention of King Lucius in the Vatican Library.

Yet there do remain important qualifications to a simplistic take on this 'discovery'. Did Nothelm not anticipate this finding, or was it something he already expected and verified? Benedict Biscop could also have gathered the information on his many trips to Rome in the late seventh century (a link that is further developed in Chapter 6) and presumably he might have alerted Nothelm. One should imagine the encounter with the *Liber Pontificalis* a very great revelation to an unexpecting historian or researcher, but there is nothing in Bede's tone in either of his works to suggest this as a new historical discovery. Instead, the person of King Lucius of Britain is summarily presented in a very few lines. This raises the question of whether Bede and the British educated religious of the eighth century were already well aware of Lucius through oral tradition and now-lost written sources.

It is entirely plausible that King Lucius in the *Liber Pontificalis* was not a 'discovery' made by Nothelm so much as a verification while he was in Rome. Although the *Liber* has no direct relation to the collected letters of Gregory the Great to St Augustine of Canterbury, Bede or his researcher could be expected to seek out the precedents. At any rate it is anything but established that Bede's information about Lucius came *solely* from the *Liber Pontificalis* and Nothelm's research trip to Rome.

NENNIUS (*HISTORIA BRITTONUM*, 829/30)

The original version of the *Historia Brittonum* was probably 'written in Wales by a multilingual cleric in the year 829/30',[27] drawing upon both English and Irish sources. The work was ascribed to Nennius but the true author remains unknown. The pertinent citation in the *Historia Brittonum* reads:

> Post centum et sexaginta septem annos post aduentum Christi, Lucius bryttannicus rex com omnibus regulis totius bryttanicae gentis baptismum suscepit, missa legatione ab imperatoribus Romanorum et papa romano Euaristo.[28]

The date given for Lucius and all his realm submitting to baptism is 'post 167' and the Pope's name, at least in some of the manuscripts, has been mistakenly replaced with 'Evaristus', who held the pontificate much earlier, from *c.*98 to 105. Except for the name Euaristo, the details and date of this statement closely follows Bede's *Ecclesiastical History* of 731.

Two later additions to Nennius' *Historia* include a note after the name Lucius: '*agnomine Leufer Maur, id est magni splendoris propter fidem, que in eius tempore venit*' – 'with the surname Leufer Maur, that is of great honour on account of the Faith, which came (to Britannia) in his time'. This additional information is included also in the body of writing known as *Trioedd Ynys Prydein* (*The Welsh Triads*) discussed below in Chapter 3. Suffice it to say here that this additional note most likely dates from the twelfth or thirteenth century and that the name 'Leufer Maur' may be rendered 'Great Light'.

THE CHRONICLE OF AETHELWEARD (C.988)

Aethelweard's *Chronicle* has been placed within the decade 978 to 988 and 'a latish date within that limit is to be preferred'.[29] Aethelweard held the position of ealdorman of Wessex and the early years of his *Latin Chronicle* are based on the *Anglo-Saxon Chronicles*, but with one important difference. Aethelweard relates that Pope Eleutherius made contact with King Lucius via a mission rather than Lucius contacting the Pope. This reversal of the standard story has been interpreted by Campbell[30] as Aethelweard having 'ill translated' Bede. Be that as it may (and in Chapter 4 we encounter evidence that there was at least a letter back from the Pope, although extant copies are later than 988) the *Chronicle* is an important example from the late tenth century of the story's transmission.

THE CHRONICLE OF MARIANUS SCOTUS (1028–1082/83)

Marianus Scotus was born in Ireland in 1028 and appears to have secluded himself from the world in 1052; four years afterwards he quitted his own country and became a monk in the Irish monastery of St Martin at Cologne; he was ordained a priest in 1059 by Sigefrid, Abbot of Fulda, at Wurtzburg; he retired to Fulda as a recluse, where he died in 1082 or 1083. Marianus is part of what is known as the Hiberno-Scottish missionary efforts of the eleventh century, discussed further in Chapter 5. In the Frankish kingdom he and companions founded St Peter at Regensburg in 1072. He is also known to have composed a general chronology and for the earlier portion of the work his chief authorities were Eusebius, Cassiodorus and Bede.[31] As a whole his work does not offer any additions to his sources, but illustrates that by the mid eleventh century Bede's statement about King Lucius was being adhered to. As we have already seen, there was growing confusion over the exact years in which to locate Lucius and what else he may have done for the British Church. In the years after the Norman Conquest, monasticism and the financial growth of the wool trade affected the political claims made by some religious foundations over their neighbours. The churches of western Britain vied for primacy over each other to such a degree that forged documents were produced in order to provide grounds for ascendancy. Unfortunately for the credit of King Lucius, who represented the earliest dependable precedent of British Christianity – by the Venerable Bede no less – his story became embroiled in this intrigue, and so began a long career of embellishment that bordered on mythologising. One such embroidery was the old *Book of Llandaff*.

THE OLD *BOOK OF LLANDAFF* (*DE PRIMO STATU LANDAUENSIS ECCLESIE C.*1125)

In the context of monastic foundations vying with each other and attempting to prove one was older than a rival, in *c.*1125 a great dispute finally erupted over diocesan property boundaries between the church of Llandaff, St David's and Hereford. That wrangling produced the querulous *Book of Llandaff* (in Welsh the *Llyfr Llandaf*)[32] containing much that is dubious in the section dealing with the land grants given to Llandaff by ancient kings including Lucius. However, like all effective allegories, it incorporates considerable history of substantial veracity. The passage of present interest reads:

> In the year of our Lord's incarnation CLVI [156] King Lucius sent Elvanus and Medwinus to Eleutherius, the twelfth bishop of Rome, to desire that he might be made a Christian by his instruction. Upon which, the Pope gave God thanks that such a heathen nation were so earnest in their applications for Christianity. And then, by the advice of the priests of the city of Rome, they first baptized these ambassadors, and afterwards instructing them more fully in the principles of the Christian faith, they proceeded to ordain them, making Elvanus a bishop, and Medwinus a teacher; and they, being thus qualified, returned to king Lucius, who, with the chief of the Britons, was baptized: and then, according to the form of Eleutherius's instructions, the ecclesiastical order was settled, propagated among the inhabitants.

This Welsh is the first extant source to mention the names of the native British ambassadors sent to Rome by King Lucius. Elvanus and Medwinus are key figures in the history of these events carried forward by Welsh oral tradition.[33] They are mentioned again and much later by Raphael Holinshed in 1586 as 'Eluanus Aualonius' and 'Medguinus Belga'; there is a thin but important path between fabrication and embroidery.

As part of a counter-claim to that of the church of Llandaff, the brethren of St David's appealed to Pope Honorius II (1124-1130) in *c.*1125. In this letter they claimed there were three archbishops in Britain in the time of King Lucius. It seems at present lost to history what Rome's response was, but it is noteworthy that this detail predates Geoffrey of Monmouth's treatment of the same idea by about 11 years.

We have seen how in the early twelfth century Lucius, a king, was abused as a pawn in claims to ancient rights. Whoever could best argue that Lucius was their original benefactor would gain the benefit and sanction of Rome, creating a contentious process whereby King Lucius was reduced for pliable uses, giving one establishment precedence over another. As unfortunate as this proved to be for the future credibility of all that relates to Lucius, it does reveal how important he had become. After all, he did represent the official introduction of Christianity into British royalty and civic society. Through each age much was subsequently associated with him for contemporary political reasons, which led at last to cynicism about his historical reality. For the moment, in the twelfth century he was championed throughout Britain with a stature he could do nothing to oppose, much to his demise. As we will see, this mythical stature became grist for the fabulous mill of Geoffrey of Monmouth.

HENRY OF HUNTINGDON (*C.*1088–*C.*1156)

Henry of Huntingdon, while he was active as late as the mid twelfth century, is of special importance as a primary source because his first drafts of the *Historia Anglorum* were not influenced by the work of Geoffrey of Monmouth, as so many later sources were. Henry was Archdeacon of Huntingdon from 1110 to *c.*1156 and composed his *Historia* between 1129 and 1154.[34] His first book was completed by 1133 and it was not until he travelled in 1139 to Le Bec in northern France that he encountered Geoffrey's writing. Henry then made several alterations to the first book of his own *Historia* but there remain, thankfully, important differences between Henry and Geoffrey's details.

Henry's *Historia* comprises the following sources, approximately 25 per cent following Bede, some 40 per cent the *Anglo-Saxon Chronicle*, and about 10 per cent other written sources.[35] Unlike the majority of writers one encounters citing Bede, Henry was using the fuller account in Bede's *Chronica maiora* of 725 rather than the abridged version in the later *Historia ecclesiastica*. Henry also revised and supplemented his Book I using Paul the Deacon's *Historia Romana*.[36] Another source appears to have been a *Life of St Helena* and Henry calls her the daughter of King Cole of Colchester.[37] Tatlock has regarded this as 'a reliable case where Geoffrey borrowed from Henry and not vice versa'.[38] Henry of Huntingdon's actual entries read:

> 27: Antoninus Pius held the monarchy of the world for twenty-two and a half years[39]
>
> 28: Marcus Antoninus Verus [Marcus Aurelius], with his brother Aurelius Lucius Commodus [Lucius Verus], nineteen years and two months. These men were the first to govern the Empire with equal authority, as up to that time emperors had ruled one at a time. They conducted a war against the Parthians with marvelous courage and good fortune. In their time, when Eleutherius presided over the pontificate of the Roman Church, Lucius, king of the British Isles, sent a letter

to him beseeching that on his authority he might be made a Christian, and before long he achieved his pious request. The Britons preserved the faith which they had received, inviolate and entire, in peace and quiet, until the time of the emperor Diocletian. In praise of Antoninus Verus, from The Roman History: [Paul the Deacon's work] 'After his partner Antoninus [Lucius Verus] died of apoplexy [Paul viii. 10], he remained in imperial authority and worthy of the highest praise. He never changed his facial expression for either joy or sorrow. He was dedicated to the Stoic philosophy. He was a supreme philosopher in moral conduct and in erudition [Paul, c. 11]. Very learned in Latin and Greek literature. Kind to all, never haughty, very readily generous. Benevolent and moderate towards the provinces. He successfully fought the Germans. He conducted the Marcomannic War [Paul, viii. 12] against the Quadi, the Vandals, the Sarmatae, the Suevi, and all the barbarian peoples, although no record is left for comparison with the Punic wars. So the saintly man, the victor of this great conflict, made his triumph with his son Commodus. When the treasury was exhausted, he sold the royal ornaments, but afterwards he paid the prices of the items to those who were willing to return them, and was not annoyed with those who were unwilling [Paul, c. 13]. He permitted noblemen to present entertainments in the same style as himself, and with similar attendants. He was so lavish in providing games after his victory that it is said that a hundred lions were exhibited at one time [Paul, *c.*14].

29: Commodus, son of the aforesaid Commodus [Commodus was the son of Marcus Aurelius, not of Lucius Verus], reigned imperially for thirteen years. He conducted a successful war against the Germans. He ordered the head of the Colossus to be replaced with a representation of his own head.[40]

Book I

Henry's surprising mistake over the identity of Commodus is however not repeated in his Letter to Henry I:

*c.*95: Marcus Antoninus et Lucius Aurelius fraters[41] …

*c.*96: Antoninus Commodus[42] …

*c.*97: Helius Pertinax[43] had so brief an empire that there was no chance for anything to be written down.

*c.*98: [Septimius] Severus Pertinax acquired your kingdom, King Henry, after great battles, and he died in it.[44]

*c.*99: Antoninus Caracalla, son of Severus, exhibited nothing similar to his father's virtue and righteousness.[45]

*c.*100: While Macrinus ruled the empire, King Abgar, a very holy man, reigned at Edessa.[46]

The final note about King Abgar of Edessa shows that Henry of Huntingdon was not only using Bede's *Chronica maiora* but that he, and presumably his royal audience, understood that Abgar was a separate and different person to the previously mentioned King Lucius.

Before meeting with Geoffrey of Monmouth's *History of the British Kings* it is important also to first briefly consider the work of Ordericus Vitalis (1075-1141), *The Ecclesiastical History of England and Normandy*, completed in 1136, the same year Geoffrey finished his own book. Ordericus Vitalis was born in Shrewsbury and at the age of 32 became a priest at Rouen in Normandy, where he wrote his *History*. In Book I, Chapter XXIII he says:

> On the demise of his brother Commodus, Antoninus took his own son Commodus as his colleague in the government. Melito, bishop of Sardis, in Asia, wrote an apology for the Christians, addressed to the emperor Antoninus. Lucius, king of Britain, sent a letter to Eleutherius, bishop of Rome, soliciting admission into the Christian church. Apollinaria of Hierapolis in Asia, and Dionysius of Corinth, are ranked amongst the most illustrious bishops of the age.

The wording of Ordericus exactly follows Bede's *Chronica maiora* of 725 whereas most other writers, except for Henry of Huntingdon, limit themselves to Bede's *Ecclesiastical History* of 731. In northern France then, at least a more accurate rendition of events was retained. This source and those we have encountered above are completely at odds with Geoffrey of Monmouth's ambitious work and what followed it, as discussed in the next chapter.

CHAPTER 3

THE EMBROIDERED TALE

The extant primary sources relating to King Lucius of Britain were critically sampled in the last chapter. However they may be intertwined and linked in complex ways, they all ultimately relate to the *Liber Pontificalis* and tend to credit that document by according with its essential statement. Yet the textual sources from the early twelfth century and specifically Geoffrey of Monmouth (*c.*1100–*c.*1155) bring out a new set of details and complications augmenting the comparatively simple records of Bede and Nennius. Geoffrey's *Historia Regum Britanniae* (*The History of the Kings of Britain*) was completed in *c.*1136 while he was resident at Oxford. We may consider this date as between the transformation of a fascinating historical conundrum into a fabulous tale. Certainly not everything written about Lucius 'post-Geoffrey' is to be discounted as incredible, but the sources require extra care and increased scrutiny in order to identify and separate important new information from mere reiterations of Geoffrey.

The contemporary reaction to Geoffrey's *History* ranged widely among all who found it and it was received variously as bewildering, amusing, exasperating and worthy of serious attention.[1] Parodying the literature that supported the postures of contemporary society may have been a motivation, but not Geoffrey's primary one. Rather, the evidence is that he sought to play upon the literary culture of certain canons, both regular and monks, going so far as to produce not one history but a parody of many. In so doing he aimed to defend secular virtues as a powerful alternative to the prevailing monastic literary culture.[2]

One effect of Geoffrey's work was an increased popular interest in British secular history at large, and embellishments on Lucius in particular insured his longevity, if at the expense of his credibility. In this respect it was a dramatic turning point; although Geoffrey was displaying skill as a storyteller by embroidering received historical facts, all subsequent pursuit of these became increasingly thwarted. Nonetheless, Geoffrey and his followers at least exhibited a palpable interest in the reality-behind-the-myth of this early Christian king, but as will be seen in Chapter 4 a long legacy of the fanciful led the academics of the nineteenth century to 'solve' the problem of an over-mythologised figure, ultimately by declaring the earliest credible sources in error. Thereafter all scholarly pursuit of Lucius was rendered moribund. If Geoffrey of Monmouth warmed too much to his subject, Adolph von Harnack would put it into a deep freeze.

Embellishments and embroideries, where they can be distinguished from mere imprecision,[3] are themselves interesting cultural artefacts of how a singular story was discursively transmitted across British and European society. The ways in which it was injected into contemporary ecclesiastical and political dimensions served both to ensure, and at the same time limit, its longevity. The handling of King Lucius by Geoffrey through to Wace's *Roman de Brut* of *c.*1155, Layamon's *Brut* of *c.*1215 and Matthew Paris' *Chronica Maiora* of 1240-53 (see Appendix C), is one particular aspect of how Romance literature made fabulous myth out of historical legend.

The legacy of the *Historia Regum Britanniae* was both widespread and influential. Nevertheless, Geoffrey's historical accuracy did not go unquestioned among his scholarly contemporaries. Gerald of Wales for example, in his *Journey Through Wales* (1188) opposed Geoffrey by relating the tale of how Meilyr could tell the untruth of a book by occult methods:

> When he [Meilyr] was harassed beyond endurance by these unclean spirits, Saint John's Gospel was placed on his lap, and then they all vanished immediately, flying away like so many birds. If the Gospel were afterwards removed and the History of the Kings of Britain by Geoffrey of Monmouth put there in its place, just to see what would happen, the demons would alight all over his body, and on the book, too, staying there longer than usual and being even more demanding.[4]

Geoffrey sewed so much confusion that his name would henceforth be associated with fabrication, rather than with reliable history, and by 1685 Stillingfleet was able to confidently refer to another author, Hector Boethius, as a 'Geffrey of Scotland … so many and so improbable are his fictions'.[5] In accordance with Geoffrey's repute, it is best to handle all traditions that emanate from his pen as suspect, despite there being truths clothed as riddles wrapped in mystery inside an enigma,[6] making it still worthwhile to quote in full his passages regarding Lucius.

Table 3.1 below lists the authors, where known, and titles of works mentioning Lucius, between Geoffrey's *History* and John Hardyng's *Chronicle*. Not all these works are discussed in depth in this chapter, but the avid reader will be able to use this table and the full catalogue in Appendix C as a starting point for independent research.

GEOFFREY OF MONMOUTH (*THE HISTORY OF THE KINGS OF BRITAIN*, COMPLETED *C.*1136)

Apart from the debate over Geoffrey's intentions, a study of King Lucius would be remiss not to include his influential passages. Following are those deemed pertinent.[7]

Table 3.1: List of works referencing King Lucius from Geoffrey of Monmouth to John Hardyng

Date	Author	Title/Instance
Completed 1134–1138	Geoffrey of Monmouth (*c*.1100–*c*.1155)	*Historia Regum Britanniae (The History of the Kings of Britain)*
Between 1129 and *c*.1143	William of Malmesbury (*c*.1096–*c*.1143)	*De Antiquitate Glastoniensis Ecclesiae*
c.1143	Alfredus (Alfred) of Beverley (?–1154/7)	*Annales sive Historia de gestis regum Britanniae*
1122–1154		*The Anglo-Saxon Chronicle* (Laud MS)
c.1155	Wace (*c*.1115–*c*.1183)	*Roman de Brut*
c.1177	Joceline/Jocelyn of Furness (mid 12th c.)	*The Life of St Kentigern*
Mid 12th c.	Joceline/Jocelyn of Furness	*De Britonum Episcopum* (Only in Stow's 1598 *Survey of London*)
Mid 12th c.	Joceline/Jocelyn of Furness	*Vita Helena*
1188	Gerald of Wales (*c*.1146–*c*.1223)	*The Journey Through Wales*
1193	Gerald of Wales (*c*.1146–*c*.1223)	*The Description of Wales*
c.1202	Ralph de Diceto (?–*c*.1202)	*Chronicle*
1213	Radulphus Niger (*c*.1140–1217)	*Chronicon succinctum de Vitis Imperatorum et tam Franciae quam Angliae Regum, a Christo ad Anno 1213*
c.1214	John of Wallingford (John de Cella) (1195–1214)	*Chronica Joannis Wallingford*
c.1217	Prince Alexander Neccham/ Neckam (1157–1217)	*De sapientia diuina*
?*c*.1166–1216		Letter from Eleutherius to Lucius (included among the *Leges Edwardi bonis Regis*)
c.1236	Roger of Wendover (?–1236)	*Flores Historiarum*
1240–53	Matthew Paris (1200–1259)	*Chronica Maiora*

*c.*1250–75		*The Welsh Triads*
*c.*1268	Martinus Polonus/Martin of Troppau or Oppaviensis (?–1278)	*Chronicon Pontificum et Imperitorum*
?*c.*1224		*Annals of the Church of Rochester* (cited by Jeremy Collier)
Before 1313	Ralph de Baldoc/Baudake (flourished 1294–1313)	
13th c.	Robert of Gloucester (mid-late 13th c.)	*Chronicle*
Between 1231 and 1513		Brass Plaque in St Peter-upon-Cornhill, London
*c.*1333	Unknown; reworking of Wace	*Le Brut* (*Brut d'Engleterre*)
*c.*1338	Robert Mannyng (Robert de Brunne) (*c.*1275–*c.*1338)	*Chronicle*
*c.*1350	Richard of Cirencester (*c.*1335–*c.*1401)	*Chronicle*
*c.*1351	(Claudius) Henricus de Erfordia (flourished *c.*1351)	
*c.*1399		The '*Short Chronicle*' of Kirkstall Abbey
Before 1400/6	Petrus de Natalibus (?–1400/6)	*Legends of the Saints*
*c.*1440s	Reginald Pecock (*c.*1395–1460)	*Repressor of Overmuch Blaming the Clergy*
1443	John Flete (*c.*1398–1466)	*The History of Westminster Abbey*
1454	Thomas Rudborne jnr (flourished 1447–1457)	*Historia major … ecclesiae Wintoniensis*
	John Capgrave (1393–1464)	*Chronicle of England*
*c.*1465	John Hardyng (1378–*c.*1465)	*Chronicle* (printed by Richard Grafton in 1543)

A single son was born to Coilus. His name was Lucius. When Coilus died and Lucius had been crowned King of the country, the latter imitated all his father's good deeds, with the result that he was considered by everyone to be a second Coilus. His great wish was that he should end in even greater esteem than he had begun; and he therefore sent a letter to Pope Eleutherius to ask that he might be received by him into the Christian faith. The miracles which were being wrought by young Christian missionaries among different peoples had brought great serenity to Lucius' mind. He was inspired with an eager desire for the true faith. What he asked for in his pious petition was granted to him: for the Holy Father, when he heard of the devotion of Lucius, sent him two learned men, Faganus and Duvianus, who preached the Incarnation of the Word of God and so converted Lucius to Christ and washed him clean in holy baptism, they were made members of the Kingdom of God. Once the holy missionaries had put an end to paganism throughout almost the whole island, they dedicated to the One God and His Blessed Saints the temples which had been founded in honour of a multiplicity of gods, assigning to them various categories of men in orders.

At that time there were twenty-eight flamens in Britain and three archflamens, to whose jurisdiction the other spiritual leaders and judges of public morals were subject. At the Pope's bidding, the missionaries converted these men from their idolatry. Where there were flamens they placed bishops and where there were archflamens they appointed archbishops. The seats of the archflamens had been in three noble cities, London, York and the City of the Legions, the site of which last, by the River Usk in Glamorgan, is still shown by its ancient walls and buildings. The twenty-eight bishops were placed under the jurisdiction of these three cities, once the superstitions practiced there had been purged away. Parishes were apportioned off, Deira being placed under the Metropolitan of York, along with Albany, for the great River Humber divides these two from Loegria. Loegria itself was placed under the Metropolitan of London, together with Cornwall. The Severn divides these last two provinces from Kambria or Wales, which last was placed under the City of the Legions.

(Book iv.19)

At last, when they had arranged everything to their liking, the missionaries journeyed back to Rome and asked the most holy Father to ratify all that had been done. He gave them his approval; and they then returned once more to Britain. In their company came a great number of other religious men, and by their teaching the faithful among the Britons were soon fully established as Christians. Their names and deeds can be found in the book which Gildas wrote about the victory of Aurelius Ambrosius. All this Gildas set out in a treatise which is so lucidly written that it seemed to me unnecessary that it should be described a second time in my more homely style.

(Book iv.20)

When this famous King Lucius saw that worship of the true faith had increased within his kingdom, he was very pleased indeed. He turned to better use the goods and the lands which the idolatrous temples had hitherto owned, permitting them to remain in the hands of the churches of the faithful. Feeling that he ought himself to find the money for some mark of distinction that should be greater than this, he rewarded the churches with even larger lands and houses, and increased their power by giving them every possible privilege. In the end Lucius died in the town of Gloucester while still occupied with these matters and with other moves which formed part of his plan. In the year 156 after the Incarnation of our Lord he was buried with all honor in the church of the Archdiocese. He had no heir to succeed him, so that after his death dissension arose between the Britons, and the power of Rome was weakened.

(Book v.1)

Once the fact of the death of Lucius was known in Rome, the Senate sent Severus as its delegate, and two legions with him, to restore the country to Roman domination …

(Book v.2)

Here Geoffrey has offered a much-embellished account of King Lucius including several details that have not been encountered before, so far as the record of extant works allows us to tell. A major problem is that Geoffrey cites a work written by Gildas, presumably composed in the sixth century, on the victory of an Aurelius Ambrosius. This work seems to be unknown to Geoffrey's contemporaries: other than his mention there survives no independent reference to it. To contemplate the reality of this lost primary source has long been alluring, but since Geoffrey's credibility is generally so suspect, his reference to a lost work of Gildas can give us no great assurance about the information he apparently gleaned from it. But *if* this work by Gildas existed and *if* Geoffrey had a unique monopoly over it, an inestimable importance attaches to much of what he adds to the story of Lucius.

Since, from what evidence survives, this single work by Gildas disappeared as rapidly as it had appeared for Geoffrey's eyes alone, it has seemed reasonable to discount it and the information it supposedly contained. However, we do not by any stretch have a complete record of primary sources once in existence and stranger things have happened than a jealously guarded source appearing, only to be lost again.[8] Indeed, the information given by Geoffrey is difficult to proscribe because upon it rests so much of the subsequent embroidery enveloping King Lucius.

The additions to the story include Pope Eleutherius sending two missionaries named Faganus and Duvianus to Britain having first received a letter from Lucius requesting formal conversion to Christianity. Nothing is said of the messengers who carried the letter to the Pope (Elvanus and Medwinus) mentioned in the old *Book of Llandaff*. The names of the two missionaries Geoffrey does give vary during the succeeding centuries. For example Johannes Beverus, known also as John Fiberius and John of London, who wrote a condensed version of Geoffrey's work in the early fourteenth century has the latter name as Dunianus.[9] The later version of *Le Brut* (1333) and its abridgement (*c.*1367) also alter them even further as 'Pagan', either a word play on their pre-Christian beliefs or simply a transcription error,

Table 3.2: Name spellings of the missionaries sent from Rome to Britannia

Author/Title	Date	Missionaries from Rome
Geoffrey of Monmouth	1136	Faganus, Duvianus
Jocelyn of Furness	c.1177	Faganus, Divianus
Gerald of Wales	c.1193	Faganus, Duvianus
Ralph de Diceto	c.1202	Faganus, Duvianus
Annals of Rochester	c.1224	Fugatius, Damianus
Johanne Beverus/Fiberius (John of London)	c.1310	Faganus, Dunianus
Le Brut	1333	Pagan, Elibrayne
'Brute Abridgment' of MS 306	c.1367	Pagan, Olibane
John Capgrave	c.1464	Fugan, Damian
John Hardyng	c.1465	Faggan/Phagane, Dubyan/ Dirvyen/Duvyen
John Leland	c.1552	Fugatius, Damianus
Raphael Holinshed	1586	Faganus, Dinaw/Dinauus

and 'Elibrayne' or 'Olibane', remarkably different from Damian/Duvian. Table 3.2, above, provides a listing of the various spellings given for these two missionaries.

The year Geoffrey assigned to the death of Lucius was AD 156, most likely a misappropriation of Bede's *Ecclesiastical History* dating of the king's conversion to that year, whereas Bede assigns the death of Lucius to the year 167. Geoffrey gives no date for Lucius' conversion, which seems curious if he was consulting Bede. Similarly an investigation into the historical veracity of Lucius need not pay serious heed to the replacement of 28 *flamens* and three *archflamens* with bishops and archbishops, except that this was perhaps Geoffrey's attempt to tie in the existence of known metropolitan sees in Britain by 314. His attempt has remained problematic, and in 1845 Brewer scathingly remarked:

> … the imagination of Geoffrey … has converted a petty king into a Roman monarch, and these twenty bishops are but the coinage of his brain.[10]

Nevertheless, the 'invention' of early bishoprics associated with Lucius may just amount to a nod of approval from Geoffrey to the community of St David's, whose letter of *c.*1125 to Pope Honorius II (1124-1130) argued there were three archbishops in the days of Lucius. The additional idea that Faganus and Duvianus returned to Rome to obtain ratification from the Pope and journeyed a second time to Britannia with a large number of religious people, would seem to be part of the 'lost' work by Gildas.

THE ANGLO-SAXON CHRONICLE (THE LAUD MS, 1122-1154)

Within the great Saxon compilation of historical notices known as *The Anglo-Saxon Chronicle*, there appear the following succinct entries:

> 155: Marcus Antonius and Aurelius his brother rose to power.

> 167: Eleutherius became bishop of Rome. For 15 years. To him, Lucius Brytwalana cing sent men …

> 189: Severus rose to power.

These bare facts are listed with such brevity that we gain only one insight, namely that the Anglo-Saxons used Bede's *Ecclesiastical History* as their primary source for these early years, referring to Lucius in an anachronistic form: 'Lucius Brytwalana cing', a Saxon expression of his monarchy. However, one particular version of *The Anglo-Saxon Chronicle* known as *The Peterborough Chronicle*, expresses the same information in a fuller and slightly differently way:

> 155: Here Marcus Antoninus and his brother, Aurelius, succeeded to the throne.

> 167: Here Eleutherius succeeded to the bishopric of Rome and held it honourably for fifteen years. Lucius, king of the Brito-Welsh, sent men to him and asked for baptism, and he sent to him at once; and they continued afterwards in the orthodox faith until the reign of Diocletian.

> 189: Here Severus succeeded to the throne and went with an army to Britain and conquered a great part of the island by battle; and then for the protection of the Britons he built a rampart of sods with a board wall on top of it from sea to sea. He reigned seventeen years, and then died at York. His son, Bassianus, succeeded to the throne. His other son, who died, was named Geta.

> 202: Here Pope Victor, like his predecessor, Eleutherius, decreed that Easter be celebrated on a Sunday.

Although Bede's mistaken *Historia* dates again appear, an important difference is the detail that Lucius sent men to Eleutherius rather than just a letter. This agrees with another body of work known as *The Welsh Triads*. Set in groups of three, the *Triads* record (set in writing in the thirteenth century[11]) an ancient oral tradition of the history of the Britons. The second of the noted kings of the Isle of Britain has this entry:

> Second was Lleirwg ab Coel ab Cyllin Sant, who is called Lleufer Mawr, who built the first church in Llandav, and that was the first church in the island of Britain: he granted the privilege of nationality, judgement and oath to every one of the Christian faith.[12]

From this British oral source we are provided interesting information about King Lucius. His full name is given as Lleirwg of Coel of St Cyllin, naming Coel as the father, himself the son of Cyllin. This record unwittingly sets up a lore of lineage for Lucius of previous saints and Christian rulers, even entangling Joseph of Arimethea, St Paul, Simon Cyrene and a host of others. The fabric of the developing embroidery would, with enough imagination, weave and connect such figures as Constantine, his wife Helen (refigured as a Briton), Arthur and Merlin into one de-contextualised and tightly knit anachronistic garment, hung on fabulous genealogical pedigrees in which Lucius became progressively ensnared.

What is entirely plausible is the emissaries of Pope Eleutherius baptising Lleufer (or Lles) and he took on the name Lleirwg (Lucius). Eleutherius was subsequently remembered in Welsh as 'Pab Elidir'.[13] Lleufer became locally known and entered oral tradition as Lleufer Mawr, the latter word akin to 'maior' or 'major', possibly with the sense of 'Great'. This important testimony from the oral tradition in the Brythonic language provides an independent verification of the events elsewhere described, as in Rome and British monastic literature.

Along with the multiplicity of names and deeds reported by Geoffrey, there appears to be some continuity with an indigenous oral tradition that was newly written down. However so much 'new' information on Lucius (not to mention the wealth of other additions and alterations applied by Geoffrey to the persons and doings of later British rulers) had the effect of confusing, for the purpose of entertainment by lambasting contemporary literature, the subsequent telling and retellings of the ancient king.

GERALD OF WALES (*THE JOURNEY THROUGH WALES C.1188; DESCRIPTION OF WALES C.1193*)

As we have seen, Gerald of Wales made it quite clear that he was no supporter of Geoffrey's *History*. However, in his *Description of Wales* (*c.*1193), Gerald made the following curious statement, originally in Latin, that requires some attention:

> Praeterea olim, longeque ante excidium Britannicum, quia per annos circiter ducentos, per Faganum et Duvianum, ad petitionem Lucii Regis ab Eleutherio papa in insulam transmissos, in fide fundati sunt et solidati.

> About two hundred years ago, long before the fall of Britain, the Welsh were instructed
> and confirmed in the Christian faith by Faganus and Duvianus who, at the request of
> King Lucius, were sent to the island by Pope Eleutherius.[14]

Perhaps surprisingly, this substantially agrees with Geoffrey and supports our
earlier consideration of Geoffrey's statements about Faganus and Duvianus as
based on a common ancient source, possibly Gildas, since lost. There is added
interest in how Gerald dates the mission of Faganus and Duvianus: 'About two
hundred years ago, long before the fall of Britain'. At first sight this translation
seems a vague way for a twelfth-century historian to refer to the times of King
Lucius, for his contact with Eleutherius could not have surpassed 192 (the year
that Pope died) which would set the locus of a phrase 'about two hundred years
later' to around *c.*392. That date is not far from 'the fall of Britain' if we pin
this to the traditional *c.*407 when Flavius Aetius left the Britons to their own
defences against invading Saxons, Angles and Jutes. If, therefore, we read 'ante'
as 'before' or 'ere' instead of 'ago' – an entirely feasible shift in translation – the
idiomatic phrase makes eminent sense. Indeed the illogic of 'ago' tying to a
point of reference in the twelfth century is a strong internal argument for this
re-rendering of Thorpe's 1978 translation.

Gerald reiterates and confirms Geoffrey while at the same time complaining about
him. Other writers such as Jocelyn of Furness assimilated the 'new' information
with their own additions, also ascribed to lost ancient sources.

JOCELYN OF FURNESS (THE *LIFE OF SAINT KENTIGERN*: C.1177, *BOOK OF
BRITISH BISHOPS*, MID TWELFTH CENTURY; IN STOWE'S *SURVEY OF
LONDON*)

Jocelyn, or Joceline, a monk of Furness, flourished between the years 1177 and
1185, and is known as the compiler of biographies and the author of several *Lives
of Saints* including St Kentigern, St Helena,[15] David, King of Scotland, and St
Waldef (*Waldeu*, the second Abbot of Melrose). Stowe mentioned that Jocelyn
also composed a now-lost *De Britonum Episcopis* (*History of the Bishops of Britain*)
which apparently contained a comprehensive list of the Archbishops of London
from the time of King Lucius. This list is dealt with in Chapter 6 in the discussion
of the London church St Peter-upon-Cornhill. Regarding the *Life of St Kentigern*,
Jocelyn included some details about Lucius as follows under Chapter XI:

> Now this Cambrian region, over which Kentigern presided as bishop, had once on a
> time, with all Britannia, accepted the Christian faith in the time of Pope Eleutherius,
> when Lucius was king; but in consequence of the Pagans from time to time infesting
> the island, and asserting dominion therein, the islanders, lapsing into apostasy, had cast
> away the faith which they had received.[16]

Further, in Chapter XXVII, Jocelyn wrote:

> For Britain, during the reign of the most holy king Lucius, in the papacy of Eleutherius,
> by the preaching of the most excellent teachers Faganus and Divianus and others,
> whom Gildas the wise, the historian of the Britons, commemorateth, received the faith
> of Christ. It preserved that Christianity thus received whole and undefiled till the time
> of the Emperor Diocletian.[17]

Again we encounter mention of the lost work of Gildas relating to the Roman
missionaries and this is probably Jocelyn reiterating Geoffrey, but it does remain
plausible that the northern monk had access to ancient sources no longer extant,
perhaps indeed one was the lost work of Gildas. In any case Jocelyn is an example
of how widespread and influential Monmouth's work had become soon after its
completion.

THE ANNALS OF THE CHURCH OF ROCHESTER (C.1224)

John Leland (1506-1552) mentioned in his *De Rebus Britannicus Collectanae*,
published much later in 1770/4, an intriguing document he called the *Annals
of Rochester*. In 1688 Jeremy Collier also cited this document in his *Ecclesiastical
History of Great Britain*. It is most probably the *Textus Roffensis* compiled by Ernulf
(Ernulphus/Amulphus), who is mentioned in the *Anglo-Saxon Chronicle*. Ernulf
was Prior of Rochester until his resignation in 1096, then Prior of Canterbury
(1096-1107) and Abbot of Peterborough (1107). Finally in his capacity as Bishop
of Rochester (*c*.1114-1124) he compiled the various documents relating to the
ancient Church of Rochester.[18] However, as discussed further in Chapter 4, the
Textus Roffensis does not include consular dates for when Lucius contacted Rome,
whereas the document Collier was consulting apparently fixes upon a year for
King Lucius' contact with the Pope, in the consulship of Severus and Herennianus,
and in the eleventh year of the Emperor Marcus Aurelius when Eleutherius was
Bishop of Rome.

The original author obviously managed to unearth a more accurate way of relating
King Lucius' contact with Pope Eleutherius, rather than only quoting the inaccurate
date 167 from Bede's *Ecclesiastical History*. He may have found from a now-lost Latin
history that it was contemporary with Severus and Herennianus, whose consulship,
he related, was in the eleventh year of Marcus Aurelius when Eleutherius was Pope.
If the author was working from Marcus' sole reign, after Lucius Verus' death in 169,
then the eleventh year would have been 179 (otherwise the eleventh year of shared
rule would be March 7, 171 to March 7, 172). Of the two consuls named, presumably
Severus is the future emperor, while Herennianus is Herennius Nepos who was
executed, along with many other Roman nobles, by Severus as emperor at the close
of the second century. It is not impossible that Herennius Nepos was consul in the

year 171-172, but of the two options for the 'eleventh year of Marcus Aurelius', 179 is to be preferred as this was within the papacy of Eleutherius.

A provisional surmise might be appropriate regarding this interesting source. The historian of Rochester seems unaware of Bede's mistake, and reused his date of 167 to 'clarify' material from an older source. The Latin source from which he was presumably working may not have given a numerical year of King Lucius' contact with the Pope, but rather may have expressed it in terms of consulships and papacy with a detail that lent it historical veracity. Roman historians chronicling major events regularly expressed dates by consular years so it is reasonable to conclude that the historian of Rochester had access to a manuscript of great antiquity.

If this primary source did bear record of King Lucius' contact with Pope Eleutherius, it would be of prime value. It is evident that Bede did not use such a source since he has a completely different form of expression. It may be that this source was not annotated by the ecclesiastics at Canterbury for Bede's use in 725 or 731, strongly suggesting that the church was unaware of this old Latin text. Its use in the thirteenth century, by a member of the religious community at Rochester, could mean several things. The text may have remained hidden for centuries in some unknown corner of Rochester, assumed to be other than what it was. This supposed original Roman chronicle, which included an entry regarding King Lucius, is of course not extant. However, the implication that a Latin source of some great age included the episode of King Lucius' contact with Pope Eleutherius is of greater value than any other of our surviving primary sources from Britain.

I propose that the transcribing done by the historian of Rochester, being possibly the only citation from a now-lost source would be of priceless value to our written evidence of King Lucius. Of course, this is all based on the idea that John Leland and Jeremy Collier were indeed citing an authentic source rather than adding more fictitious threads to the embroidery.

LE BRUT (WACE C.1155)

Geoffrey of Monmouth began his *History* with the chapter *Brutus Occupies the Island of Albion*. By using Bede and Nennius for the description of Britain[19] he was able to weave together legend and credible historical writing in such a way that we might now consider the *History* good storytelling[20] and a beginning of historical fiction. The story of Brutus of Troy and his people the Britons is a subject for another study, but since it provided the fictive context for a series of poetic works from the twelfth to fourteenth centuries, poems that elaborated upon King Lucius, the subject is of interest here. Hard upon its completion, Geoffrey's work caused an immediate reaction on the continent. Even before Gerald of Wales could make his snide comments, Wace (*c*.1115-*c*.1183) had, by 1155, already written his *Roman de Brut* in Anglo-Norman. Further, the English poet Layamon, who wrote his *Brut* in *c*.1215, quickly drew upon this handling of the legendary founder of Britain and he received widespread acclaim. Layamon's *Brut* in turn influenced Sir Thomas Malory's *Le Morte d'Arthur* (first published by William Caxton in 1485). In *c.*1333 a new version of Wace's poem appeared called *Le Brut*, or *Brut d'Angleterre*.[21] The way it covers the episode of King Lucius is worth discussing.

> How Kyng Lucye regnede after Coel his fader, that was a gode man; and after, he bicome cristen.
>
> After Kyng Coel, regnede Lucie his sone, that was a gode man to God and to al the peple. he sent to Rome, to Apostle Eulenchie, that tho was, and seide that he wolde bicome a cristen man, and resceyue baptisme in the name of God, and turne to the ryyt [right] bileue. Eulenchie sent ij legates, that me callede Pagan and Elibrayne, into this lande, and baptisede the kyng and alle his menye (mene), and after went fro toune [a margin note in an ancient hand reads: [fir]st cristes Kynge] to toune, and baptisede the peple til al that Lande was baptisede, and this was in the c. lvj yere [156] after the Incarnacion of Ihesu Crist. and this kyng Lucye made tho in this lande ij erchebisshoppes, on at Kaunterbery and anothere at York, and othere meny bisshopes that yit bene in this lande. And when thise ij legates hade baptisede al the lande, thai ordeynede prestes forto baptisen childern and forto make the Sacrament; and after, thai went ayeyne [again] to Rome, and the kyng duellede in his lande, and regnede with michel (mych) honour xiij yere [13 years], and after deide, and lith [lieth] at Gloucestre.
>
> Chapter XLIV

> How this lande was longe withouten a kyng; and how the Britons chosen a kyng. This kyng Lucie hade none heire of his body bigeten, that was afterwarde grete harme and sorwe to the lande; ffor, after this kyng Lucies deth, none of the grete lordes of the lande wolde suffren (soffre) an-othere to bene (be) kyng, but leuede in werre and debate amonges ham l. yere [50 years] withouten kyng. but tho it bifel aftirwarde that a grete Prince come fro Rome into this lande that me callede Seuerey [Septimius Severus]; nouyt forto werr', but forto saue the ryght of Rome …
>
> Chapter XLV

The works we have been reviewing are ostensibly chronicles of history (excepting Gildas' extant polemical sermon) but *Le Brut* represents a concerted contemporary effort to write history in a new and fashionable, partly secular, way and therefore owing more to Geoffrey than to Bede. Amongst these colourfully embroidered retellings of King Lucius are several details worth highlighting. For instance, Pope Eleutherius is called 'Eulenchie' and, as noted earlier, the names of the two *legates* sent by the Pope are spelled 'Pagan' and 'Elibrayne'. King Lucius is related as baptised in 156, a reiteration of Geoffrey's error or intentional alteration of Bede's *Ecclesiastical History*. Curiously, only two Archbishoprics are mentioned, one at Canterbury, the other at York.

The statement that King Lucius ruled for 13 years (apparently to 169), died and was buried at Gloucester is a misreading of Geoffrey and receives further discussion in Chapter 6 regarding the traditional locations of Lucius' burial. Additionally, since

Lucius had no progeny, *Le Brut* has it that there was war and faction for 50 years until the arrival of Severus. The unrest over the succession apparently created the violent conditions Severus had to settle first-hand, but in fact, from the supposed death of Lucius in 169, half a century of conflict brings us to 219, a full eight years after the recorded death of Septimius Severus and eleven years after he had arrived in Britannia. Obviously, twelfth-century attempts at temporally locating Lucius in second-century history remained a serious difficulty.

The poetic verses illustrated above do at least show how King Lucius was assimilated into the popular genre of Romance legend; this increased his popularity but ultimately damaged his historical credibility. We thus move away from the blatantly mythic poesy of courtly verse and return to sources that at least intended to chronicle and comment upon the deeds and events of actual history.

RICHARD OF CIRENCESTER (*CHRONICLE* WRITTEN C.1350)

Richard of Cirencester wrote his *Chronology of Principal Events* about the year 1350 and although it does not add anything new and noteworthy, it represents the continuing transmission of the story of Lucius into the fourteenth century:

> XXV. 4160. Britain was enlightened by the introduction of Christianity, during the reign of Lucius, who first submitted himself to the cross of Christ.

JOHN HARDYNG (1378–C.1465; *CHRONICLE*)

The rhyming *Chronicle* of John Hardyng (1378–c.1465) received great popularity within the court of King Henry VI, reaching an even wider audience when Richard Grafton later printed it in 1543. In Chapter 51 Hardyng relates the history of King Lucius:

> Lucius, kyng of Britayn, reigned
> Liiii yere, and was the seconde christened kyng of Britayn, by
> Faggan & Dubyan, that baptized all
> this lande; and for thesame
> cause bare the same armes
> after he was baptized. Also
> he made of iiii archeflamynes
> in Britayn, three archebyshoppes,
> at London, Yorke and Carlion.

Hardyng states that Lucius' reign lasted 54 years. If Lucius died in 201, then Hardyng believes he came to the British throne in 147. He calls Lucius the 'seconde christened kyng of Britayn', as Hardyng has Coilus, Lucius' father, as the first. A difference from Geoffrey is Hardyng's report of four 'archeflamynes' made into three archbishops, at London, York and Caerleon-upon-Usk. Numbering four *archflamines* rather than the usual three may simply be a mistake, rather than an embellishment.

> After kyng Coile his sonne, then Lucius,
> So crowned was with royall diadem,
> In all vertue folowed his father Coilus;
> To compare hym in all that myght beseme,
> He put his will after, (as) his witte could deme,
> In so farre forth that of Christentee,
> He contynued so a Christen man to bee.

> And in the yere of Christes incarnacion
> An. C. foure score and tenne,
> Eleuthery [the] first, at supplicacion
> Of Lucyus, sent hym twoo holy menne
> That called wer Phagane and Dirvyen [Faggan and Duuyen],
> That baptized hym, and all his realme throughoute,
> With hertes glad and laboure deuoute.

Hardyng dates the sending of 'Phagane and Dirvyen' to Britain and Lucius' baptism as 190 (100 + four score and ten) which appears one score of years too late for these events. Hardyng's source seems to have been unique. Undoubtedly he was using Geoffrey, but the minor and major differences may add up to another, unidentified, source. For example, 'Eleuthery the first' is a unique way of referring to this Pope. There was a Pope Lucius I (253-254), but Hardyng's source, certainly written after 254, would have distinguished the latter Pope from the ancient British king who shared the Latinised name Lucius, otherwise known as Lleufer Mawr. Perhaps harking back to the early Britons, Hardyng and his fifteenth-century audience may have had a penchant for the Greek name and the expression 'Eleutherius the first' may have been an attempt to clarify between him and Lucius the first who could popularly have been hailed as Eleutherius the second.

> Thei taught ye folke ye lawe of Christ eche daye,
> And halowed all the temples in Christes name,
> (All mawmentes) and idols caste awaye
> Through all Britayn, of al false goddes thesame,
> The (temples flamynes), the idols for to shame.
> They halowed eke and made bishoppes sees
> Twenty and viii at dyuers great citees.

Again, here we have Hardyng's poetic version of information straight from Geoffrey, including the 28 bishops' sees being at diverse great cities.

> Of (iii acheflamynes) thei made archbishoprikes;
> One at London, (Troynouaunt that) hight,
> For all Logres, with lawes full autentikes
> To rule the church & christentee in right:
> Another at Carlyon, a towne of might,
> For all Cambre: at Ebranke (Eboranke) the thirde,
> From Trent North for Albany is kyde.

That three *archflamines* were made into archbishoprics accurately follows Geoffrey but Hardyngs' occasional mistaken rendering of a fourth may be the result of his many rewrites provided for different patrons, or it may be due to alterations made by Richard Grafton in the sixteenth-century edition.

Other details echo Geoffrey, for example where London is also called Troynouaunt, Geoffrey had mentioned the city of Trinovantum and translated it as Troy Nova, or New Troy.

> All this workes the Pope gladly (Eugeny then) confirmed.
> The kyng then gaue to (Faggan and Duuyen)
> The ysle of Analoon, and by cherter affirmed,
> That was called otherwyse Mewtryen (Inswetryan),
> Also (as) frely as Ioseph and his holy men
> Had it afore (then forth) for theyr dispence,
> Wherof (thei) wer glad, and thought it sufficience.

(Based on the Harleian manuscript, the alternative words in brackets are from the Seldon manuscript). Hardyng now has Eugeny for the name of the Pope concerned, when it should be Eleutherius, whom he already poetically called Eleuthery. Eugeny (compared with Eulenchie in *Le Brut*) probably refers to Pope Eugenius or Hyginus (139 to 142), about 35 years before these events. Again, it could be a simple blunder, but if Hardyng's source had King Lucius ascending the British throne in 147, and, as we have already seen, refers to him as the second christened British king, there may be a buried detail worth uncovering. King Coilus, Lucius' father, was styled as the first christened British king. If we are to understand 147 to date the end of Coilus' reign, then it is likely that his monarchy at least covered the times of Popes Eugenius\Hyginus (139-142), and the first five years of Pius I (142-157). The mistake may have come about by the source drawing some parallel between King Coilus' christening by Pope Eugenius and the baptism of his son, Lleufer, but of course this can only remain conjectural.

The Isle of Avalon is referred to as Analoon, likely an exercise of Hardyng's poetic licence. However, he tells us it 'was called otherwyse Mewtryen', and in another version Inswetryan, this seems further to point towards ancient British oral tradition and possibly lost records at Hardyng's disposal.

> (But when this kyng had reygned in cotenplacion,
> Fyftie and iiii yere in all prosperitee,
> He departed to God, desyryng his saluacion,
> In heaven to dwell with all felycytee,
> Where the aungelles synge incessauntely
> Glory, honoure, and euerlastyng prayse
> Be to the lambe of God, nowe and alwayes.)

Instead of this stanza the Harleian and Seldon manuscripts have:

> The yere of Crist an hundreth four score and sixtene
> The crucifixe whiche Ioseph made and sett
> at Caierlion, euermore to haue honoured bene,
> In Themmys come up, withoute any lette,
> Wher Poules qwarfe is now with flodes bett;
> Whiche Lucius, with Troynovaunte cite,
> With procession brought with solempnyte,
>
> And sett it up at Poules with reuerence,
> At the North dore by inspiracionn,
> Wher long it stode whiles Britons had regence;
> But whan the kynge had reigned, in contemplacion,
> Fifty and four yere in grete prosperacion,
> He passed to Gode whome he hade alwaye serued,
> To haue the blisse that he hade euer deserued.

The event of Lucius bringing the crucifix to London is a new detail and dated to the 'hundreth four score and sixtene' or 196. It may derive specifically from local London tradition, perhaps related in a source once held at old St Paul's. Several London traditions regarding King Lucius existed and these are further discussed in Chapter 6. The chronicle continues:

> At Cairglowe buried, after his dignitee,
> For whom all men made great lamentacion;
> Who bare before the (his) baptyme of propertee,
> His auncestres armes, and after with consolacion,
> He bare the armes, by (of) his baptizacion,
> Whiche Ioseph gaue vnto Aruigarus.
> As saith the Briton called Mewynus (As the Briton saith, that hight Mewynus).

(Taken from the Harleian manuscript, the words in brackets are the alternative wordings from the Seldon manuscript). Here Hardyng relates that Lucius was buried at Gloucester, citing his source: the Briton Mewynus. If this writer is to be identified as Medwy, known as Medwynus, and venerated as a Saint at Glastonbury, then Hardyng had access to and use of an important document originally written by one of the two great British Saints who travelled to and from Rome purportedly at the behest of King Lucius himself.

> For cause he had no (ne) heire to kepe the lande,
> Through all Britayn the barons gan discorde,
> Vnto the tyme that Romayns toke on hande
> To chese a prince by there stedfaste accorde,
> But iiii yere were gone or (then) they could accorde;
> In whiche tyme then Seuer the senatour,
> Hether came to be theyr gouernoure.

Hardyng states that because Lucius had no heir, the Britons were in 'discorde' for four years. Then Severus, the senator, came to Britain to take over the British government. From Lucius' death in 201, this brings Severus to Britain in *c.*205 when, in fact, he became emperor in 193 and arrived in Britannia to quell rebellion in 208. The related unrest following Lucius' reign is consistent with Wace's *Le Brut* but the not unreasonable time-span is completely at odds with Wace's 50 years.

In Chapter 71, Hardyng fancifully described the heraldic arms borne by Uther Pendragon as being the same as:

> … the armes also of good kyng Lucius, whiche after baptyme his armes alwaye ware the
> same armes that kyng Constantynus, at his batayll against Maxencius, so (he) bare alwaye,
> yt Saynt George armes we call, whiche Englyshemen nowe worshippe ouer all.

In Chapter 78, John Hardyng goes on to weave the legend of Arthur into the history of Lucius, further demonstrating a desire to align his style with legendary Romance after the manner of Wace and Layamon. He again draws a figure of Arthur's shield, of the same arms:

> … which armes Aruiragus, Lucyus, and Constantyne bare of silver, a crosse of goules.

One should not surmise that this was, in fact, Lucius' heraldic crest, for Hardyng is too apparently concerned with working the fashionable courtly and political sensibilities of the twelfth-century Arthurian legends into an historical context. What it does illustrate is that his choice of known historical figures such as King Arviragus, King Lucius and the Emperor Constantine the Great is intended to provide a less unbelievable historical context. The inclusion of King Lucius at least shows that Hardyng and his readers recognised him as a historical King. The arms described are of course those of St George, obviously symbolising these ancient kings as prefiguring the English crown.

The third stanza of Hardyng's Chapter 88, on St Augustine of Canterbury, reads:

Gregory hym made archebishop of Caunterbury,
Of all Englande hiest then primate,
And had the paule (palle) with hyest legacye
By Gregorye sent to hym and ordinate
Fro London then, thus was that tyme translate,
To Caunterbury, the sea (cee) metropolitan,
And London sette as for his suffrigan.

This relates how the *pallium* was sent to St Augustine from Pope St Gregory I, and that the metropolitan see was translated to Canterbury from London, where it had been abandoned or lost to the invading Angles.

Hardyng's work then locates King Lucius into the same courtly milieu as does Layamon, and although he may have been accessing some important ancient documents and local traditions, his work is largely informed by Geoffrey of Monmouth and styled according to fifteenth-century sensibilities.

JOHN CAPGRAVE (1393–1464; *CHRONICLE OF ENGLAND*)

John Capgrave included in his *Chronicle of England* the following short notices:

163 – Marcus Antonin the trewe, with Lucye, his brother Lucy, regned XIX yere.

In the XIX yere of Antoni was Eleutheri Pope, a Grek of nacion. He receyved a letter fro the kyng of Grete Britayn, cleped Lucius, that he schuld send summe prestes to this lond to baptize him, and his puple. And the Pope sent hedir Fugan and Damian, whech performed this dede. Summe Chronicles sey this was in yere of oure Lord 165.[22]

Capgrave has the correct number of years that Marcus Aurelius was emperor if starting, as implied, when he and Lucius Verus first shared rule of the Empire. However, this took place in 161 rather than 163. The nineteenth year of Marcus also represents his final year, 17 March 179 to 17 March 180. Within this year, Capgrave reports that Eleutherius received a letter from King Lucius. The discovery of this letter in the Guildhall archives of London in the sixteenth century is fully discussed below in Chapter 4 and Appendix A (see *4.1*).

It is also interesting to note that Capgrave's rendering of the names of the missionaries sent by the Pope, Fugan and Damian, is substantially different from Faganus and Duvianus provided by Geoffrey but, as with most of the other writings discussed of the twelfth to the fifteenth century, some of these authors and works follow Geoffrey almost verbatim, although there are other details and influences that could be much older than even Bede's work. Our problem is that several of the sources surmised, not least a supposed work of Gildas, are no longer extant. Generally, as time progressed, attempts were made to place an accurate date upon the events associated with King Lucius. There was considerable variety in the dates provided with barely a consensus, but they all do fall within the late second century, and therefore accord roughly with Bede and ultimately the *Liber Pontificalis*.

We have also seen how the simple note made by Bede in 725 and 731 became much embroidered, embellished and coloured by contemporary styles of legendary Romance. In many respects this ensured the longevity of the story by rehearsing it for popular culture, but it also decreased its historical credibility. The next chapter follows how Lucius was suddenly taken boldly out of the legendary fabric he had been progressively woven into, and used as a pawn of important political and religious issues in the Tudor and Elizabethan Ages. He had a new importance, but his ever more devalued historical status as mythical legend, from a compounding of deeds attached to him by the fashions of courtly Romance in the twelfth century, would continue to hamper him.

CHAPTER 4

CONTINUED DISPUTATION

The vital air, the sighs which first I breath'd, were all informed,
were all inspired by Lucius[1]

A debate over the role of King Lucius in British history, particularly regarding ecclesiastical history in general, reached a peak during the Tudor and Elizabethan era. He was argued about, dissected, contested and championed by opposing religious and political factions. Disputed claims had begun as early as the twelfth century between rival monastic foundations in Britain. Yet in the sixteenth century, with the move toward Protestantism, elements of the ancient story were adduced by those wanting to maintain established orthodoxy, but also by their opponents who backed reforms and a final split with Rome. The Christian humanism of sixteenth-century Britain became radically polarised over national concepts of origin. An attempt to crystallise revered elements woven more or less into myth by Geoffrey, or other efforts to demystify the legendary past, became – and has largely remained – a controversy between belief and scepticism. This tension was recently best summed up by Ferguson:

> Where little or no hard evidence can be found either to support or reject a legend, it becomes necessary to make the most of hypothesis based on reasoned conjecture.[2]

The problem with a view of necessity for conjecture, unaided by archaeology, is who should arbitrate, or decide, what is sufficient to attain 'the most' of hypothesis while being reasonable? With regards to King Lucius in this chapter, we shall see what results when 'hypothesis based on reasoned conjecture' is unsupported by the evidence that archaeology and philological scholarship would be able to provide later in the twentieth century.

As can be seen from the literary works listed in Appendix C, at least 90 between 1492 and 1904 made reference to King Lucius. Most of them will not be explored in this chapter, we will rather consider the broader context in which they appeared. The century spanning the 1530s to the 1630s saw a notable increase of citations of the ancient king, to borrow authority and the weight of tradition. After the mid eighteenth century there appear more critical concerns over Lucius' historical reality, although even these were swept up in renewed polemics between 'Romish' and National conceptions of Church. However, since Harnack's 1904 article no serious amount of ink has been spent on Lucius, with one exception, Felicity Heal's 2005 article entitled *What can King Lucius do for you? The Reformation and the Early British Church.*[3] This is an incisive paper on the many ways the story of King Lucius became embroiled in the religious-political wrangling of the Protestant Reformation and Catholic counter-Reformation. Heal's thesis is that King Lucius *as a story* (i.e. without discussing its probative content) can be revisited in the context of how identity was contextually constructed:

> Origin myths and archaeology have long since parted company ... but engagement with foundation myths has not wholly vanished, and indeed has experienced something of a revival in recent years as the study of ethnicity and nationhood has burgeoned. Moreover, the current intellectual interest in representation and the construction of identity through narrative might indicate that historians could once again benefit from visiting the territory of ... King Lucius. It is not the content of the stories of origin, rather their function and ability to express beliefs in very different environments that suggests the value of such a re-reading.[4]

Our focus is in fact on both the content as well as the expressive function of Lucius' story and how it was transmitted through the shifting issues of successive centuries. However it is also important to understand, as Heal aims to show, how the contemporary conflicts over authority, and not merely the pursuit of origins *per se*, 'makes the Lucius legend so intriguing'.[5] King Lucius

> ... had a plasticity that could be moulded to different ideologies. He could be explained, and explained away, from a variety of perspectives. His tale obviously aided the papal cause because of his appeal to Rome and the consequent assumption that mission triumphed in the name of the pope. At the same time the king's conversion demonstrated both the precocity of British Christianity and its royal imprimatur. This, and the story of the early beginnings of episcopacy had visible charms for establishment Protestantism. Lucius's abiding importance therefore lies precisely in his ability to represent and reproduce discourses of difference so successfully.[6]

The specific context of King Lucius' place in Tudor debate revolves around Henrician legal research, which combed ancient documents in order to provide a precedent for the anticipated split from Rome. What they uncovered was so important it would imprint an indelible mark on the subsequent concepts of the monarchy in Britain: a letter from Pope Eleutherius to Lucius! This epistle might with some confidence be attributed, at least in penmanship, to thirteenth-century political intrigue, but discovered when it was, it would ensure for some time Lucius' role in defining sacrosanct responsibilities of British monarchy: bolstering Henry VIII's title, 'Defender of the Faith'.

THE EPISTLE FROM POPE ELEUTHERIUS TO KING LUCIUS

Henry VIII's researchers made what would seem an auspicious discovery in the archives of London's Guildhall – a letter purported to be from Pope Eleutherius to King Lucius. The history of this document is fascinating. It is included in the earliest London custumal, the *Liber Custumarum*, within the section concerned with the duties of kingship, the *Leges Edwardi bonus Regis* (the Laws of Edward the Confessor) bound together in the volume now known as *Cotton Claudius DII*. In 1913, Liebermann established a history for this letter dating to the reign of John (*c.*1166-1216).[7] As such it may well have been a product of the same political crisis that produced the *Magna Carta* in 1215.

In 1205 King John (1199-1216) came into conflict with Pope Innocent III (1198-1216) over the candidacy for the next Archbishop of Canterbury, leading to the Interdict of 1208 and deposition in 1211 of John's candidate. In 1209 John was excommunicated, but agreed to hold the kingdom as a fief of the papacy. As the Pope's vassal, John was obliged to accept the papal nominee, Stephen Langton (Archbishop 1207-1228), although John would not officially recognise Langton

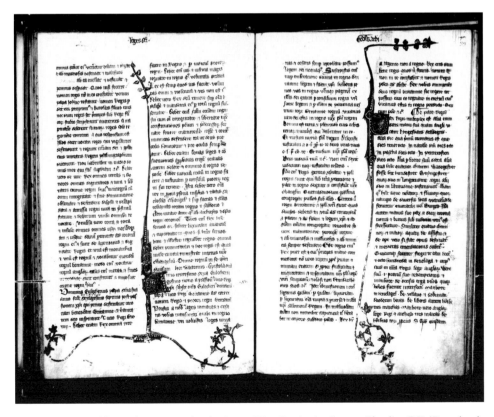

4.1 The purported letter from Pope Eleutherius to King Lucius in Cotton Claudius DII (*Reproduced by permission of the British Library*)

4.2 Portrait of King John (*From Cassell's History of England, 1902*)

until 1213. The following year Archbishop Langton urged John's confirmation of Henry I's *Charter of Liberties* (the *Coronation Charter*), a proclamation of 1100 binding the king to obligations toward church officials and nobles. By confirming this important charter in 1214, Langton substantially armed the Barons of England to draft the *Magna Carta* and oblige John to sign it at Runnymede on June 15, 1215. Ironically, in that same year Langton was suspended by the Pope for not enforcing the papal censure which had made John only a vassal.

If there is an apt period to ascribe for the theory that a letter of Eleutherius was transcribed (or, indeed devised) it could well have been in 1214/15 at the instigation of the Lord Mayor of London, William Hardel, for his signature appears on the *Magna Carta* and this could explain how a copy of the purported epistle ended up in London's Guildhall.

The letter's rediscovery in the early sixteenth century prompted its immediate use. The first comprehensive translation appeared in James Pilkington's 1568 *Confutation of an Addition* and was subsequently used by John Foxe in his 1570 edition of *Acts and Monuments.*[8] In 1568 William Lambarde printed an abridged version of the Latin transcription in his compilation of the Saxon laws, *APXAIONOMIA, sive de priscus anglorum legibus libri.*[9] In 1661 Fuller reproduced it with the scriptural quotations italicised, and in 2005 Heal reprinted the 1601 translation by Francis Godwin. In the present work (*4.1*) is the first image of the document ever to be published and several observations about it can be made (see Appendix A for a full treatment).

In the *Cotton Claudius* epistle from the Guildhall of London, two identical copies of the letter appear strikingly adjacent to one another, something not mentioned by any of the writers referencing it. In both letters and also in the chapter headings at the beginning of the section, the Pope's name is consistently written 'Euletheri' rather than the more accurate 'Eleutheri'. This is an odd and unique mistake, perhaps suggesting the source letter was copied incorrectly and the mistake was repeated. The reason for exact, immediately adjacent copies is a question beyond the scope of this work, but it is relevant that Raphael Holinshed indicated several copies of the letter extant in his day (1586), some partially destroyed and some partially intact.

The letters Holinshed consulted were dated to the consulships of Commodus and Vespronius, an ancient style of dating, whereas the letter(s) in *Cotton Claudius DII* (apparently the only instances now extant) say nothing of consulships. They simply begin with:

Dominus Euletherius papa … Anno centesimo sexagesimo nono a passionem xpi …

(See Appendix A for translation). The date is given as AD 169, having no accurate relation to any of the consulships debated in the sixteenth century. The fact of

Table 4.1: Publication history of the Epistle from Pope Eleutherius to King Lucius

Date	Author and Title
*c.*1216	Unknown author; during the reign of King John (*c.*1166-1216)
1563	James Pilkington (1520-1576); *Confutation of an Addition*
1565	John Stow (1525-1605); *A Summarie of Englyshe Chronicles*
1568	William Lambarde (1536-1601); *ΑΡΧΑΙΟΝΟΜΙΑ*
1570	John Foxe (1516-1587); *Acts and Monuments*
1586	Raphael Holinshed (?-*c.*1580); *Chronicle*
1586, 1607	William Camden (1551-1623); *Britannia*
1601	Francis Godwin (1562-1633); *A Catalogue of the Bishops of England*
1618	John Speed (1552-1629); *History of Britain*
1655, 1662	Thomas Fuller (1608-1661); *The Church History of Britain*

sixteenth-century debate over which consular year should date a letter that plainly states the year speaks negatively of the originality of the Cottonian letters in hand. A second-century epistle from Rome would have been dated according to the consular year. The *Anno Domine* method of dating was devised by Dionysius Exiguus (*c.*470-*c.*544) in 525 to calculate Easter and only received wider usage between the eighth and eleventh centuries. The letter(s) in *Cotton Claudius DII* uses the form 'Anno … passionem Christi'. Yet were this is a medieval transcript of an older manuscript employing the ancient method of dating, the consuls for AD 169 were Q. Pompeius Senecio Roscius Murena Coelius and P. Coelius Apollinaris. Clearly then, the letter extant in the British Library is not one of the versions discussed by Holinshed and his contemporaries. The two copies in *Claudius DII* are intact, not in accord with Holinshed's notice of differing states of dilapidation, nor indeed Usher's having five different manuscripts.[10] Other examples of the purported letter must have existed and each may have begun with the consular year of the communication, but it seems no two of these independently agreed.

William Camden, for instance, while not citing the full letter in his 1607 edition of *Britannia* does state that it was 'dated in the second consulship of Aurelius Commodus and Vespronius'.[11] Vespronius is most likely Lucius Vespronius Candidus Sallustius Sabinianus who was consul in *c.*174-176, before he was the consular legate for the province of Dacia in *c.*182.[12] Lucius Aurelius Commodus Antoninus (Lucius Aelius Commodus Augustus) was emperor from 180 to 192 and his first consulship began on January 1 of 177 with his brother-in-law M. Peducaeus Plautius Quintillus.[13] His second consulship was held in 179 with Martius Verus[14] and not Vespronius. Therefore, Camden's information is rather muddled and although the general time-period of *c.*174 to 179 is consistent with several other sources, not all agree on the names of the consuls for the year when the epistle was supposedly composed or sent to Britannia.

As noted in Chapter 3, John Leland claimed he had seen a version of the letter in what he identified as the *Annals of Rochester*,[15] which apparently dated it:

> … in the consulship of Severus and Herennianus, and in the eleventh year of the emperor Marcus Aurelius.

These consular names most probably represent Titus Statilius Severus and Lucius Alphidius (Alfidius) Herennianus (Gerennianus), who held that post in AD 171-172.[16] The eleventh year of Marcus Aurelius refers to the year 172, counting forward from his accession, with Lucius Verus, to the throne in 161. As mentioned in Chapter 3, the *Annals of Rochester* to which Jeremy Collier also later referred was most probably the *Textus Roffensis* compiled by Ernulf. Yet the extant versions of this ancient collection do not include this epistle to Lucius, so Leland and perhaps Collier may both have been consulting a version of the *Textus* that no longer survives. Since the consuls Leland cites from his *Annals of Rochester* are not mentioned in the *Liber Pontificalis* in relation to Lucius, it is possible one of the versions of the letter extant in Britain was of considerable age and our only witnesses to it are the comments made in the sixteenth and seventeenth centuries.

It is intriguing that the epistle lay dormant and undiscovered for so long, from probably as early as the thirteenth century to its discovery in the Guildhall archives of London in the period of the Tudors, apparently remaining forgotten and unnoticed for three centuries.

One highly significant phrase found for the first time in this letter refers to a king in Britain as 'the vicar of God in your kingdom' ('Vicarius vero Dei estis in regno') and David's Psalm 24[17] (Greek numbering 23:1) is used for scriptural support:

> The Lord's is the earth, and the fullness of the world and all that dwell in it.

This phrase and the associated concept that a monarch should be godly, as he represents God within the kingdom, has had a long and deep tradition in Britain. The implied responsibility of the sovereign to the people is certainly a tone that rings true to thirteenth-century troubles with King John and this might afford a theoretical reason for such a letter, if it existed, being brought to his attention, possibly all the way from Rome. As for Lucius, he might well have wondered how newfound religious principles should be expressed in his rule. A letter such as this from Eleutherius would have been a rather heartening answer concerning the personal example a king can give to his realm, which is one of peace; a reply that seems quite pertinent to a second-century king whose territory was open to threat by Roman political manoeuvres, let alone military encroachments should the Christians under his rule prove troublesome and uncooperative with the secular administration.

4.3 Henry VIII silver half groat, second coinage (1526-44) minted in Canterbury

Yet in fact the story of King Lucius was used to support Henry VIII's claims of 'spiritual supremacy and provincial self-determination'[18] and in an early draft of the 1533 *Statute of Restraint of Appeals*, reference was made to kings as 'called and reputed vicars of god with the same [realm]'.[19] This version and the final published statute, were written by Thomas Cromwell, the Chief Minister to Henry VIII from 1532 to 1540, but the finished draft does not include this line, rather a much more general statement:

> Where by divers sundry old authentic histories and chronicles, it is manifestly declared and expressed that this realm of England is an Empire …[20]

Heal has suggested the reason for its omission may be due to the idea resting on one papal letter. At any rate, a consequence of this omission was movement of the jurisdictional debate onto other ground, overlooking the value of Eleutherius' letter.[21] Henry had wished to annul his marriage to Catherine of Aragon and wed Anne Boleyn, sending his secretary, William Knight, to Rome to petition Pope Clement VII, but the pontiff withheld consent. In 1530, a friend of the Boleyn family, Thomas Cranmer, three years before he was unexpectedly promoted to the position of Archbishop of Canterbury (1533-1556), compiled together with Edward Foxe (c.1496-1538) the unpublished *Collectanea Satis Copiosa* known also as the *Second King's Book*.[22] This collection of historical documents would provide evidence for royal supremacy, giving examples of historic kings who had no superior on earth, thus providing precedence for Henry's decision to divorce without papal consent. The *Collectanea* included Old Testament quotations and excerpts from the works of Ivo of Chartres (c.1040-1115), Hugh of St Victor (c.1078-1141),[23] Bede, William of Malmesbury, Geoffrey of Monmouth and Matthew Paris, but it was the letter of Eleutherius to Lucius that was favoured. Cranmer and Edward Foxe quoted it 'three times in full',[24] the second quotation entered under the section entitled *Institutio officium et potestas Regum Anglie*. Although the *Collectanea* was not published, further use of the letter in the original draft of the statute by Cromwell does indicate a consensus among Henry's officials that it might usefully be construed to show 'that kings of Britain, and by extension of England, had possessed general authority over the Church, which they had then lent in specific circumstances to clergy and papacy'.[25] However, this particular construction on King Lucius ultimately could not work, as Cromwell must have recognised, for the instruction had come from the Bishop of Rome.

During this same period, apart from the buzz of partisan argument and interpretation of the nature of Lucius' kingship, the problem of reliably dating him and his contact with Pope Eleutherius reached a new pitch. Caesar Baronius (1538-1607), head of the Vatican Library, raised uncertainties on how these events had been dated in the past. The Archbishop of Armagh in Ireland, James Usher/Ussher (1581-1656), in his *Ecclesiastical Antiquities of Britain* (1639) collated some of the sources we have been considering. In 1685 Edward Stillingfleet (1635-1699) completed *Origines*

Britannicae (*The Antiquities of the British Churches*) expanding upon Usher's work. Commenting on traditions and discrepancies in the dates and deeds of Lucius, he railed against the 'British tradition', writing:

> ... although in the most ancient times here was Monarchical Government, yet it was not extended over all Britain, as the Monkish Tradition pretends concerning King Lucius, and I know not how many Predecessours of his, even from the coming of Brutus to his days. But neither our Religion, nor our Government need such Fictions to support them.[26]

Regarding the letter itself he opined:

> ... the original tradition of the British Church; which Geffrey of Monmouth hath corrupted with his Flamines and Archiflamins; and others afterwards made an Epistle for Eleutherius to King Lucius, but could not avoid such Marks in the way of Writing as evidently discover the Imposture.

In view of the letter(s) in *Cotton Claudius DII*, it is not clear what 'Marks' Stillingfleet was referring to, though of course the 'Anno ... passionem Christi' dating form and the style of handwriting is certainly not second century and the misspelling of Eleutherius' name may have fuelled his charge of 'Imposture'. Be that as it may, after Stillingfleet the epistle from Pope Eleutherius to King Lucius quickly fell out of interest as a historical document. There had been so much derision and misuse of the letter that it is hardly surprising that historians have neglected it. Other than Heal's recent publication of Francis Godwin's 1601 translation, it remained unnoticed. This is unfortunate in light of the fact that among the several versions mentioned by Holinshed one may have been of considerable age, possibly even to within the Roman period. Although the Tudor and subsequent use of this correspondence, and the invoking of King Lucius in general, was contentious if not biased and polemical, it demonstrates how vital the events surrounding this ancient king could be to a construction of another king's identity.

After Henry VIII, the purported letter of Eleutherius, and especially its statement that the king was God's vicar on earth, continued to have some currency. In 1598 James VI of Scotland (subsequently James I of England) published *The Trew Law of Free Monarchies*, setting out the doctrine of the Divine Right of Kings in England and Scotland. Also in 1598 James completed his *Basilikon Doron* (Royal Gift),[27] published in 1599. It was intended as a guide for his son Henry Frederick, Prince of Wales on succession to the throne, but Henry died in 1612 and the Gift went to Charles (later King Charles I, 1625-1649). Writing in Scottish, James warned equally of Puritans and Papists and further expounded the Divine Right as a royal prerogative in a work that certainly influenced Shakespeare's *Macbeth*. Importantly *The Trew Law* and the *Basilikon* are ultimately related to a now-ancient philosophy that the monarch is God's vicegerent upon earth, the point made at a superficial level by the purported letter from Eleutherius. James was, apparently, taking its known statement out of the context of papal advice to a British king and reworking the Divine Right for his own policy of autocratic rule.

A King James scriptural basis for the Divine Right of Kings is *Romans* 13:1-2:

> Let every soul be subject unto the higher powers. For there is no power but from God: the powers that exist are ordained of Him.

However, as detailed in Appendix A, this is not the biblical support adduced in the purported letter, but rather Psalm 24:1.[28]

To this day the monarch of Britain is anointed with sacred oils, as a remembrance of Godly responsibilities so succinctly stated in the Letter of Eleutherius.

RAPHAEL HOLINSHED (*CHRONICLE* COMPLETED 1586)

Another notable work from this period worth discussing is the *Chronicle* of Raphael Holinshed, completed in 1586. His work was influential and is perhaps best known as the source for several of Shakespeare's plays including *Cymbeline* and *King Lear*. In dealing with the subject of King Lucius, Holinshed utilised several important sources. From the *Chronicles of Burton* he quoted:

> Under the yeare of Grace 141 and time of Hadrian the emperor that nine scholars or clerkes of Grantha or Granta [Cambridge] were baptised in Britaine, and became preachers of the gospell there.

When dealing with London traditions of Lucius (see Chapter 6 for the particular case of St Peter-upon-Cornhill) Holinshed cited William of Malmesbury:

> ... Westminster to be the place where Lucius builded his church upon the ruines of that Flamine 264 yeeres before the comming of the Saxons, and 411 before the arrivall of Augustine.

He referred the interested reader to:

> Read also his appendix in Book 4 Pontif where he noteth the time of the Saxons, in the 449 of Grace, and of Augustine in the 596 of Christ ... [185 AD]

And, as mentioned above, he included notice of:

> ... letters to Lucius and his Nobilitie, dated in the consulships of Commodus and Vespronius.

Among his multitude of other sources Holinshed also made mention of Haermannus Schedelius, Prince Alexander Neccham (Alexander Neckam 1157-1217), Jean Bouchet (1476-c.1558), and the *Annales of Aquitaine*. Concerning the chronological sequence of events reported in the *Chronicle* it is possible to reconstruct Holinshed's scheme for the main events in Lucius' life:

177: Lucius sent Eluanus Aualonius and Medguinus Belga of Belga to Rome.

178: Eleutherus sent Faganus and Dinaw/Dinauus to Lucius.

c.181 [The third year of receiving the gospel]: Lucius sent messengers to Eleutherus requiring some briefe epitome of the order of discipline then used in the church.

post-c.181: Eleutherus sends letters to Lucius and his Nobilitie, dated in the consulships of Commodus and Vespronius.

185: [using William of Malmesbury] Lucius builds a church in London at Westminster, although other historiographers think it was at St Peter Cornhill.[29]

The above sequence of dates is consistent with a few of the more important earlier sources. Yet while focusing on the British tradition, Holinshed goes so far as to cite Schedelius' *Nuremburg Chronicle*, introducing to an English readership another tradition of King Lucius. This Raetian tradition of Luzius von Chur, and the connection between Britain and Switzerland is the focus of Chapter 6.

Before we move on to the Raetian tradition, it is worth noticing how finally, in the seventeenth and early eighteenth century, perhaps due to the high proportion of writings about the ancient king, a piece of dramatic art was produced with him as the subject.

John Ross, a barrister of the Inner Temple published a collection of short poems (*Britannica, sive de Regibus Veteris Britanniae*) in 1607 based upon each of the British kings mentioned by Geoffrey of Monmouth. His rendering of King Lucius:

Sic valet exemplum Regis cum plebe, quod audit
Vel videt, in sensum pronior usque trahit.
Promptius intuitu sequimur, quam mente receptum:
Ista per Idaeas, ille per acta probat.

So strong is the king's example for the people, they are always more ready to accept what he sees and hears. We always more readily follow what has been received by observation than by reason: the latter is manifested through ideas, the former through deeds.[30]

As, arguably, seeing is indeed believing, with realities of Lucius drifting rapidly out of sight by this point, Lucius had truly entered mythology. Yet the fruits of the embroidery begun by Geoffrey of Monmouth would come to their most grotesque expression a century after Ross' poem, when Mary de la Rivière Manley's (c.1667/1672-1724) farcical play *Lucius, the First Christian King of Britain* premiered on

11 May 1717 at Drury Lane. It was a limited success for Manley, as she received 600 guineas upon its delivery, and three years later the play was once more performed,[31] but in terms of popular success it was a flop.

Manley's voice before this effort had been as a highly political commentary disguised in romantic prose. She had, for example, previously lambasted members of the Whig party in her 1709 play *The New Atlantis* and she had endured a period in prison because of it. However, *Lucius* the play does not offer the same kind of commentary of contemporary issues, although it was clothed in eighteenth-century anachronisms based on the warped reading of history by Sir Richard Baker (1568-1645), Aylett Sammes (*c.*1636-*c.*1679) and James Tyrrell (1642-1718).[32] In the context of the present work there is nothing to recommend Manley's *Lucius*, for Vortigern is made his stepfather and Rosalinda of Albany and Avalon his lover, though one silver thread can be retrieved, placed at the heading of this chapter.

What is significant is that Manley's treatment of Lucius shows how he was thought amenable, like King Leir (Lear),[33] to the oblivion of fiction, albeit that Manley's is the only English piece of literary art based on the king. Manley's cloying script aside, perhaps the parody's unpopularity is due to Lucius retaining coinage through the eighteenth century, for his was a name generally known and he had lately been much spoken of. However, with the rhetorical and polemical problems over King Lucius we have outlined, the days of belief in the content of his story were definitely drawing to an end. So we approach an understanding of intolerant nineteenth-century academic attitudes and invective assessment of Lucius, for this was the context within which Harnack eventually wrote his article of 1904.

ONE SIDE OF TWO COINS

In the same year that Holinshed's *Chronicle* appeared (1586), the College of Antiquaries was founded and debate was encouraged until James I forbade it in 1614. Scholars interested in archaeology continued some discourse at the Royal Society and then on 5 December 1707 within the smoky rooms of the Bear Tavern in The Strand, the inaugural meeting of the Society of Antiquaries was held. A little over a century later a paper was read before the Society on 21 March and 11 April, 1850 by the historian Henry Hallam (1777-1859) entitled: *Observations on the Story of Lucius, the first Christian King of Britain.*[34]

Hallam praised the scholarship of Usher, Stillingfleet and Jeremy Collier, but questioned how these men of learning could have agreed to Lucius' conversion and 'unite in receiving this as an authentic fact'.[35] There had been those, he argued, who had not been convinced, including Rev. Thomas Dunham Whitaker (1759-1821) and Robert Henry (1718-1790)[36] but again, certain contemporaries were inclined to believe the story. In this category Hallam mentioned John Lingard (1771-1851), a Roman Catholic priest and author of *The History of England, From the First Invasion by the Romans to the Accession of Henry VIII*, published in 1819. Hallam continued:

I confess myself unable to attain the slightest degree of belief as to the entire story, taking it as recounted in the usual authorities. The Society will permit me to lay before them the reasons which have led me, first to doubt, and finally to reject, the conversion of Lucius.[37]

Making a comparison of the Latin of Bede's *History* and *Chronica*, he added:

The great difficulty that occurs in the passages from Bede which we have just extracted is, that more than half a century after the island, as far as the Firth of Forth, if not beyond, had been reduced into a Roman province, we find Lucius roundly called Britanniarum rex; the very style of our gracious Sovereign at this day.[38]

This remark of Hallam highlights the general problem that nineteenth-century academics had with understanding Roman Britain, as they projected their own contemporary context of the British Empire anachronistically back onto the Roman Empire. This attitude is evident from Hallam's statement, which, more accurately could have been rendered *our gracious Sovereign at this day is roundly called Britanniarum rex; the very style used by Bede in describing Lucius*, at least putting the horse before the cart. In an attempt to identify which British tribe Lucius may have ruled, the antiquaries of the prior century had argued for the *Regni* (the *Regnenses* of Chichester, West Sussex), with Lucius the successor of 'Cogidunus', but in support for such a theory Hallam found 'not the smallest particle of testimony'.[39] His convincing scepticism is shown in questioning whether a 'native prince' could reign autonomously at the heart of a Roman province and, if so, why Gildas hadn't recorded in his 'briefest history' this immensely important ruler? As we have seen, mistaking Gildas' sermon as a brief a history caused significant problems of this sort.

After praising Usher in his introduction as one writer 'on our ecclesiastical antiquities who [has] most claim to deference of learning',[40] Hallam continued:

The accumulation of obscure and modern testimony which we find in Usher's long disquisition on the tale of Lucius is a curious specimen of omnivorous and misplaced erudition. A single grain of critical good sense is worth all this chaos of chaff, so frequent in the learned men of the sixteenth and first part of the seventeenth centuries.[41]

Finally Hallam arrived at the subject of the two coins. In 1618 John Speed, in his *History of Britain*, had included an engraving of a coin above what Hallam called 'a manifestly spurious letter from the Pope Eleutherus to Lucius'.[42] The coin had apparently been in the possession of Sir Robert Bruce Cotton (1570/1-1631) and this was known both to Usher in 1639 and Stillingfleet in 1685 as well as a second example. Stillingfleet stressed that each coin bore 'the image of a king with a cross, and the letters LUC, as far as they could be discovered'.[43] One of these coins was then added to Edmund Gibson's 1695 edition of William Camden's *Britannia*.

William Henry Anderdon (1816-1889) even noted a third coin of Lucius, with supposedly his full name and an emblematic star.

Although these coins were subsequently identified as Iron Age Gaulish issues, it is important that Hallam and other nineteenth-century critics assessing the evidence in support of a King Lucius showed openness to material artefacts and archaeological evidence such as numismatics and place-names, rather than the literary evidence alone.[44] Yet against this nascent trend, the scepticism against Lucius of Britain was mounting, from such respected persons as Louis Marie Olivier Duchesne (1843-1922) and Christian Matthias Theodor Mommsen (1817-1903).[45] Duchesne concluded that the story was a fifth-century invention, while Mommsen attempted to demonstrate that it had originated in Rome and had nothing to do with Britain. In the wake of these two scholastic giants, Francis J. Haverfield (1860-1919) confidently stated in 1896 that 'the story is certainly untrue: it is wholly irreconcilable with general history and is rejected by historians of all creeds and schools', though conceded that its history was nonetheless 'worth sketching'.[46]

Of course, when Hallam was giving his paper to the Royal Society (the mid nineteenth century) it was still far too early in the development and practice of archaeology to provide much in the way of examples of fourth-century Christianity in Britain, let alone second-century examples. Yet regrettably, after Haverfield's 1896 opinion, and certainly Harnack's conclusions in 1904 as discussed in Chapter 1, archaeologists stopped looking for Lucius altogether and instead assigned early evidence of Christianity in Britannia to the period of the fourth century and the Council of Arles in AD 314.

Archaeology is now a mature discipline, with over 150 years of methodological and theoretical development and redoubtable discoveries. It is well worth pausing to reflect on how recent many of our famous discoveries are: excavations at Silchester (Calleva Atrebatum) between 1890 and 1909, Lullingstone Villa (1939), Fishbourne Palace (1960), the mosaics at Hinton St Mary (1963), the Londiniensium inscription (2005) and a multitude of others including continuous research in such Roman cities as York (Eboracum), Canterbury (Durovernum Cantiacorum) and Colchester (Camulodunum).

In light of recent discoveries, and having put Harnack's conclusions into serious question, we can move on to explore whether, despite the lack of effort to find them, there are at present any material traces of Lucius.

CHAPTER 5

WHAT ARE WE LEFT WITH? THE ARCHAEOLOGICAL EVIDENCE OF KING LUCIUS OF BRITAIN

Lucius in tenebris prius idola qui coluisti,
Es merito celebris ex quo baptisma subsisti
Coelestis medici merito quam meruisti
Omine felici lotus baptismati Christi[1]

Central to the story of King Lucius is the concept of Christianity becoming formally practised in Britannia by the late second century. Jumping ahead a century, we know that the year AD 314 has been a pivotal benchmark in all discussions of early Christianity in Britain, when it was recorded that three British bishops attended the Council of Arles in southern Gaul, called by the Emperor Constantine to address the Donatist heresy and settle the date of Easter. From the several versions of the *acta* of this council we have the names of the three bishops and two of their companions (a presbyter, Sacerdos, and a deacon, Arminius). The bishops were: Eborius de civitate Eboracensi, Restitutus de civitate Londinensi and Adelfius de civitas Londiniensium/colonia Londiniensium.

In 1896 Haverfield suggested the last entry was a mistake for Lindensium (Lincoln)[2] but it is interesting that an inscription discovered in 2002 at the intersection of Tabard Street and Long Lane in Southwark, London, and associated with late second-century material refers to the people of this city as 'Londiniensium'.[3] As Restitutus was also Bishop of Londinensi(um) the question must remain as to the relative locations of these two bishops' parishes (*colour plate 3*).

The name Restitutus (*restituo*) literally means 'restore, rebuild, and renew',[4] a name one might associate with the contemporary progress of Christianity in Britain. By all accounts, the Christian religion must have been present for some time prior to AD 314 for it to have been organised to the extent of having several (three at the least) bishoprics. Quite plausibly, by the early fourth century soon after persecutions under Diocletian, the Church in this country was enjoying renewal and restoration.

This historic evidence of British clergy at Arles has strongly influenced the study of Romano-British Christianity and although the religious presence must have been significant at least a generation prior to 314, the archaeological evidence is as yet extremely spare.[5] There may be an explanation, albeit an uncomfortable one, for this apparent invisibility; archaeological interpretations of Romano-British Christianity have long been unduly influenced by this historic date. A reassessment of the evidence and abundant material is much needed. We have seen in Chapter 4 how Henry Hallam and his contemporaries were beginning to consider archaeological evidence at the birth of this discipline, but this interest was overwhelmed by internecine polemics. As a contribution to recent research into Romano-British Christianity[6] I will focus on the site of St Peter-upon-Cornhill in London as evidence of the continuity and/or reuse of a high-status Roman building for Christian worship, the forum-basilica of Londinium.

ST PETER–UPON–CORNHILL

Pancakes and fritters
Old shoes and slippers
Say the bells of St Peter's[7]

In 1661 Thomas Fuller included in his *Church History of Britain* a list of those churches thought to have been founded by Lucius: in AD 179, St Peter-upon-Cornhill in London; the chief Cathedral church in Gloucester; in AD 180 a church at Winchester; a church and college of Christian philosophers at Bangor; in AD 187, the church dedicated to Mary in Glassenbury (Glastonbury), 'repaired and raised out of the ruins by Faganus and Duvianus, where they lived with 12 associates; a chapel in honour of Christ in Dover Castle; and St Martin in Canterbury, before new named to that saint'.[8] In 1685 Stillingfleet highlighted what he believed to be the fraudulent claims that had corrupted the story of King Lucius, from some chroniclers:

> For some of them carry Faganus and Diruvianus (as some call him) to Glassenbury; others make him Consecrate the Church at Winchester, to which they say King Lucius had a particular kindness, and gave all the Lands and Privileges which the Flamins had, to the Bishop and Monks. (A gift that would never make them the richer or the safer.) Others make King Lucius to found St. Peter's Church at Westminster, the Church in Dover Castle, St. Martin's by Canterbury, St. Peter's in Cornhill, where the Metropolitan Church, they say, was placed by him, and Theanus made the first Bishop, who was succeeded by Eluanus, who went on the Embassey to Eleutherius; and, besides these, they make him to found and endow so many Churches, with such unlikely circumstances, as hath made others question, whether there was ever such a

5.1 Engraving of St Peter-upon-Cornhill by Charles John Mayle Whichelo (1784-1865) (*Reproduced by kind permission of the Guildhall Library, London*)

Person in the World as King Lucius: That being the common effect of saying much more than is true, to make what is really true more doubtfull and suspicious.[9]

In 1979 Alan Smith[10] counted 11 examples of 'Lucian' dedications within England and these are listed below in Table 5.1. In addition to these might be added four churches in Gwent dedicated to the memory of the bishops associated with Lucius.[11]

Considering the example of St Mary in Castro, John Lyon included in his 1781 *History of Dover Castle* the following short statement:

Our monkish chronicles and several of our old historians after them have ascribed the building of this church and St. Martin's in the city of Canterbury … to Lucius whom they suppose to have been a provincial king in Britain, by the courtesy of the Romans. He probably reigned in Kent between the years of Christ one hundred and seventy seven and one hundred and thirty one.[12]

From what authority Lyon concluded Lucius ruled in Kent is a mystery and the dates he ascribed to Lucius' reign (177-131) make no sense, not least because they go backwards in time! In 1797 William Darrell reiterated the idea that Lucius founded

Table 5.1: Churches and locations purported to be founded by King Lucius

1	St Peter-upon-Cornhill, London (AD 179)
2	St Paul's Cathedral, London
3	Westminster Abbey, London
4	St Mary, Glastonbury (AD 187)
5	Winchester (AD 180)
6	Cambridge (AD 141)
7	St Martin's, Canterbury
8	Bangor
9	Llandaff
10	St Mary in Castro, Dover (AD 161)
11	St Mary de Lode, Gloucester

this ancient church and provided the date AD 161. Again, in an already complex variety of possible dates for Lucius, the late eighteenth century witnessed several comparable cases of the practice of plucking a second-century date out of the ether and applying it to Lucius. The cause of general confusion and wariness over the king is perhaps best exemplified in Darrell's closing invention:

> This pious prince … having no issue, appointed at his death … the Roman Emperor Severus his successor[13]

which gives us little wonder why by the nineteenth-century the veracity of this ancient king came to be questioned, rather to excess.

In the twentieth century, Smith expected as proof of Lucius that his stories should be conspicuous at such places as Colchester and Lincoln, but because they are not, he considered the king's absence a proof of his non-existence. Yet, as is well known, the absence of proof is no proof of absence. It is curious to expect popular memories of a king so ancient departed. Indeed any consistent memories, in a surviving oral tradition, would be especially valuable precisely because they are *un*expected. At any rate, Smith included York in this category but omitted the presence in the Minster of an early fifteenth-century stained glass representation of Lucius (cover of this book and *colour plate 2*) and Eleutherius.

Among the sites listed in Table 5.1, the most developed in evidence for the presence of Christianity in Britain prior to 314, with a direct connection to King Lucius, is the London church of St Peter-upon-Cornhill, situated on the corner of

Cornhill and Gracechurch Street. The original structure was destroyed in the Great Fire of 1666 and replaced by Sir Christopher Wren (1632-1723) between 1675 and 1681. He is known to have rebuilt the church upon the older foundations, preserving the original alignment.

Two years before Harnack's influential article of 1904, Canon William Benham (1831-1910) curtly stated in his *Old St Paul's Cathedral* (1902) that 'the story of King Lucius and that of the church of St Peter Cornhill are pure myths, without any sort of historical foundation, and so may be dismissed without more words'.[14] Consequently, investigation has only recently been made into the archaeological connections between the church and the Roman Basilica of London.

THE LUCIUS INSCRIPTION OF ST PETER-UPON-CORNHILL

Merrifield pointed out that St Peter-upon-Cornhill (*colour plate 4*) has a traditional claim to Romano-British origin but that this is based upon the inscription 'on a tablet that hung in the church until the seventeenth century'.[15] The tradition is not wholly dependent upon this tablet for 'in 1417, the rector of St Peter's, Cornhill, was confirmed by the Mayor and Aldermen in his customary right to precedence in the Whit Monday processions, on the ground that St Peter's was the first church founded in London'.[16] Nevertheless, since the plaque hanging in St Peter's has never received thorough study, it and the inscribed text deserve a fuller exploration (*colour plate 5*).

Transcription of the brass plaque presently in St Peter-upon-Cornhill:[17]

BEE IT KNOWNE TO ALL MEN THAT IN THE YEARE OF
OVR LORD GOD 179, *LVCIVS* THE FIRST CHRISTIAN KING
OF THIS LAND, THEN CALLED BRITAINE, FOVNDED Y^E FIRST
CHVRCH IN LONDON, THAT IS TO SAY, Y^E CHVRCH OF S^T. PETER
VPON CORNEHILL AND HEE FOVNDED THERE AN ARCHBIS=
HOPS SEE, AND MADE THAT CHVRCH Y^E METROPOLITANE AND
CHEIFE CHVRCH OF THIS KINGDOME, AND SO IT INDVRED Y^E
SPACE OF 400 YEARES AND MORE VNTO THE COMING OF S^T.
AVSTIN THE APOSTLE OF ENGLAND, THE WHICH WAS SENT
INTO THIS LAND BY S^T. GREGORIE Y^E DOCTOR OF Y^E CHVRCH IN
THE TIME OF KING ETHELBERT AND THEN WAS THE ARCH=
BISHOPS SEE & PALL REMOVED FROM Y^E FORESAID CHVRCH
OF S^T. PETER VPON CORNEHILL VNTO DOROBERNIA, THAT
NOW IS CALLED CANTERBVRIE, & THERE IT REMAINETH
TO THIS DAY, AND MILLET A MONKE WHICH CAME INTO
THIS LAND WITH S^T. AVSTIN, HEE WAS MADE THE FIRST

BISHOP OF LONDON AND HIS SEE WAS MADE IN PAVLS
CHVRCH, AND THIS *LVCIVS* KING WAS THE FIRST
FOVNDER OF Sᵀ. PETERS CHVRCH VPON CORNEHILL, &
HEE REIGNED KING IN THIS LAND AFTER BRVTE
1245, YEARES. AND IN THE YEARE OF OVR LORD GOD
124. *LVCIVS* WAS CROWNED KING AND THE YEARES
OF HIS REIGNE WERE 77 YEARES · AND HEE WAS BV=
RIED (AFTER SOME CHRONICLES) AT LONDON: AND AFTER
SOME CHRONICLES HEE WAS BVRIED AT GLOCESTER, IN THAT
PLACE WHERE Yᴱ ORDER OF Sᵀ. FRANCIS STANDETH NOW.

This plaque was purportedly saved from the original church during the destruction of the building and ensuing panic caused by the Great Fire of 1666. It presently hangs in an ornate oak frame under glass in the North Vestry and has been displayed in the church since Wren's rebuild.

According to documentation, Ralph de Baldoc/Baudake first mentioned a plaque when he was Dean of old St Paul's Cathedral or else during his capacity as the Bishop of London from 1304 to 1313. Although the brass plaque has long been associated with St Peter-upon-Cornhill, by *c.*1513 Robert Fabyan wrote:

> Of this Lucius it is shewed in a Table hangynge vpon the wall of ye North side of ye Ile in ye back of ye Quere of seynt Poules Churche of London, that the sayd Lucius reigned ouer the Brytons lxxvii yeres.[18]

In 1586 Holinshed also mentioned an alternative plaque:

> Howbeit by the tables hanging in the reuestrie of saint Paules at London, and also a table sometime hanging in saint Peters church in Cornehill, it should seeme that the said church of saint Peter in Cornehill was the same that Lucius builded.[19]

Table 5.2: Pre-1666 references to and citations of the inscribed plaque of St Peter-upon-Cornhill

Date	Reference
1294-1313	Ralph de Baldoc/Baudake
*c.*1513	Robert Fabyan: *The Concordance of Histories*
1586	Raphael Holinshed: *Chronicle*
1598	John Stow: *Survey of London*
1631	John Weever: *Ancient Funerall Monuments*
1639	James Usher: *Ecclesiastical Antiquities of Britain*

Therefore it seems there were two plaques, one in St Peter-upon-Cornhill and the other in old St Paul's Cathedral. The plaque within St Paul's seems by 1586 to have been moved to the vestry from 'the wall of the north side of the aisle behind the Choir' (Fabyan cited above), where it was in *c.*1513. Within this 73-year period it is known that old St Paul's was heavily restored following a severe fire in 1561 and completed five years later.[20] This may explain why the plaque was moved to the vestry, but unfortunately it does not appear to have survived the Great Fire of 1666. The only indication we have of the contents of the plaque in old St Paul's comes from Robert Fabyan's remark (*c.*1513) that it mentioned King Lucius reigning for 77 years. This 77-year reign of Lucius was also earlier mentioned in the *Chroniculi S. Pauli* of 1399:

> Post mortem Bruti Rex Lucius extat anno graciae Cxxiiij. Lucii primi Regis Christiani regnantis lxxvij annis, London sepultus est.[21]

> After the death of Brutus, King Lucius lived in the year of Grace 124. Lucius was the first Christian King and reigned 77 years, and is buried in London.

Within the archives of Lambeth Palace is the *Short Chronicle*, known as MS 306, a collection of three short chronicles bound together in a sixteenth-century folio volume. The first of them is a brief abridgement of the *Chronicle of the Brute*, the earliest books of which were written by 1333. The entire *Short Chronicle* may have been penned in the reign of Edward IV in the year *c.*1483. However, this 'abridgement', ends with the first year of Henry IV in 1367 and reads:

> After hym [Goran the grete] regned his sonne Lucye, that was a gode kynge and a trewe, and welbelovyd with all the comyne peple of the londe, and he sent to Rome to Pope Eleuthie and desired to be a Cristenman; and so the pope was joyfull therof and sent heder ij legates that highte Pagan and Olybane for to baptice Kynge Lucye and his peple, and so he was the first cristen kynge that ever was in this londe. And fro Brute unto Lucye is Mclxv yere. Tho was Kynge Lucye crowned and regned kynge xxiij yere or he was christened aftyr that he regned liiij yere. Summa of his regne lxxvij yere; than he dyed and lithe enterred att London.
> The yere of oure Lorde Jhesu Crist Ccj, A°
> After the dethe of Lucye …[22]

A marginal note beside the above entry is written in a later, Tudor hand:

> Anno Domini C[l]xiij erat prim[us] Christianissimus Re[x] Angliae, nomine Lucium[23]

The 'abridgement' mentions a span of 1165 years between Brutus and Lucius, providing Brutus with the fabulous date of *c.*1041 BC, but the plaque in St Peter's has 1245 years (*c*.1121 BC). Thus they both mention Brutus, albeit with dates not otherwise attested, and they agree on the year 124 as the beginning of Lucius' reign. The manuscript goes on to claim that Lucius reigned for 23 years until his baptism and a further 54 years after, a total reign of 77 years ending with his death in 201 and burial in London. These estimates place his baptism at AD 147, 30 years too early for the pontificate of Pope Eleutherius. It is not unreasonable to believe the epochs have been mistakenly reversed, giving the revision that Lucius converted to Christianity in his fifty-fourth year of reign, in AD 177/8 (in the pontificate of Eleutherius) and ruled for a further 23 years, until 201. This reversal might indicate the information had been inserted and incorrectly copied from an older source. The adjustment has been made for the 'abridgement' in Table 5.3 opposite.

Table 5.3 illustrates that while the first chronicle in the *Short Chronicle* may be an abridgement of *Le Brut*, the dates and years it provides for the details of Lucius' life in particular are completely at odds with that of earlier romance. In fact, they do not agree on any of the five events they describe in common. MS 306 is undeniably based on *Le Brut*, and they both offer unique respective spellings for the legates sent to Britain by Eleutherius: Pagan and Elibrayne (Le Brut), Pagan and Olybane (MS 306), but with Lucius' dates they diverge dramatically. Whoever penned the 'abridgement' in *c*.1367 may have resided in and been partial to London, as this document gives one of the earliest claims for Lucius' burial in that city.

That claim does not derive from Geoffrey of Monmouth, for he stated (V.I):

> In the end Lucius died in the town of Gloucester … In the year 156 after the Incarnation of our Lord he was buried with all honour in the church of the Archdiocese.[24]

He identified Britain's three archbishoprics as London, York and Caerleon-upon-Usk, and Thorpe took the passage quoted above to mean Lucius died in Gloucester and was buried in London.[25] However, it seems more likely that Geoffrey meant Caerleon-upon-Usk as he had just mentioned Gloucester and associates the burial with the Archdiocesan church. If indeed Geoffrey located Lucius' burial in Caerleon, then MS 306 appears to be the earliest extant source for locating it in London. This brief document also dates more of the events of Lucius' life than any other source, but as we have seen it appears to be based upon an older source that had Lucius' conversion in AD 177/8. It is from that earlier pre-1367 source that the information on the plaque in St Peter-upon-Cornhill may derive.

John Bale[26] (in 1557-60) and later Thomas Fuller (1661) both assigned the conversion of Lucius to the year 179, a date found only on the plaque of St Peter-upon-Cornhill, implying the pre-1666 inscription was generally known. Indeed by 1586 Raphael Holinshed, responding to his associate William Harrison, used the plaque inscription to offer a resolution to confusion current in London as to whether Lucius had founded St Peter-upon-Cornhill or Thorney Island, Westminster.

Thus the plaque was certainly in St Peter-upon-Cornhill by 1586 when Holinshed made his comments, and still in 1598 when John Stow mentioned it in his *Survey of*

Table 5.3: Dates and years given by relevant sources of the events in King Lucius' life

Event	Le Brut: 1333	MS 306	Chroniculi S. Pauli	Plaque in St Peter-upon-Cornhill	John Leland	John Bale
		'abridgment' c.1367	1399	pre-1586	c.1552	1557–9
Birth/Coronation	X	124	124	124	X	X
Reign before Conversion	X	23 [54]	X	X	X	X
Conversion	156	147/163 [177/8]	X	[c.179]	186	179
Foundation of St Peter-upon-Cornhill	X	X	X	179	[186]	X
Reign after Conversion	X	54 [23]	X	X	X	X
Total length of reign	13 yrs.	77 yrs.	77 yrs.	77 yrs.	X	X
Death	[169]	201	[201]	201	X	X
Burial place	Gloucester	London	London	London/Gloucester	X	X
Period without a ruler	50	62 yrs.	X	X	X	X

London. In 1631 John Weever, in his *Ancient Funerall Monuments* gave the first full transcription of the inscription:

> Be hit known to al Men that the yeerys of owr Lord God An. CLXXIX, Lucius, the fyrst christen king of this lond, then callyd Brytayne, fowndyd the fyrst Chyrch in London, that is to sey, the Chyrch of Sent Peter apon Cornhyl; and he fowndyd ther an Archbishoppys See, and made that Chirch the Metropolitant and cheef Chirch of this kingdom, and so enduryd the space of CCCC yeerys and more, unto the commyng of Sent Austen, an Apostyl of Englond, the whych was sent into the lond by Sent Gregory, the Doctor of the Chirch, in the tym of King Ethelbert, and then was the Archbyshoppys See and Pol removyd from the aforeseyd Chirch of Sent Peters apon Cornhyl unto Derebernaum, that now ys callyd Canterbury, and ther yt remeynyth to this dey.
>
> And Millet Monk, whych came into this lond wyth Sent Austen, was made the fyrst Bishop of London, and hys See was made in Powllys Chyrch. And this Lucius, Kyng, was the fyrst Fowndyr of Peters Chyrch apon Cornhyl; and he regnyd King in this Ilond after Brut MCCXLV yeerys. And the yeerys of owr Lord God a CXXIIII Lucius was crownyd Kyng, and the yeerys of hys reygne LXXVII yeerys, and he was beryd aftyr sum cronekil at London, and aftyr sum cronekil he was beryd at Glowcester, at that plase wher the ordyr of Sent Francys standyth.

The wording of the present plaque exactly matches this pre-1666 transcription by Weever, but whereas he maintains archaic spelling and Roman numerals, the present inscription employs later standardised spelling and Arabic numerals. Therefore, it is likely that the inscription Weever transcribed was of a different origin and appearance to the brass plaque now in the North vestry of St Peter's. What we see today in St Peter's must be an updated inscription based on his wording of an original, copied from a plaque/tablet or monument that was not saved from the conflagration of 1666.

The opening form, 'Bee it knowne' is found in the mid seventeenth century[27] (as expected if Weever was rewording into a contemporary style) but other information conveyed by the plaque is certainly earlier. The final sentence 'at Glowcester, at that plase wher the ordyr of Sent Francys standyth' refers to the monastery of Greyfriars in the city of Gloucester, founded in 1231. Greyfriars was dissolved in 1538, during the Reformation, and became a brewery. The information therefore dates the source's origin to between *c.*1231 and 1538.

The line 'he was beryd aftyr sum cronekil at London, and aftyr sum cronekil he was beryd at Glowcester' refers to two different chronicle traditions. We have seen that assigning Lucius' burial to London may derive from a tradition older than the fourteenth-century MS 306. The second chronicle is most likely the early thirteenth-century *Chronicle* of Robert of Gloucester or the *Flores Historiarum* by Roger of Wendover, who died in 1236.[28] Certainly a tradition grew up around Lucius' burial in the Roman city of Glevum, indeed at least one representation of

King Lucius seems to have been extant in the Lady Chapel of Gloucester Cathedral prior to the Dissolution.

One piece of information not given on the St Peter's plaque appears conspicuously absent as it avoids concluding that Lucius was buried at St Peter-upon-Cornhill. There is a balance of information describing his other burial tradition at Gloucester, which suggests even the earlier source was unable to decide between the chronicles. As for a claim of primacy, the plaque merely asserts that Lucius founded St Peter-upon-Cornhill in AD 179, which would certainly be one of his earliest Christian acts.

GLOUCESTER AND KING LUCIUS

In 678/9 Osric, ruler of the Hwicce and viceroy to King Ethelred of Mercia founded the Benedictine Abbey of Saints Peter and Paul at Gloucester. By the time of Abbot Serlo (1072-1104) the abbey expanded and became the city's cathedral. By the early fourteenth century the inscription opening this present chapter was noted at the Abbey by the Benedictine monk John Fiberius or Bever (John of London), who died *c.*1311.[29] The quatrain cited appears in stained glass in the west window in the north aisle of the cathedral; a window in bold Gothic-style stained glass depicting the major events in Lucius' life (*colour plates 6, 7, 8, 9, 10 & 11*). John Hardman Powell (1828-1895), a Catholic working for Hardman & Co. of Birmingham, created the window in either 1862 or 1865.[30] Powell, an associate of the famous architect Augustus Welby Northmore Pugin (1812-1852), appealed to nineteenth-century Anglo-Catholic tastes, following a lineage of several eighteenth-century artists who had depicted Christianity being brought to the ancient Britons. For example, there was Simon Francois Ravenet's (after Francis Hayman, 1708-1776) engraving of 1752 entitled *The Druids; the Conversion of the Britons to Christianity*, John Hamilton Mortimer's (1740-1779) 1764 painting of *St Paul preaching to the Ancient Britons*, and Joseph Haynes' 1780 etching of a Mortimer canvas entitled *St Paul preaching to the Britons*.[31] The nineteenth-century, contemporary and direct influences upon Powell's work included T.H. Maguire's (after Edmund Thomas Parris, 1793-1873) lithograph of 1847 *Joseph of Arimathea Converting the Britons* and, in the same year, Charles George Lewis' (after John Rogers Herbert, 1810-1890) engraving of *The First Preaching of Christianity in Britain*.[32] However, at present, and without further research, it appears as though Powell was the first artist in many centuries to depicted King Lucius.

Powell's Lucius window is partitioned into several panels. Beneath the inscription four armoured figures head the scenes below. On the far left appears Robert 'Curthose' III, Duke of Normandy (*c.*1051/4-1134) who was involved in the First Crusade and siege of Antioch in 1097-8. Next is Thomas (de Woodstock) Plantagenet (1355-1397), youngest son of King Edward III, becoming Duke of Gloucester in 1385. Beside him is Humphrey of Lancaster (1390-1447), son of King Henry IV and brother of King Henry V, who was created Duke of Gloucester in 1414, a year before

5.2 John Hardman Powell

being wounded at the Battle of Agincourt. Finally, on the far right stands an as yet unidentified figure wearing an Earl's coronet.[33]

The scenes below these figures represent Lucius' coronation by Druids, messengers being sent to Eleutherius, the King's baptism and his funeral procession. Druids crowning the King, emphasing Lucius' movement from paganism to Christianity, is somewhat of a visual corollary to Geoffrey of Monmouth's 'embroideries'.

Elsewhere in the cathedral one of the missing statues from the Lady Chapel reredos, dating to about *c.*1457,[34] exposes a mason's graffiti (*5.3*) reading LUCI, King Lucius, according to Roland Short.[35] This further highlights the fact that statues and monuments of Lucius existed in Britain at least before the Dissolution. Further research and, indeed, archaeology are required to ascertain examples beyond these.

Tradition usually identifies the ancient Gloucester church of St Mary de Lode as Lucius' resting place, though in the church his supposed effigy appears more like a medieval knight (*colour plate 11*). Excavations in 1978-9[36] revealed an early second-century Roman building interpreted by Heighway and Bryant as a villa, with associated bath complex, that was replaced in the fifth century by a cemetery[37] and a timber mausoleum containing three burials. This mausoleum was destroyed by fire

5.3 Mason's graffiti luci[us] in reredos of Gloucester Cathedral Lady Chapel; identified as lucius rather than lucia by Short (After Short 1946-48:35-36 17.c)

and its alignment was subsequently preserved by a series of churches, the medieval St Mary de Lode being the latest. Heighway has suggested:

> It is not impossible that this 'mausoleum' was a Christian structure, and that it survived as a burial chapel until the Middle Ages when it was appropriated by St. Peter's Abbey and used as the latter's parish church. One can speculate further that the origins of the burial chapel may have lain in a private chapel within the large Roman house, and that this is the explanation of the persistent Roman alignment.[38]

What of the Gloucester burial mentioned by the plaque of St Peter-upon-Cornhill? It identifies the place where Greyfriars subsequently stood. The Franciscan establishment of Greyfriars (c.1231), situated in the south-east intramural corner of the city, underwent several phases of expansion in 1239, 1285 and 1365. Controversy surrounded the Greyfriars' acquisition in 1285 of land formerly owned by the Benedictine Abbey of St Peter and St Paul. Of particular interest is the rebuilding of Greyfriars shortly before the Dissolution between 1515 and 1525, when the remains of an earlier church were incorporated. This earlier church may have been in that place where 'ye order of St. Francis standeth now' identified by the St Peter's plaque. This poses a question – whether the earlier church was newly discovered from hidden remains in the 1515-1525 renovations, or if this church was already known and traditionally associated with King Lucius' burial.

ST MARY DE CRYPT, GLOUCESTER

Very close to Greyfriars is the ancient church of St Mary de Crypt, identified as a late Saxon church with an immense parish incorporating the entire southern half of the walled area of Gloucester. The crypt of St Mary de Crypt may have been supposed the site of Lucius' burial. The earliest recorded church was known as the Church of the Blessed Mary in 1140. The name 'de Crypt' apparently refers to the crypt of St Mary's:

> Which now consists mostly of brick, but it was once stone, and was thirteenth century or earlier. It is a curious feature for which there seems no explanation.[39]

The Order of St Francis was also established in London in 1224. Significantly, in Cornhill a house was hired from the Sheriff John Travers and sectioned into monastic cells receiving novices such as Gilbert de Wyke and Joce of Cornhill.[40] By the summer of 1225 they had begun to take up residence near Newgate. This early association between the Greyfriars of Gloucester and at Cornhill highlights one route of communication between Franciscan houses regarding local information; discoveries made by the community at Gloucester would obviously be known in London. In particular, the location of King Lucius' burial in Gloucester can have been of Franciscan authorship.

THIRTEENTH–CENTURY (OR EARLIER) ROOTS

As we have seen, the information expressed in the St Peter-upon-Cornhill inscription could date to anytime between 1231 and 1538, but the echo of an older trace in the early thirteenth century is not excluded. The details of King Henry III's reign are particularly relevant here. His father, King John (1199-1216), had infuriated his barons over the rights of the monarchy and in 1215 the *Magna Carta* was drawn up. The King was required to respect legal procedure and accept that the law bound his will while his subjects' rights were protected. Upon John's death in 1216 Henry, aged nine, was crowned in the Abbey of Saints Peter and Paul, Gloucester, and his regents ruled by the reissued *Magna Carta* from 1217 to 1227. When Henry reached maturity he was keen to restore royal authority.

As already mentioned, the purported letter from Eleutherius to Lucius discovered at the Guildhall may relate directly to these tense years of regal unruliness, baronial unrest and the drafting of the *Magna Carta*. The origin of the information in the plaque of St Peter-upon-Cornhill can itself stem from these years, since the primacy of this place could explain why the mayor of London was invited to sign the *Magna Carta*. Yet this begs the question as to why St Peter's is linked to the antiquity of King Lucius.

One link is the intriguing list of Archbishops of London prior to St Augustine's arrival in England in 597. Although it may be a further instance of medieval and/or sixteenth-century embroidery to establish the primacy of St Peter's over St Paul's, the evidence deserves to be revisited.

THE ARCHBISHOPS OF LONDON

Information about the relationship between St Peter-upon-Cornhill and King Lucius comes from Stow's quotation of the now-lost *Book of British Bishops* by Jocelyn of Furness (mid twelfth century). Nothing more is known of this book than Stow's use of it in his *Survey of London*, published in 1598. In 1639 Archbishop Usher (1581-1656) noted that Jocelyn, who died in 1177, was a monk of the Cistercian abbey of Furness in the county of Lancashire, adding that 'It is doubtful whether his work [*Book of British Bishops*] be now extant'.[41] Jocelyn also wrote a *Life of St Helena*, a topic for Chapter 6, and a *Life of St Kentigern*[42] in which he mentions King Lucius twice.[43] Stow, regarding the Archbishops of London, says:

> The Archbishops names I find only to be set down by Joseline of Furness, in his book of British bishops, and not elsewhere:
>   1: Thean {saith he} was the first archbishop of London, in the time of Lucius, who built the said church of St. Peter, in a place called Cornhill in London, by the aid of Ciran, chief butler to King Lucius.
>   2: Elvanus was the second, and he built a library to the same church adjoining, and converted many of the Druids to the Christian faith.
>   3: Cadar was the third; then followed,
>   4: Obinus
>   5: Conan
>   6: Paludius
>   7: Stephen
>   8: Iltute
>   9: Dedwin
> 10: Thedred
> 11: Hillary
> 12: Guidelium
> 13: Vodimus, slain by the Saxons
> 14: Theanus, fled with the Britons into Wales, about the year of Christ 587.[44]

This is a wellspring of information and even though there is not yet any way of verifying the authenticity and/or veracity of Jocelyn's cited list nor even Stow's accompanying comments, Table 5.4 offers a useful comparison between the

Table 5.4: Names of the Archbishops of London according to Stow (Jocelyn of Furness), Raphael Holinshed, Geoffrey of Monmouth and Martyrologies

Date	Jocelyn of Furness (according to Stow): *c.*1170s	Geoffrey of Monmouth: 1134–1138	Raphael Holinshed: 1586	Martyrologies
*c.*179–185	Thean		Theon	
	Eluanus		Eluanus	
	Cadar		Cadocus	
	Obinus		Ouinus/Owen	
	Conan		Conanus	
	Paludius		Palladius	
Martyred 17 Sept. 304	Stephen		Stephanus	Stephen
Martyred 7 Feb. 305				*Augulius/ Angulus/Argulius*
314 (Council of Arles)	Iltute		Iltutus Restitutus	
	Dedwin		Theodromus/ Tadwinus/ Theodwinus/ Tacwinus/ Tatwinus	
	Thedred		Tidredus/ Theodredus	
*c.*367	Hillary		Hilarius	
*c.*431			Fastidius Priscus	
*c.*410	Guidelium	Guithelinus	Guittelinus	
Martyred 23 July 436	Vodimus		Vodinus	St Vodine
*c.*587	Theanus	Theonus	Theonus Iunior	

information Stow attributed to Jocelyn, and names given by Geoffery of Monmouth, Raphael Holinshed and the Martyrologies.

Several details can be gleaned from this comparison. Stow mentions that 'Thean, the first archbishop of London, in the reign of Lucius, built the said church [of St Peter-upon-Cornhill] by the aid of Ciran, chief butler to King Lucius'.[45] Three years after Stow's *Survey*, in 1601, Bishop Francis Godwin[46] reiterated that 'Theanus, helped by Cyranus, pincerna to King Lucius, built St. Peter's Cornhill'. Likewise Cressy, in his *History of the Church of Brittany*,[47] added 'Theanus, the first Bishop of London, died A.D. 185, the year in which Origen was born'.

The name Conan probably relates to Constans meaning 'reliable' in Latin. If Conan were a contraction of Constantine, then perhaps this bishop should be listed later, since one might expect the name to appear after the reign of the Emperor Constantine (280-337) and after the publication at Milan of the *Edict of Toleration* (*The Peace of the Church*) in 313.

Martyrologies list Stephen as 'Bishop of London, martyred, in the Diocletian Persecution, September 17, 304, in Monmouthshire'. Likewise, following Stephen, they list Augulius/Angulus 'Argulius, Bishop of London, martyred 7 February 305, in London'. His time as Bishop of London only amounted to ten days short of five months, perhaps explaining his exclusion from other historical sources.

Iltutus Restitutus, more correctly known simply as Restitutus, is historically known to have attended the Council of Arles in 314,[48] providing us with a secure date in the sequence of names. Hillary probably gets his name after Hilary/Hilarius of Poitiers (c.315-367). Guidelium/Guithelinus/Guittelinus of c.410[49] may more correctly be Vitelinus or Vitelius.

Holinshed inserts here Fastidius Priscus, a Pelagian Archbishop of London visited by Palladius in 431. Neither Jocelyn (Stow) nor Geoffrey mentions him, indicating Holinshed had other sources not otherwise known or used. He provides five variations of the name – Theodromus, Tadwinus, Theodwinus, Tacwinus, and Tatwinus, all different to the Dedwin of Jocelyn (Stow). This implies that from 1586, when Holinshed was writing, and 1598 when Stow first completed his *Survey of London*, there may have existed up to six versions of a list of Archbishops of London, not all written by Jocelyn. Francis Godwin in 1616, Archbishop Usher in 1639, and John Le Neve in 1716 all mention Jocelyn's list of Archbishops of London, but no other source.

In the Martyrologies, after mention of 'St Vodine, Bishop of London martyred by the Saxons July 23, 436' there is a gap of approximately 151 years, then it is noted that Theanus (the second/'junior') was archbishop of Gloucester,[50] then occupied the See of London from which he fled in c.587. The abandonment of the See of London would have been reported in Rome, and St Gregory (Pope from 590-604) reacted by deputing the monk Augustine to head a mission to re-establish the Church in Britain. This mission famously arrived in Kent in 597, and upon verifying that the *pallium* of London – the symbol of an Archbishop's office and position – had been lost, the Pope advised creating a third Archbishopric in a more fitting location. Augustine decided upon Canterbury.[51]

A PLAQUE IN OLD ST PAUL'S

Returning to the plaque in London centuries later, Robert Fabyan noticed the tablet in old St Paul's, London, not long before the final expansions at Greyfriars in Gloucester. Fabyan became an Alderman and then Sheriff of London who lived, and in 1513 was buried, at St Michael Cornhill, only a few metres west of St Peter-upon-Cornhill. Being an antiquarian, Fabyan, it is reasonable to assume, had a very good knowledge of his neighbourhood, making it curious that while mentioning the plaque at St Paul's he was silent concerning its connection to St Peter-upon-Cornhill. Some rivalry may have existed between St Michael Cornhill and St Peter-upon-Cornhill, but no argument of ancient supremacy seems to have arisen between them. A reasonable inference is that by 1513 the plaque was not at St Peter's and that perhaps a second plaque was produced for the Cornhill church by 1586 when Holinshed mentioned both.

It is also plausible to deduce that the wording of our present plaque is not that used on the plaque in old St Paul's, since an inscription claiming the antiquity of St Peter-upon-Cornhill would hardly be hanging in the latter church – not, at least, if there was incipient rivalry at the time. A rivalry may well have existed; old St Paul's was set up in AD 604 as the 'new' seat of the archbishop of London while, if the implications

5.4 Old St Paul's in ruins following the Great Fire of 1666, by Thomas Wyck *c.*1673 (*In Adrian Tinniswood's* By Permission of Heaven: The Story of the Great Fire of London; *London: Jonathan Cape, 2003; pp. 204-5)*

1 J.B. Segal on Mount Tektek, near Edessa, 1983
(*Reproduced by kind permission of Mrs Leah Segal
and Dr Naomi Segal*)

2 Early fifteenth-century panel 16 from the
Great East Window of York Minster; King Lucius
(*Reproduced by kind permission of the Dean and
Chapter of York*)

3 Londiniensium inscription, found amid second-century material at Long Lane, Bermondsey (*Museum of London*)

Above left: 4 St Peter-upon-Cornhill looking north (*Photograph by the author, 2007*)

Above right: 5 Brass plaque in the west vestry of St Peter-upon-Cornhill (*Photograph by the author, by kind permission of St Helen's House, Bishopsgate; Martin Fitzsimons*)

Above left: 6 Hardman window of King Lucius' life at Gloucester Cathedral (1860s) (*Photograph by Richard Cann; by kind permission of Mark Beckett and Robin Lunn of Gloucester Cathedral*)

Above right: 7 Detail of Hardman window; Coronation of Lucius by Druids (*Photograph by Richard Cann; by kind permission of Mark Beckett and Robin Lunn of Gloucester Cathedral*)

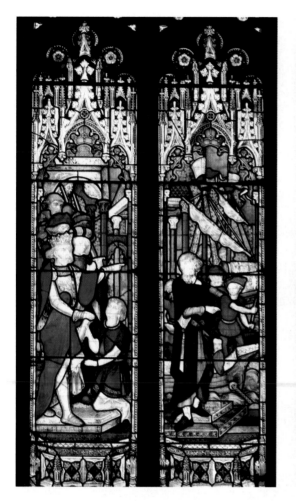
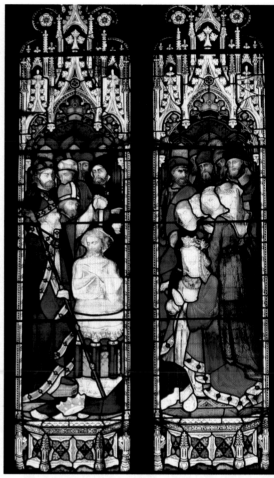

Above left: 8 Detail of Hardman window; Messengers being sent from Britain (*Photograph by Richard Cann; by kind permission of Mark Beckett and Robin Lunn of Gloucester Cathedral*)

Above right: 9 Detail of Hardman window; Baptism of King Lucius (*Photograph by Richard Cann; by kind permission of Mark Beckett and Robin Lunn of Gloucester Cathedral*)

Above left: 10 Detail of Hardman window; Funeral procession of King Lucius (*Photograph by Richard Cann; by kind permission of Mark Beckett and Robin Lunn of Gloucester Cathedral*)

Above right: 11 Detail of Hardman window; Lucius being crowned (*Photograph by Richard Cann; by kind permission of Mark Beckett and Robin Lunn of Gloucester Cathedral*)

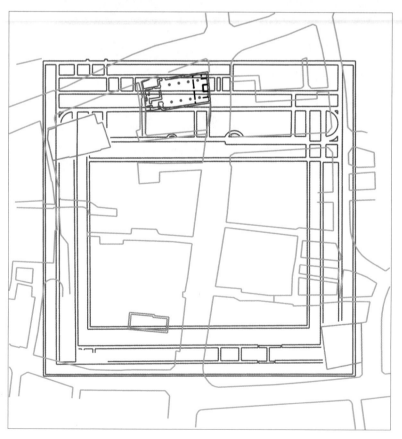

Right: 14 Google Earth view of Chur and Trimmis looking south-west (*Dominic Barker 2007*)

Below: 15 The Raetian *limes* in the third to fifth century (*After Tanner 1978:269, Map 7; D.J. Knight 2007*)

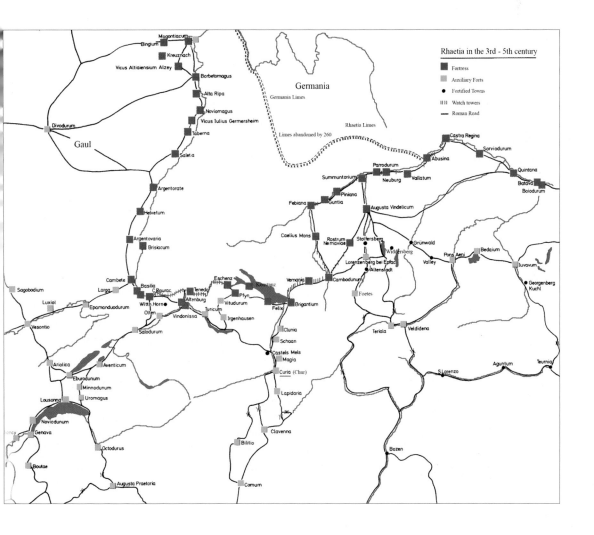

Rhaetia in the 3rd - 5th century

- ■ Fortress
- ■ Auxiliary Forts
- ● Fortified Towns
- IIII Watch towers
- — Roman Road

Left: 16 Bust of St Luzius von Chur (*Reproduced by kind permission of the Raetische Museum of Chur, Switzerland*)

Below: 17 St Luzius reliquary (*Reproduced by kind permission of the Raetische Museum of Chur, Switzerland*)

on the plaque are to be heeded, St Peter's was the original basilica. A rivalry may have erupted, spurred by Reformation and stoked by the ministers of Queen Mary between 1553 and 1558, with Saint Paul championed by the Protestants and Saint Peter by the Catholics. Sixteenth-century allegiances could be as black and white as that.

At any rate, it is not altogether strange that by 1586 there was mention of two distinct plaques. What the two would have shared in common were the essential details regarding King Lucius. It may be that during Mary's reign, a second inscription was prepared for St Peter's and St Paul's respectively, and by accident of history or fire only one plaque survived, the second and reworded one that has been in St Peter's since *c.*1586. Any such conjectural history of the plaque(s) does not, however, settle the veracity of the inscription regarding King Lucius.

Again, why is Lucius specifically associated with St Peter-upon-Cornhill? He had admittedly been forced into a Davidic metaphor for divine kingly authority, of great interest to thirteenth-century history, but as we've seen there remained tangible historical reality behind the medieval English story of Lucius. It may be further evidenced by assessing the archaeology of the site of St Peter-upon-Cornhill.

THE SECOND–CENTURY ROMAN BASILICA OF LONDINIUM AND ST PETER–UPON–CORNHILL

One of the most striking features of Roman Londinium was its forum basilica. By *c.*100 it had become immense even by Roman standards, measuring 166m x 167m; approximately five times larger than the original structure. This may have been in response to Londinium advancing from the status of *municipium* to *colonia*.[52] Of interest to our study is a sequence of observations regarding the relationship between St Peter-upon-Cornhill and the Roman basilica.

In 1934 Sir Robert Eric Mortimer Wheeler made an important point: there is every likelihood that the London basilica and forum were of the type represented at Silchester, Caerwent and elsewhere, and so approximated to the normal plan of the headquarters-building of a Roman fortress. In the military headquarters the central room at the back of the basilica was the official regimental shrine and it is likely enough that the corresponding room (emphasised at Silchester by an apse) at the back of the civil basilica fulfilled an equivalent function, as a sort of municipal chapel. Today, the high altar of St Peter's, Cornhill, stands over the site of the central room at the back of the London basilica. Does St Peter's thus represent, in all topographical literalness, a continuous tradition from the time when Christianity first became the official religion of Roman London, with an official altar in the old municipal shrine?[53]

In 1969 Merrifield wrote that the Roman basilica 'served as courts of justice, town hall, and public meeting-place, and would also have contained the *curia*, or local senate house, the position of which is not yet known'.[54] In 1987 Peter Marsden published a composite plan of the early medieval structures on the forum and basilica site of London. Including the Saxon church of All Hallows he commented

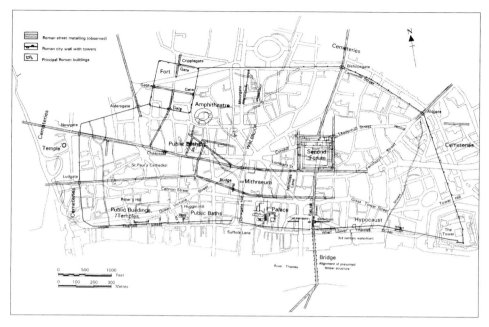

5.5 Plan of Londinium (*After Wacher 1974:89, figure 37*)

that St Dionis Backchurch, St Michael Cornhill and St Peter-upon-Cornhill 'were constructed on the ruins of the basilica and forum, though whether or not they reused standing Roman walls is not known', adding 'However, it is interesting that St Peter upon Cornhill church was allegedly founded in AD 179'.[55]

The northern extent of the basilica was not discovered until 1982 during excavations at 68 Cornhill, and subsequent excavation has established that by the early second century the northern range 'comprised a single row of offices and a long portico which ran the length of the Nave and North Aisle, sub-divided by non-structural partitions'.[56] One particular room (number 13 in Marsden is number 2 in Brigham, measuring 7.5m square[57]) had in situ dark blue wall plaster. Immediately west of this is a room (number 12 in Marsden[58]) underneath Gracechurch Street and overlain to the west by the eastern wall of St Peter-upon-Cornhill, covered in 'yellow panels with a black border, on a yellow ground with touches of red'.[59]

This room was given a tessellated floor at a raised level, suggesting it 'may have had a higher status than normal, possibly acting as an antechamber for the *aedes* or shrine-room'. It is possible this *aedes* 'occupied a central position in the Northern Range ... beneath the east end of the church of St Peter's, Cornhill'.[60] Indeed, Marsden further suggested that:

It may be significant that St. Michael's church, Cornhill, lies on the presumed site of the western tribunal of the basilica, and that St. Peter's church lies in the centre of the northern part of the basilica, a place sometimes reserved in other basilicas for a

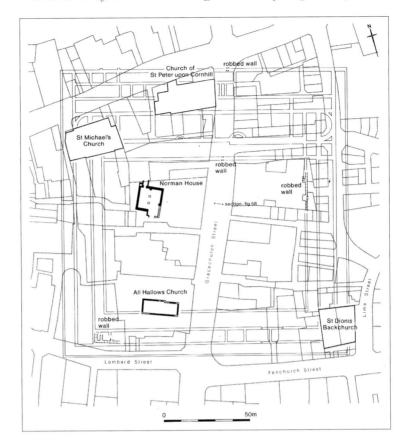

5.6 Plan of London's basilica (*After Marsden 1987:69, figure 57*)

municipal shrine.[61] Merrifield has suggested that a Christian chapel could have been established in the basilica at this point, and was later adapted as the church of St. Peter. This might account for the later medieval tradition that the church of St. Peter had been founded by a King Lucius in AD 179.[62]

If Merrifield, Marsden and Brigham's interpretations are correct then the church of St Peter-upon-Cornhill, if not also St Michael's, has continuity with the second-century basilica. As noted earlier, Wren retained the original alignment of St Peter's when he rebuilt it between 1675 and 1681. The church straddles the basilica municipal shrine-room or *aedes* and it is feasible for the under-structure to have utilised the dry solid Roman basilica wall fabric for support. The eastern end and the situation of the high altar of St Peter's stands exactly upon the middle of the northern range of rooms, and the east wall itself is a mere two degrees off the basilica alignment (*colour plate 13*).

Gracechurch Street, undeniably a later Saxon pathway through the forum and basilica ruins, respects the eastern wall of St Peter's as it slightly kinks at the church before intersecting with Cornhill, firmly implying St Peter's is earlier than the Saxon street. However, it must remain for a future archaeological investigation in the crypt of St Peter-upon-Cornhill to ascertain whether the church simply sits upon Roman walls or whether the earliest phase of the church is indeed Roman. That day may be some time in coming as the entrance to the crypt was bricked up in the nineteenth century and the present custodians believe this is because plague victims were interred there. Intriguingly, there is an eighteenth-century anecdote that three 'London Tavern Apprentices' explored a passage leading from under the belfry at an unknown distance and direction before the entrance was bricked up, a passage also supported by lore as leading to St Helen's.[63]

It is an important break from the 314 straightjacket that the interpretations offered by Merrifield, Marsden and Brighman, informed by archaeological investigation, consider the antiquity of Lucius or Christianity.

Colour plate 13 illustrates the physical relationship between the second-century basilica and the church of St Peter-upon-Cornhill. The eastern wall is aligned north-south over the Roman rooms while the central nave piers straddle the south wall of the northern range, all perhaps visible during the nine years between the church's destruction in 1666 and the start of Wren's work in 1675.

The material evidence of Londinium's Roman basilica remained hidden until the last three centuries, and the northern range in particular was not revealed until 1848 when a sewer was dug immediately east of St Peter's, under Gracechurch Street, and later in 1881-2 when Leadenhall Market was built. When Holinshed mentioned the plaque in St Peter's in 1586, there was at that time no clear knowledge that

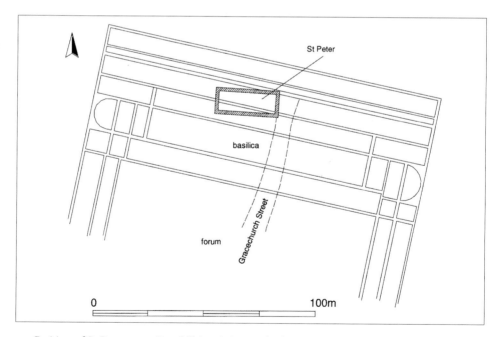

5.7 Position of St Peter-upon-Cornhill in relation to the basilica of Londinium (*Bell 2005: 94, figure 51; after Rodwell 1984, fig. 3c*)

the church stood directly upon the second-century Roman basilica. Therefore, the tradition of locating Lucius' Archdiocesan church at St Peter-upon-Cornhill could at best have echoed an indistinct memory of the reality; the *aedes* of Londinium's basilica is directly below St Peter's and at some date the patron goddess and imperial image gave way to Christianity. However, could this conversion of creed at the heart of Britannia have happened as early as AD 179?

It has often been noted that the archaeological evidence for pre-314 Christianity in Britain is extremely sparse, but this statement naturally depends upon what we agree is 'evidence'. Charles Thomas' 1981 work[64] has remained a valuable archaeological study of Christianity in Britain during the Roman era and has fuelled debate as to whether a portable artefact such as a chalice can provide us with a sure indication of organised Christian practice in Britain at these remote times. Since a portable and personal object may have changed hands often, and with intentions differing at each transaction, recent emphasis has been on identifying more permanent types of Christian artefacts such as buildings and graves, in an attempt to uncover religious belief and praxis. There is a small number of such buildings in Britain including the 'church' at Silchester, St Mary de Lode in Gloucester and St Martin's at Canterbury. The villa chapel at Lullingstone was discovered in 1939 and excavated from 1949-1961 while excavations between 1976 and 1988 at Butts Road in Colchester revealed what has been interpreted as a Roman Christian church.[65] These and many more minor discoveries were obviously not available for discussion when Lucius was being cast as myth. The archaeological investigation and debate over Christianity in Britannia continues. Let us return briefly to another ancient building associated with St Peter-upon-Cornhill.

THE LOST LIBRARY OF ST PETER–UPON–CORNHILL

A library that once adjoined St Peter-upon-Cornhill is no longer extant and its exact location is not certain. In 1598, Stow wrote:

> Eluanus, the second archbishop, built a library to the same [St Peter-upon-Cornhill] adjoining … True it is, that a library there was pertaining to this parish church of old time, built of stone, and of late repaired with brick by the executors of Sir John Crosby, alderman, as his arms on the south end doth witness. This library hath been of late time, to wit, within these fifty years, well furnished of books; John Leyland viewed and commended them; but now those books are gone, and the place is occupied by a schoolmaster and his usher, over a number of scholars learning their grammar rules, etc. Notwithstanding, before that time a grammar school had been kept in this parish, as appeareth in the year 1425, I read, that John Whitby was rector, and John Steward schoolmaster there; and in the 25th of Henry VI it was enacted by parliament, that four grammar schools in London should be maintained, namely, in the parishes of Allhallows, in Thames Street, St. Andrew in Oldbourne, St. Peter's upon Cornehill, and St. Thomas of Acars.[66]

The repairs to the original stone library were executed shortly after Sir John Crosby's death in 1476. The library was 'well furnished of books' 50 years prior to Stow's comment and, therefore, until at least *c.*1548, when John Leland (*c.*1506-1552) used its facilities. In 1530 Leland became Henry VIII's chaplain and librarian with the special honour of being the King's antiquarian. What Stow is indicating is that during the Reformation the library of St Peter-upon-Cornhill was emptied and all that remained was incorporated into the existing grammar school. It is not inconceivable that the purported letter from Eleutherius to Lucius (see Chapter 4) was not in some way linked to this library and its removal at the time of Leland. Certainly, many manuscripts from this *scriptorium* are now lost, except for one example; in the ownership of 'St. Peter's is a rare and beautiful manuscript copy of St. Jerome Vulgate':

> This Bible, written on fine white vellum, is the work of a scribe, at one time attached to St. Peter's, and was completed by him in 1290. It is the only manuscript Bible written specially for a City church that remains still in the possession of that church. On the last page is a note in the same hand stating that the Bible was made specially for the Church of St. Peter-upon-Cornhill. Consisting of 586 leaves of parchment, adorned with 160 illuminated initials showing a close similarity to the work of the schools of St. Alban and Sarum.[67]

It is not impossible that the Franciscan Greyfriars, upon their move from Sheriff Laver's house in Cornhill to Newgate in 1225, maintained a connection with Cornhill and either instituted or continued an ancient library next to St Peter's. However the library was founded, its existence as a centre of study with its own characteristic manuscript-copying style appears to have had some renown. This would certainly add to the connection between the Gloucester Greyfriars and their transmission to London of the details of King Lucius' burial place.

One final pertinent word comes from the literate neighbourhood of Cornhill, from William Makepeace Thackeray's short *Roundabout Papers* essay *On A Lazy Idle Boy* written for the first instalment of the *Cornhill Magazine* in 1863:

> I had occasion to pass a week in the autumn[68] in the little old town of Coire or Chur, in the Grisons, where lies buried that very ancient British king, saint, and martyr, Lucius, who founded the Church of St. Peter, on Cornhill. Few people note the church now-a-days, and fewer ever heard of the saint. In the cathedral at Chur, his statue appears surrounded by other sainted persons of his family. With tight red breeches, a Roman habit, a curly brown beard, and a neat little gilt crown and sceptre, he stands, a very comely and cheerful image: and, from what I may call his peculiar position with regard to Cornhill, I beheld this figure of St. Lucius with more interest than I should have bestowed upon personages who, hierarchically, are, I dare say, his superiors.[69]

The strange connection between Britain and Chur in Switzerland will be explored in the following chapter.

CHAPTER 6

OUR MAN IN RAETIA – ST LUZIUS VON CHUR

William Makepeace Thackeray, after a journey to Switzerland in a bid to regain his health, wrote a short piece entitled *A Very Idle Boy* for the first edition of the *Cornhill Magazine* (1863). In Chur, he noted that contrary to King Lucius' burial in Britain:

> Alban Butler,[1] in the "Lives of the Saints", v. xii., and Murray's "Handbook", and the Sacristan at Chur, all say Lucius was killed there, and I saw his tomb with my own eyes![2]

Thackeray was citing an alternative tradition that King Lucius gave up his British crown and became a missionary on the continent, journeying with his sister Emerita to the Roman province of Raetia where both died. To the present day King Lucius, known as St Luzius, is venerated at Chur and Emerita at the small neighbouring Alpine village of Trimmis (*colour plate 14*). We can call this version of Lucius' life the 'Raetian tradition'. Such an extraordinary connection between King Lucius of Britannia and Raetia[3] was thought to be so that strange it was generally (perhaps until Thackeray) dismissed as medieval imagination and folklore, but it will prove interesting to explore a little more seriously.

It is important first to understand the sixteenth-century context in which Luzius von Chur entered into the English consciousness, and then proceed to the literary and historical roots of the story. As a working hypothesis, for the sake of argument we will posit Lucius of Britannia as just a story, and try to identify the possible ways and reasons why it could have been transferred to Raetia. Several contradictions will lead us to modify this position, whereby Lucius is not just the product of story transmission and transmutation, allowing for the plausible reality of a Luzius who ventured to Chur and is at least believed to be a British king. Then a discussion of the church of St Luzius at Chur and the age of its dedication will be supplemented with the eighth-century *Vita Lucii*, leading to an assessment of whether the tradition of Luzius von Chur concurs or remains irreconcilable with that of the Lucius of British tradition.

6.1 Portrait of William
Makepeace Thackeray
(*F. Holl after Samuel
Lawrence; steel engraving,
published by Smith, Elder
& Co., 1853*)

There are indications that details from the Raetian tradition had arrived in Britain before the sixteenth century. Jocelyn of Furness (1130-1199), whom we have already encountered, wrote a *Life of St Helena*, newly translated and published.[4] It is likely that Henry of Huntingdon consulted this Life, which says that Emerita was the daughter of Helena. Now, St Helena actually hailed from Bithynia in *c.*250 and might never have visited Britannia, but pertinent here is that Jocelyn, in distant Furness, had become informed of the Raetia tradition and Emerita's supposed relation to Lucius.

Nonetheless, it remained for the development of printed books and other circumstances for the story of Lucius of Chur to claim a wider British awareness. The notice of Luzius von Chur in Schedelius' *Nuremburg Chronicle* (printed in 1492) and Holinshed's subsequent citation of that work in his own *Chronicle* of 1586 is part of a broader context based not only on the written word; several English Protestants in Switzerland for the reign of Mary (1553-1558) had encountered the tradition first-hand.

ENGLISH PROTESTANT EXILES IN SWITZERLAND (1553–1558/9)

As seen in Chapter 4, references to Lucius became more frequent in the sixteenth century, partly in the writings of English Protestant clerics living in exile in Switzerland during the Stuart reign. In Zurich and the surrounding cities they encountered the tradition of St Luzius and some, like John Foxe, commented on this Swiss tradition at a time when debate in England over the purported letter from Eleutherius to Lucius was still fresh.

The Reforming churches of Switzerland offered safe haven to English Protestant clerics and the city of Zurich became an important centre due to the fame and influence of Huldrych Zwingli (1484-1531) of Wildhaus, St Gallen. The Reformation quickly spread from Zwingli's headquarters in Zurich to five other cantons of Switzerland.[5] One notable Zwinglian was Martin Bucer (1491-1551), of whom Henry VIII had requested advice in connection with his divorce from Catherine of Aragon. Bucer was hailed to Augsburg in 1548 to

6.2 Engraving of Huldrich/Ulrich Zwingli by von Ludwig Bechstein, 1854. (*Zweihundert deutsche Männer. Leipzig*)

counter-sign an agreement between Catholics and Protestants, known as the *Interim*, but unhappy with having done so, he accepted Cranmer's offer to live in England. Arriving in 1549 he was appointed regius Professor of Divinity at Cambridge.[6]

Pietro Martire Vermigli (Peter Martyr) (1499-1562), an intriguing Italian theologian of the Reformation, was particularly affected by Zwingli's writings.[7] Vermigli fled Italy in 1542 and found refuge in Zürich, Basel and Strasbourg. In 1547 he too was invited to England by Archbishop Thomas Cranmer and given a pension to support himself. In 1548 he was made regius Professor of Divinity at the University of Oxford, where he gathered about him several promising young men including John Jewell (1522-1571), future Bishop of Salisbury. He gained immense respect and influence in sixteenth-century England and by 1552 was instrumental in many of the modifications made in the *Book of Common Prayer*. During Mary Stuart's reign, Vermigli was allowed to return to Strasbourg, and in 1556 he accepted the Chair in Hebrew at the University of Zürich, where many of his devotees followed and gathered about him.[8]

The English temporarily residing in Switzerland included John Hooper (d.1555), John Jewell (d.1572), James Pilkington (d.1576)[9] and Zwingli's successor Heinrich Bullinger (1504-1575) accepted with hospitality several of the English refugees. On returning after Mary's execution they brought Bullinger's writings with them.

John Foxe, in his 1563 *Book of Martyrs*, declared it a fantasy that Lucius had given up a crown to become an aged missionary on the continent or 'Doctour and Rector of the Churche of Cureak'. Implicit in sixteenth-century disbelief in the Raetian tradition of Lucius at Chur is perhaps to be found a certain allegiance between Protestantism in Britain and the Reformed Church in Switzerland, after all, the story of Lucius in Raetia was firmly entrenched in the Catholic Bishopric of Chur.

Counter to the discrediting Protestant opinion, in the early 1580s the Jesuits commissioned a fresco for the walls of the Collegium Anglorum at Rome, the oldest English institution outside of this island, a seminary for training priests for England and Wales. The fresco depicted a cycle of martyrs, including a scene of Lucius and his martyrdom at Chur. The fresco is now lost, but an engraving of it was made by Giovanni Battista Cavalieri (1525-1597) and published in Rome (1584). The scene has been interpreted as 'a defiant reaffirmation of the traditional English religious history that Foxe's book had been designed to replace and eradicate'.[10] We will differ from this interpretation since Foxe was apparently not negating the British tradition, but the fresco does represent a Jesuit decision to equate Luzius von Chur with King Lucius. In the left background Fugatio and Damiano, the emissaries of Pope Eleutherius, baptise Lucius. The foreground dominates the scene with the violent martyrdom of Lucius near Chur, and in the right background his presumed sister, Emerita, looks on as she is bound and burned alive.[11]

A . S·Lucius Angliæ Rex à Fugatio, & Damiano S·Eleutherij·P·P·legatis bapti:
zatur, eiusq̃ regnũ tũc primum publicè fidem Chriſtj recepit

B . Idem regno composito Euangelium prædicaturus in Germaniam ſe confert.
Vbi poſt lapidationem, Churiæ Epiſcopus cum eſſet, à plebe infideli perimitur

C . S·Emerita S·Lucij Soror Tremonty pro Chriſto igne crematur

4

6.3 The martyrdom of Lucius near Chur; etching by Giovanni Battista Cavalieri, 1584. *The Bodleian Library, University of Oxford; shelfmark Antiq.c.I.5(1), folio 4*

A TALE OF TWO TRADITIONS: RAETIA AND BRITANNIA

Sebastian Munster (1488-1552) completed his *Cosmographia* in 1544 and made reference to an unpublished manuscript, *Augustanae urbis descriptione*, by the cartographer Achilles Pirmin Gassarus/Gasser (1505-1577) of Augsburg. Gasser believed that King Lucius was not the same person as St Lucius of Chur. Archbishop James Usher (1581-1607) followed Gasser's opinion in 1639 and also later Thomas Fuller (1608-1661) in his publications of 1655 and 1661, stating:

It is therefore well observed by a learned man, that Lucius the German preacher was a different person from the British King, who never departed our island, but died therein.[12]

Edward Stillingfleet (1635-1699) also cast a critical eye on the story and in 1685 commented on each of the sources known to him (see also Appendix C). Stillingfleet thus provided a wellspring of information not readily available in prior British writing, regarding what we are calling the Raetian tradition and its controversy in Britain. Table 6.1 below provides a chronological list of the sources Stillingfleet cited for the Raetian tradition.

Table 6.1: Chronology of sources regarding St Luzius von Chur cited by Stillingfleet in 1685

Date	Publication Date	Author	Title
896		Notker Balbulus (*c.*840-912)	*Martyrology*
Before 1400/6	1493 (Venice)	Petrus de Natalibus (?-1400/6)	*Legends of the Saints* (L. I. c.24)
Before 1510	1516	*Johannes Naukler* (*c.*1425-1510)	*Memorabilium omnis aetatis et omnium gentium chronici commentarii*
1528	1538	Giles Tschudi (1505-1572)	*Descript. Rhet.* [*De prisca ac vera Alpina Rhaetia*] (c.18.)
1544		Sebastian Munster (1488-1552)	*Cosmographia* (L. 3. P.518)
	1566 (Basle)	Hans Heinrich Bandlin (1522-1595)	*De Viris illustrib. Germ.* [*Prosopographiae heroum atque illustrium virorum totius Germaniae*]
1586		Caesar Baronius (1538-1607)	*New edition of the Roman Martyrology*
1590s		Marcus Velserus (1558-1614)	*Rer. Vindel.* (L. 6.)
	1657 (London)	Philippus Ferrarius (?-1626)	*Nova Topograph.* [*Novum Lexicon Geographicum*] (p. 44)

The following notes supplement Stillingfleet's commentary of these nine references and in their chronological sequence:

I   Notker Balbulus: Stated that King Lucius was baptized by Timothy, brother of Novatus, whose names, Stillingfleet comments, 'are extant in the old *Martyrology* published by Rosweyd' under July 12th. Lucius then converted all *Raetia* and part of *Bavaria*.

Stillingfleet was referring to Héribert Rosweyde (1569-1629), a Flemish Jesuit lecturer at the University of Douai, near Lille (Department of Nord, France). He collected the names of saints out of old manuscripts, one of which we know was the 1613 edition of Ado of Vienne's *Martyrology*. When Rosweyde died in 1629 his ambitious *Fasti sanctorum quorum vitae in belgicus bibliothecis manuscriptiae* was not ready for printing, but Jean Bolland (1596-1665) took up the immense task and devoted himself to continuing the work in Antwerp, now known as the *Acta Sanctorum* (the *Lives of the Saints*). Assisted by Godfrey Henschen (1601-1681), the first volume of the *Acta* was published at Antwerp in 1643:

II   *Petrus Equilinus* (Petrus de Natalibus or Pierre des Noels, Bishop of *Equilinus/ Aquila*): Noted that Lucius was not baptized by Timothy, the disciple of St. Paul, but, as with Notker Balbulus, by Timothy the brother of Novatus.

III   (Johannes) *Nauclerus* (Naukler): Declared that the relationship between King Lucius and Timothy agrees with the tradition of Chur. Here, Stillingfleet acknowledges Naukler's statement that Timotheus baptized Lucius in Britain.

IV   *Aegidius Tschudus* (Giles Tschudi):[13] Asserted that Lucius was martyred at Chur and added that there was also a place near there still [in the sixteenth century] called *Clivus S. Lucii*.

V   (Sebastian) Munster: Noted that near the Episcopal palace at Chur, there was a monastery of *Sancti Lucii*.

VI   (Heinricus) *Pantaleon* (Hans Heinrich Bandlin) in Part I of his *De Viris*, from Creation to AD 800, calls Lucius the disciple of Timothy.

VII   (Caesar) Baronius's new edition of the Roman *Martyrology* claimed Timothy and Novatus were sons of the Roman senator *Pudens* and that his wife *Claudia Rufina* was British.

VIII   Marcus Velserus/Velser/Welser, from Augsburg, cites the *Annals of the church of Chur* showing how Lucius travelled to Raetia to preach the Gospel and there suffered martyrdom, 'or, at least, ended his days; for they are not agreed about the manner of his death'.[14]

IX   (Philippus) *Ferrarius*, in William Dillingham's London edition of 1657, calls King Lucius of Britain 'one of the martyrs of Curia, which the Germans call Chur, and the Italians Choira'.[15]

Raphael Holinshed, Edward Stillingfleet and Thomas Fuller, however, omitted important sources, despite their careful treatment of the Raetian tradition of Luzius. Most significantly, none made mention of the eighth-century *Vita Lucii*, its earliest extant textual witness. The British tradition of King Lucius as we have seen is firmly based on the *Liber Pontificalis* and the works of the Venerable Bede. In this tradition, Lucius, a king in communication with the Pope, ensured the Christian religion in Britain, ruled long, died and was buried in British soil. In Raetia and the *Vita Lucii* by contrast, he abdicated a throne in Britain and, at the instigation of a Roman saint, became a missionary on the continent. Lucius in Britannia was baptised by emissaries from the Bishop of Rome, whereas in the *Vita* he was baptised in Britain by St Timotheus.

It must remain open whether the two traditions ultimately derive from the *Liber Pontificalis*, but even if there were a common root, as of the eighth and through to the fifteenth centuries, they certainly grew up independently. In the sixteenth century Holinshed and contemporaries in Britain had difficulty reconciling the differences and very quickly passed off the Raetian tradition as mere medieval fancy. However, no one wished to admit that, however at odds with Bede the Raetian details may be, the *Vita* was at least as old as his work. We therefore make a closer study of Curia Raetorum (Chur) in order to provide context to an analysis of the *Vita Lucii* and to assess how such different versions of the story of King Lucius might have arisen and propagated.

CURIA RAETORUM

Curia Raetorum (Chur) was made the Roman *civitas* capital of Raetia Prima in 15 BC by Tiberius and Drusus. At present there is no firm archaeological evidence in support of Curia being a *municipium* or the theory that it became the provincial capital, and further investigation is needed.[16] By the second century and the reign of Marcus Aurelius the province of Raetia was bounded by Belgica to the west, Noricum to the east, Germania Superior to the north, and Cisalpine Gaul to the south. Paul the Deacon (*c.*720–799) mentioned the city in his *Historia gentis Langobardum* (*History of the Lombards*) and in general Curia seems to have enjoyed a protected and prosperous existence.

Local tradition holds that the relics of Lucius have long been held in the crypt of the Luziuskirche of Chur.[17] There is certainly agreement that Christianity reached this remote region at least by the end of the third century,[18] possibly introduced by Christian units of the Roman military[19] or by gradual movement northwards from the ecclesiastical centres of Milan and Aquilea.[20] Excavations have revealed a Roman cemetery at Welschdörfli, an old district of Chur on the western bank of the Plessur, associated with an early church dedicated to St Peter, where both Christian and pagan graves were intermixed until the late fourth century.[21] However, Iso Müller has concluded that 'the historical Luzius was more likely a local figure from the Prättigau who lived during the fifth or sixth century and worked as a missionary first in an area to the north of Chur known as the *Luziensteig*, and later in Chur itself'.[22]

THE CHURCH OF ST LUZIUS

The earliest evidence of St Luzius von Chur is the church dedicated to him, the original cathedral of Chur. Between 530 and 546 St Valentinian enlarged the church at Chur. This early sixth-century expansion predates Bede by almost 200 years and the very time when the Lucius' entry in the *Liber Pontificalis* was supposed to have been made. However, it is not recorded whether the church that Valentinian enlarged was already dedicated to Lucius. We can only know that it was dedicated sometime before *c*.753/4. In that year Pope Stephen II (p. 752-757) apparently visited Chur on his journey to the Carolingian royal court of Pepin the Short (r. 751-768)

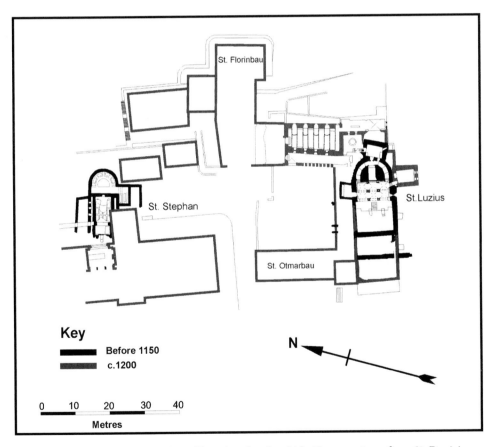

6.4 Plan of St Luzius at Chur and neighbouring churches (*After Tanner 1978:155, figure 68; Dominic Barker 2007*)

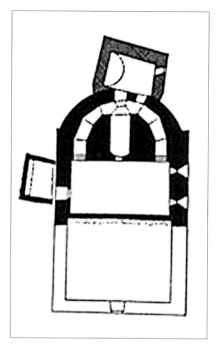

6.5 Plan of the oldest part of St Luzius von Chur with ring-crypt (*After Jacobsen 1997: figure 18*)

at Ponthion, south-east of modern Châlons-en-Champagne. It could have been dedicated to Lucius some time before this, but the documentation is wanting.

The church has been archaeologically investigated (*6.4*), and dated with provisional reference to the time of Stephen's visit[23] but there is evidence to indicate that it predates this historic event. Stylistically the church's ring-crypt (*6.5*) has been noted as the earliest example north of the Alps and has been interpreted as an imitation of the early western example of the ring-crypt at San Apollinare in Classe, which dates to 549. Therefore, the church of St Luzius at Chur may be older than the sixth century when Raetia was Ostrogothic territory until the downfall of Witigis (536-540).

At any rate the earliest mention of the church being dedicated to Lucius is in *c*.820, when his tomb was stolen from the crypt, upon which in 821 Bishop Victor II of Chur wrote a petition to Emperor Louis the Pious:

> Nec etiam illud sacratissimum corpus beati Lucii confessoris nobis reliquerunt, qui ipsam ciuitatem de diabolico errore ad cultum ueri dei praedicando conuertit.[25]

Further research is needed into this intriguing event to establish whether the thieves were ever apprehended, or what became of the tomb, but the petition at least provides early evidence of the importance of Lucius at Chur.

Bishop Tello built a new cathedral at Chur in the ninth century by reusing a former Roman fortress, and the Benedictine Abbey of Pfäfer administered the old church of St Luzius. Although a Bishop of Chur is not mentioned before AD

Table 6.2: The known early Bishops of Chur

Date	Bishop of Chur
452–455	Asimo
*c.*460	Pruritius
*c.*470	Claudian
*c.*485	Ursicin I
*c.*495	Sidonius
*c.*520	Eddo
530–546	Valentinianus
548–?	Paulinus
*c.*590	Theodore
*c.*614	Victor I

451/2 when St Asimo attended the Synod of Milan, the See of Chur could well have existed long before. Certainly the Christian religion already had influence in the area, for there was a Christian Roman prefect in the Valais in AD 377, and in 381 a bishop of Martigny attended the Council of Aquileia.[26] Closer to Chur, the fourth- or fifth-century church of St Peter at Schaan (presently in Lichtenstein) utilised a Roman fortress of the second half of the fourth century, built to secure the principal route between Curia and Brigantium (Bregenz) and continuing on to Augusta Vindelica (Augsburg).[27]

One modern explanation for St Luzius von Chur is that he has been confused with Lucius, the first-century Bishop of Cyrene in Ptolemais, Africa, his name allegedly miswritten 'curiensis', or the Roman general Lucius Munatius Plancus (*c.*87–*c.*15 BC), the conqueror of Raetia. The latter is quite a stretch since the general was no Christian, and besides, the Feast Day for Lucius of Cyrene is 6 May whereas Lucius is 3 December. It is also too much to assume that the Bishops of Chur were not aware of Lucius of Cyrene who is mentioned in Acts 13:1:

> In the church at Antioch there were prophets and teachers: Barnabas, Simeon called Niger, Lucius of Cyrene, Manaen (who had been brought up with Herod the tetrarch) and Saul.

Before focusing on the *Vita Lucii* and second-century events between Britannia and Raetia relevant to the life of Lucius and/or Luzius, it may be useful to entertain a hypothesis whereby Lucius' presence at Chur is explainable simply as a product of eighth-century stories being shared and garbled. We can try to assess whether Luzius of Chur is a construction through physical contact and reflexive transmission of the story of a British king, taken as only a story based on a series of manuscripts. If, for example, the works of Bede were influential in creating the Raetian tradition, how might that process have taken place? Teasing out a plausible answer to this question requires a discussion of the points of contact made with old Raetia in the travels of several early British missionaries.

An example is Benedict Biscop (*c.*628-690) who made several journeys to Rome between *c.*653 and *c.*687. Biscop, with his companions Wilfrid[28] and Bishop Acca of Hexham, established important libraries stocked with manuscripts they had procured in Rome. It is not impossible that while in the pontifical library they made copies of the *Liber Pontificalis* and, with notice of Lucius, returned to Britain in *c.*687 or 703[29] (in the latter year Biscop visited Rome specifically to gather manuscripts to stock the new library at the church of Saints Peter and Paul, Canterbury).

In 682 Egfrith, the King of Northumbria from 670 to 685, encouraged Benedict to found a second monastery at Jarrow, which he did, and it was there that his young pupil Bede lived and wrote. Bishop Acca of Hexham stocked his own library with manuscripts from Rome and made them readily available to Bede. It is through these connections that notice of King Lucius in the *Liber Pontificalis* may well have arrived in Britain (it does not have to be Nothelm solely who gathered this information in Rome some 30 years later). By the same route, these Northumbrian men might have brought word of Lucius to the continent. In addition, there were other contemporary British missionaries and travellers who could figure in disseminating news of Lucius throughout the region of old Raetia.

SAINT COLUMBANUS AND GALLUS

Two notable waves of missionary activity went from the British Isles to the continent in the sixth to eighth centuries. The earlier is known as the Hibernio-Scottish mission, where the word 'Scottish' actually refers to the Irish Scotti who had occupied Iona on the south-west coast of what we now know as Scotland. These Irish monks were instrumental in spreading Christianity throughout Anglo-Saxon England and the Frankish Empire, which included the old Roman province of Raetia. They founded numerous monasteries known as *schottenstift* and *schottenklöster* (Scottish monasteries) in the Frankish territories, and as early as the late fifth century the Irish monk St Fridolin (or Fridold), known as the apostle of the Alamanns, had already founded a *schottenklöster* on the island of Säckingen at Baden and another at Konstanz. On his way to Säckingen, Fridolin travelled through Strasbourg and Coire (Chur) founding churches dedicated to St Hilarius, known in modern Swiss as Glarus.

Fridolin's is the earliest historic mention of anyone from the British Isles visiting Chur, whose bishops at the time were Claudian, Ursicin I and Sidonius (see Table 6.2).

After spending several years in the vicinity and founding the *schottenstift* at Konstanz, Fridolin extended his mission to Augsburg.

Of prime importance among these sixth-century Irish missionaries was Columbanus (543-615), famed for founding the monasteries of Luxeuil, Fontaines, Annegray in France and Bobbio in Italy. A hundred years after Fridolin, Columbanus visited Raetia briefly, and while preparing to continue to Rome one of his monks fell ill, unfit for the onward journey through treacherous Alpine passes. It was agreed to leave the monk, Gallus (*c.*550-*c.*646) by name, behind to recuperate. There in 612 Gallus set up a hermitage on the River Steinach at a place called Arbor Felix (Arbon), where a religious community rapidly gathered around him. In *c.*720 the Alemannian priest Othmar built an abbey on the site, calling it Sankt Gallen (St Gall) after this Irish monk. The great Abbey of St Gall became a famed centre of learning, and between 782 and 786 the Abbot Waldo[30] established an immense library of collected and copied manuscripts.

We know Bede's works were included into this seminal collection,[31] however the transmission of the story of King Lucius to Raetia must predate St Gall's library because the church of St Lucius was by 753/4 already at Chur. The *Vita* of St Lucius was produced at St Gall in the late 700s, fuelled – it is feasible – by the second major wave of missionary activity from Britain known as the eighth-century Anglo-Saxon mission. The champion of this mission was a Saxon named Winfrid from Devon, later renamed St Boniface (*c.*672-745).

NOTHELM AND SAINT BONIFACE

As already noted, Pope Stephen II (752-757) reportedly passed through Chur in *c.*755 and this occasion has been identified as the catalyst for building the Frankish ring-crypt of St Luzius von Chur, but the broader political context should be considered.

When the mechanisms of Roman administration departed from Raetia and Noricum in the early sixth century the remaining tribal groups of Marcomanni, Thuringians, Goths, Rugians, and Heruli coalesced into a collective by *c.*520 known as the *Men of Baia*, and this was the birth of Bavaria. One of the tribes, perhaps by this time completely assimilated into the other groups, may also have been the Brittones who had garrisoned the old Raetian *limes* for generations. An example of a remaining witness to these ancient tribal roots is the bagpipe still played in the Oberpfalz (Upper Palatinate) region. Augusta Vindelica (Augsburg) became the capital of the Schwaben (Swabian) region and from *c.*550 to 788, the house of Agilofing/Agilulfinger[32] ruled the duchy of Bavaria.

In 696, Duke Theodo invited a number of clerics from the west to organise churches and strengthen Christianity in his duchy. These religious people included St Rupert, the first Bishop of Juvavum (Salzburg) from 696 to 718, St Erhard of Ratisbon (d. 686), St Emmeram of Regensburg (d. *c.*652) and perhaps St Korbinian/

Table 6.3: List of the eighth-century Agilofing Dukes of Bavaria

Theodo V	680–718
Grimoald	c.715–724
Hugbert	725–736
Odilo	736–748
Tassilo III	748–788

Corbinian (c.670–c.730). Theodo had ensured the throne of the Lombard Liutprand (712–744) and Liutprand married Theodo's sister Guntrud, whence relations between Italian and Bavarian monasteries and church hierarchy grew especially close.[33] In 727, Liutprand took the cities of Emilia-Romagna (except Ravenna) including Classis (Classe) and this may be when the style and design of the ring-crypt of San Apollinare at that maritime city was brought north of the Alps and copied at Chur.

Wishing for greater independence from the Frankish kingdom, Theodo also fostered a close relationship with the Pope and travelled to Rome to confer with Gregory II (715/6–731). Later, in 739 Duke Odilo (736–748) presided over Saint Boniface's establishment of the four bishoprics of Regensburg, Freising, Passau, and Salzburg. In 741 he married Hiltrud, the daughter of the Frankish Mayor of the Palace, Charles Martel, but by 742 Odilo was at war with Martel's sons Carloman and Pepin III. He was forced to accept Frankish overlordship of Bavaria, but remained its Duke. At this time Odilo appears to have preferred the friendship of the Irishman Virgil of Salzburg, the disciple and successor of St Rupert of Salzburg, to his former Anglo-Saxon associates.[34] After 748, Grifo, the half-brother of Carloman and Pepin, attempted to establish his own rule in Bavaria, but was defeated by Pepin who installed Odilo's infant son Tassilo III as Duke, Hiltrud acting as regent until her death in 754. In 788 Charlemagne deposed Tassilo, who at the Synod of Frankfurt was made to renounce his and his family's claims to Bavaria, bringing to a close the Agilofing dynasty.

In about 740 the Agilofing house played a central role in the codification of the *Lex Baiuvariorum*, a non-Frankish legal system and series of laws empowering the *ducati* to exercise supreme judicial authority. This power was coupled with the control over local church hierarchy and monastic establishments, making the Bavarian Dukes *de facto* rulers of the *Regnum Francorum*, a fact which contemporary sources make clear when they refer to them as *princeps*.[35] The vital role the Dukes played in contemporary politics steadily decreased, as they were successively defeated and removed from office by Charles Martel, Caroloman, Pepin III and ultimately Charlemagne.[36] The powerful Bavarian dynasty of *Welf* (Guelph) would rise later in the Middle Ages.

One Anglo-Saxon religious group made an indelible mark on the Frankish court and Bavaria. Saint Walpurga was born in Wessex in c.710 and died at Heidenheim in

779. Her brothers were Saint Willibald (700/1-781/7) who was appointed Bishop of Eichstätt in Bavaria, and Saint Winebald (702-761). The father of these saintly siblings was St Richard, a Saxon King of Wessex who went on pilgrimage to Rome with his two sons Willibald and Winebald in 721/2. He fell ill and died at Lucca in Tuscany. Miracles were reported at his tomb in the church of San Frediano, and he became locally venerated (his feast day is 7 February). Subsequent embellished accounts of his life call him 'King of the English'! Willibald translated a selection of his father's relics to Eichstätt. When Boniface visited Rome in 739 he recruited Winebald for his missions, ordaining him a priest and placing him in charge of churches in Germany and Bavaria. In 742 Winebald attended the *Concilium Germanicum*, the first church council held in the eastern Frankish territories at which Boniface was made leader of the Austrasian Church.

Of all this eighth-century missionary activity, the most important Anglo-Saxon figure was undoubtedly one Winfrid (or Wynfrith). He was born at Crediton in Devon and trained in the Benedictine monastery of Nhutscelle (Nutshalling/ Nursling), 6km north-west of Southampton, where he taught in the Abbey school and wrote the first Latin grammar produced in England. Winfrid is better known as Saint Boniface (*c*.672-754), the Apostle of the Germans and Patron Saint of Germany and the Netherlands. He left Nursling in 710 for Canterbury and returned briefly in 716 before going to Germany as a missionary.

Within this missionary activity it is useful to locate the movements of Nothelm and discover when exactly he was in Rome. Albinus, who in 710 became the Abbot of the Benedictine monastery of St Peter and St Paul, Canterbury, encouraged Bede to write the *Ecclesiastical History* certainly by 731. It is known that Albinus sent archival information from Canterbury, some of which had recently been collected in Rome by Benedict Biscop, to Northumbria via Nothelm,[37] then a priest of St Paul's, London. At this time it is probable that Winfrid's six years (710-716) in Canterbury brought him into contact with Abbot Albinus and it is even possible that Winfrid and Nothelm embarked for Rome together in 718. Within the year (by 719) Pope Gregory II had dubbed Winfrid 'Bonifacius' and commissioned him to evangelise in Germany and reorganise the Church there. This, as we have seen, was partly on the request of Theodo Duke of Bavaria, and he may have been in Rome making this plea to Gregory while Nothelm and Winfrid were visiting.

Nothelm was on a 'fact-finding' mission in the pontifical library (the same library built and organised by Cassiodorus and Pope Agapetus), copying Gregory the Great's letters to the English mission of St Augustine in 597. The assumption has consistently been held that he happened upon the *Liber Pontificalis* entry regarding King Lucius, and this is how Bede received it for inclusion into his works of 725 and 731. Yet it is not necessary that Nothelm saw the early entry in the *Liber*: knowledge of it might have been held in the archives of the ancient *scriptorium* of St Peter-upon-Cornhill and old St Paul's in London, in the library of Hexham, Wearmouth-Jarrow and/or in the Benedictine library at Canterbury. If Rome was where he found the entry, it would have been a remarkable discovery, something in which Gregory II would have been greatly interested, as it could have given his plans for evangelising the Germanic tribes an essential stamp of ancient precedence and *auctoritas*.

As with Benedict Biscop's earlier journeys to and from Rome, it is significant that Winfrid, Nothelm and Theodo might all have been present in Rome at the same time, by *c.*718 and certainly before 725 when Bede completed his *Chronica maiora*.

Nothelm returned to Britain with the results of his research, passing it on to Bede at Jarrow. Then, by 735, he became the Archbishop of Canterbury. Winfrid left Rome immediately on being renamed Boniface in 719, and after working in Hesse, Thuringia and Frisia he was elevated in 722 to Bishop of the Germanic territories. He made further visits to Rome; in 732 Gregory made him Archbishop over Germany, in 737-8 he was made Papal Legate for Germany, and in 745 Mainz became his metropolitan see. Following his visit to Rome in 737-8 Boniface went to Bavaria while Odilo was duke and founded the bishoprics of Regensburg, Salzburg, Freising and Passau. In the meantime the fame of Bede's works had become widespread, and in 746-7 Boniface wrote to the Abbot of Wearmouth-Jarrow requesting copies to be sent, this too could be how Lucius was introduced into Bavaria and old Raetia.[38]

Therefore, there were several windows of opportunity for the story – supposing it just a story for the moment – of King Lucius to get to Chur from Britain. It could have found its way to old Raetia by the missionary activities of Columbanus and Gallus, or those of Boniface from 719 to his death in 754 immediately prior to Pope Stephen II's journey through Chur on his way to Pepin's court. Yet these opportunities do not satisfactorily explain why memory of a sainted British king would take root in a location so remote and seemingly unrelated to Britain. In the eighth-century *Vita Lucii*, certain British details were either elided or refigured for local tradition, for example Eleutherius' role is played by St Timotheus. However, the claim that Luzius was a King of Britannia is retained. If the Raetian tradition stems solely from Bede's works combined with an active strategy of retelling for the context of Chur, Luzius should figure as a king of more local peoples – that is, presuming the story was thought to be just a story, available for allegory. Alternatively, if the people of Chur received the story and really believed it, not wishing to do it allegorical harm, this suggests their use of Timotheus has been either misunderstood, or that they knew something more about Lucius' discipleship before his official baptism, and we can benefit from the extra information.

The Raetian emphasis of Lucius' status as a missionary saint may be significant here. He might have been characterised by the Scotti and Anglo-Saxon missionaries in the early 700s as a royal precedence for their own missionary efforts, providing them at once with ancient authority and credibility to assist in their methods of instructing the Raetian and Bavarian population. In a similar way to Fridolin's introduction of St Hilarius of Poitier to the area, Columbanus, Gall and Boniface may have likewise introduced British traditional elements of Lucius to the region.

It does remain possible the story was not transplanted to Chur at all but rather the tradition was already present there. Indeed, the case of Richard, 'King of the English', his death at Lucca in *c.*722 and subsequent entry into local devotion should be kept in mind when considering how a person's life may have different effects remembered in different countries.

Other than a twelfth-century hint by Jocelyn of Furness there is nothing in the *Liber Pontificalis*, Bede or the majority of British writers to suggest King Lucius went to Raetia. That information is only fully presented before an English readership in 1586 with Holinshed's citations of Schedelius' *Nuremburg Chronicle* of 1493. It is therefore safe to assume the tradition of Chur remained independent of the main British textual strands that we have followed in prior chapters.

The foregoing attempt to envisage how Lucius, being a missionary king who had left his British throne, could have been transplanted to Chur as a story without a basis in fact has proved unsatisfactory. It provides no more than various opportunities of contact for the histories of Bede and perhaps some oral tradition. However, there remain several counter-arguments to the claim that Lucius was simply a story wrapped up in manuscripts and discourses. Firstly, to assume that Lucius resided only in the written word ignores evidence from oral tradition in both Britain and in old Raetia. For example, making Lucius a product of the *Liber Pontificalis* and Bede discounts the king's names, Lleirwg and Lleufer Mawr as remembered in the *Welsh Triads*.

By the eighth century, the degree of importance in Chur of Luzius' tomb was to lead to the theft of his body and an impassioned appeal against the perpetrators by the local bishop. It indicates local custom was well established if not well attested by extant sources.

Another insurmountable argument against Lucius being a mere product of the quill comes from the eighth-century *Vita Lucii*; Lucius was a king of Britannia. There appears no reasonable explanation why, in Chur, he would be honoured as a king of Britannia, unless by a gross mistake to do with his leading a local tribe long since assimilated. Details regarding his conversion and baptism differ from the *Liber Pontificalis*, but not his title nor country of origin. Therefore, although much comparison of information between Britain and Chur may have occurred during the great missionary activities outlined above, the tradition of Chur cannot be explained away simply as a product of shared manuscripts. Following is a detailed analysis of the *Vita Lucii Confessoris Curiensis*[39] (see also Appendix B for the original Latin and accompanying English translation).

THE *VITA LUCII CONFESSORIS CURIENSIS*

This work, not in the 'British tradition' appears to be the earliest extant reference to King Lucius of Britain as a missionary in Raetia and dates to the eighth century. The title of the *Vita* refers to Lucius as a confessor rather than a martyr (a confessor is usually a saint who dies of natural causes) but in the text of the *Vita* he is described as martyred at Chur. There are the typical hagiographic elements employed in most *Vitae*, but the noteworthy details begin with the conversion of King Lucius in Britannia, by one Timotheus.[40] In 896 Notker Balbulus concurred that Saint Timotheus, the brother of Novatus, had baptised King Lucius of Britain. Later, in an alleged genealogy discovered by Caesar Baronius, Timotheus was referred to as the brother of Novatus and son of Rufus Pudens and Claudia, brought up on the 'knees of the Apostles'.[41]

Richard Smith/Smyth (1590-1675) discussed as apocryphal the 'story that St. Timothy baptized King Lucius of Britain, citing several versions'.[42] Smyth's contemporary, Hugo Paulinus de Cressy (1605-1674) commented in Book I of his *Church History of Brittany or England, from the beginning of Christianity to the Norman Conquest*:[43]

> Our ancient histories report that Timotheus the eldest son of Rufus (Pudens) came into Britain where he converted many to the faith, and at least disposed King Lucius to his succeeding conversion.

According to the *Vita*, Lucius at the end of his reign left Britannia and journeyed through the continent to the city of Agusta Vindalica, more correctly Augusta Vindelicorum, presently Augsburg.[44] This city was built near the Danube in *c*.14 BC and by the end of the first century was included in the province of Raetia. By *c*.AD 50 the Via Claudia Augusta ran through that city and connected Raetia with Italia by way of Summuntorium (Burghofe bei Mertingen/Burghofe an die Donau, near Donauworth, Germany), Hotilia (Ostiglia, Italy) and Altinum (Altino, Italy). This important road serviced several Alpine settlements including Curia Raetorum (Chur), the Roman capital of Raetia Prima. Following the Via Claudia, Lucius pursued his missionary activities into what is now the easternmost Swiss canton of Grisons (Graubünden) and particularly the Rhine and Plessur river valleys in the vicinity of Chur.

This is already so remarkably different from Bede's eighth-century details that one sees the *Vita* as part of an alternate and separate tradition. Significantly, the only detail shared by the two traditions is that Lucius was a King of Britannia in the second century. Pope Eleutherius is not mentioned in the *Vita* and this is intriguing because if the *Liber Pontificalis* is the original source of both versions of 'King Lucius of Britain' one wonders that an eighth-century document mentions no Pope in connection to him. In the eighth century everyone who had read the Venerable Bede mentioned the pontiff, leaving it quite plausible that the *Vita* was sourcing local traditions and information not found elsewhere, at least in Britain, for centuries.

EMERITA

The *Vita* is also silent regarding Emerita, the supposed sister of Lucius. She is not mentioned until 896, included in Notker Balbulus' *Martyrology*, a work partly based upon the 869 *Martyrology* of Archbishop Ado (Adonis Viennensis 850-874).

Holinshed's *Chronicle* of 1586 cited Hermannus Schedelius's *Nuremburg Chronicle* (printed in 1492):

> Herevnto Hermannus Schedelius addeth also how he went into Rhetia with Emerita his sister, and neere vnto the citie Augusta conuerted the Curienses vnto the faith of Christ, and there likewise (being put to death in Castro Martis) lieth buried in the same towne, where his feast is holden vpon the third daie of December, as may readily be confirmed.

To clear up a misidentification of Lucius with Lucion, 'it is now easie to see, that Lucius the king, and Lucius or Lucion the sonne of Chlorus, were distinct persons', Holinshed continued:

> The said Schedelius furthermore setteth downe, that his [Lucius'] sister was martyred in Trinecastell, neere vnto the place where the said Lucion dwelled, whereby it appeereth in like sort, that she was not sister to Lucius king of Britaine, of which prince Alexander Neccham in his most excellent treatise De sapienta diuina, setteth downe this Distichon:
> > Prima Britannorum fidei lux Lucius esse
> > Fertur, qui rexit moenia Brute tua[45]

Holinshed was referencing one of the *Grands Rhétoriqueurs* poets, Jean Bouchet (1476-1550). Bouchet wrote *Annales d'Aquitaine c.*1518-20[46] which made a connection between King Lucius and the satirist Lucian of Samosata (*c.*125-*c.*180) who travelled to Gaul and taught Rhetoric in Gallia Narbonenses, many miles to the west of Raetia. In the above passage Holinshed was able to dismiss this confusion, but in doing so on the weak evidence of proximity he associated Emerita with Lucion rather than Lucius. As we have seen, much earlier in 896, Notker's *Martyrology* associates her with Lucius of Chur and Schedelius followed this tradition. Differing also with Holinshed, by 1622 the Elizabethan poet Michael Drayton (1563-1631) wrote in his *Poly-Olbion*:

> Emerita the next [saint], King Lucius' sister dear, who in Helvetia with her martyr brother died.[47]

Emerita is an extremely rare personal name and may be simply honorific; the Latin 'emeritus' relates to a soldier who has served his time and deserved honourable discharge.[48] The female form of the name is more usually associated with the city of Emerita Augusta (Mérida), the capital of the Roman province of Lusitania (modern Spain). There is a Saint Emerita, companion martyr of Saint Digna at Rome in *c.*259, whose feast day is celebrated on 22 September, but St Emerita of Raetia is honoured on 4 December, the day following the feast of King Lucius.

Schedelius' *Liber Chronicarum* (*Nuremburg Chronicle*)[49] is partly based on the eighth-century *Vita*, for example the city of Augusta (Vindelica/Augsburg) is identified as a site of Lucius' missionary activities but Schedelius also had other sources. He has Castro Martis as the site of Lucius' death whereas the *Vita* has silva Martis.[50] Schedelius likely used the *Martyrology* of Notker in adding the detail that Emerita, who was Lucius' sister, was martyred at Trinecastell near where Lucius lived, meaning either Chur or Augsburg. Trinecastell could be the present Tiefencastel (Casti in Romansch), a village perched high in the Alps in the Grisons canton and in the district of Albula, 29km south-east of Chur. Tiefencastel is situated at the confluence of the Rivers Albula and Julia (Gelgia), and at the important intersection of roads leading south to the Julier Pass and east to the Albula Pass. However, it is in the town of Trimmis (in the district of Landquart) only 5km north of Chur that Emerita is venerated.

In this chapter we have illustrated the context in which the tradition of Raetia regarding King Lucius became known in sixteenth-century England. We have also entertained the concept that Lucius of Britannia is a mere story, and then explored by which channels it could have been transmitted from the British version to the Raetian by the eighth century, at a time when when local devotion at Chur had already dedicated a church and *Vita* to him. This exposed a substantial problem: if it was simply a story being transplanted from one region to another and interior details were accordingly altered (such as who was doing the baptising) why then was the nationality and title of Lucius retained? Why was Luzius von Chur not figured as King of Raetia or indeed Brigantium (Bregenz)? In the earlier roots (before the *Vita*) could he indeed have been figured as such, but that errors were committed by foreign missionaries in a process of hearing this tradition and transmitting it back to Britannia? Could the real person referred to as King Lucius of Britannia have travelled to Raetia?

In the second century there were the circumstances and opportunities for a person, a king of Britannia, to have direct associations with Raetia. In other words, the two traditions, one based on the entry in the *Liber Pontificalis* and its reiteration in Britain by Bede, the other represented by the dedicated church foundation and *Vita Lucii* at Chur, can have been based on one common factual context – Britons were being forcibly relocated from northern Britannia to Raetia in the latter half of the second century. The material evidence for these relocations has come to light in the archaeological record only in the last century, and could have been imperfectly understood in the eighth or subsequent centuries, their meanings and implications only surviving until then in unwritten cultural memory and oral tradition. The next chapter reconstructs the second-century context of how the person of Lucius, King of Britain, may have existed after all.

CHAPTER 7

RECONSTRUCTING KING LUCIUS OF BRITAIN

A book devoted to King Lucius would not be complete without a concise summary of what has been gleaned by following the various strands of the tradition and identifying where each literary thread originates. It will therefore be instructive to draw upon all of our sources and infer something of King Lucius of Britain. In reconstructing Lucius, we may be able to see if the fabric of a tradition almost 16 centuries old, if we start from the story traced back to *c*.430 (19 centuries to date if counting from events in the second century), hangs upon something real to some extent.

If we entertain Lucius being a King if not the King of all Britannia, can we also contemplate the context and character of his reign? For instance, can we identify which tribe he might have come from, and whether he was pro- or anti-Roman? To do this we will follow the sequence of years and known historical events that would have had a bearing on his life, using the entries of Table 7.1 as a guide.

FROM CORONATION TO CHRISTENING

If Lucius reigned for 77 years from AD 124 to 201, he must have assumed the crown in youth, perhaps at birth. In due time he would have come to power during the reign of Emperor Publius Aelius Traianus Hadrianus (Hadrian, AD 117-138) and after Aulus Platorius Nepos (122-*c*.125) was governor of Britannia, perhaps in the consulships of M. Acilius Glabrio and C. Bellicius Flaccus Torquatus Tebanianus. We know of his first 53 years of reign, but in 177 Lucius appears to have sent to Pope Eleutherius (177-193) a request to be made a Christian and receive missionaries to instruct his Britons. This was no mere request for information: to make the definitive request he would have had some conversion and preliminary mentorship, and known something of Christian culture. To have this knowledge, such as knowing who to write to as a king inviting bishops, implies first-hand contact through communication and trade with Christians in Britannia before 177.

Table 7.1: Time-line of dates and events associated with the life of King Lucius

Dates relating to King Lucius	Events relating to King Lucius	Dates of known historical persons and events	Governor of Britannia	General events
		122–*c*.125	Aulus Platorius Nepos	Hadrian's Wall phase 1 begun
124	Birth/ Coronation of Lucius			
		c.126	Trebius Germanus	
			?	
		c.131–133	Sextus Iulius Severus	
		c.133–*c*.135	Publius Mummius Sisenna	
			?	
		138–	Quintus Lollius Urbicus	Moved north of Hadrian's Wall; rebuilt Coria (Corbridge)
		c.141		Reoccupation of southern Scotland
		143		Antonine Wall begun
				Campaigned against several tribes including Brigantes
		145–147	Gnaeus Papirius Aelianus	Occupation of low-land Scotland
		154–158	Gnaeus Iulius Verus	Quelled Brigantes revolt; stripped them of their territory
		158–161	Longinus/Longus/ Lentulus	
		161–*c*.165	Marcus Statius Priscus	
		163	Sextus Calpurnius Agricola	Controlled uprisings in the north; rebuilt fort at Coria (Corbridge)
		c.175–178	Quintus Antistius Adventus	

Dates relating to King Lucius	Events relating to King Lucius	Dates of known historical persons and events	Governor of Britannia	General events
		175		5500 Sarmatian cavalry troops arrived in Britain
177	Beginning of Eleutherius' papacy	177		Martyrs of Lugdunum (Lyon)
178	Lucius requests instruction from Pope Eleutherius	178–180	Caerellius Priscus	
179	St Peter-upon-Cornhill founded			
180	Letter received from Pope Eleutherius	180–c.185	Ulpius Marcellus	Revolt breaches Hadrian's Wall; war lasts until 184
		180		Marcus Aurelius dies
		184/7		Antonine Wall abandoned; war in the north ends
		c.185–187	Publius Helvius Pertinax	
192	Pope Eleutherius dies	192–196	Decimus Clodius Septimius Albinus	
		197	Decimus Clodius Septimius Albinus (Usurper)	Defeated by Septimius Severus at Lugdunum (19 February 197)
		197–201/2	Virius Lupus	Restored forts in the Pennines to Roman control
201	King Lucius dies			
		c.202	Marcus Antius Crescens Calpurnianus	Served as Iuridicus Britanniae indicating need for legal advice
		c.202/3–205	Gaius Valerius Pudens	Uprisings by the Brigantes
		205–208	Lucius Alfenus Senecio	Last Governor of all Britain

Dates relating to King Lucius	Events relating to King Lucius	Dates of known historical persons and events	Governor of Britannia	General events
		205		Hadrian's Wall rebuilt
		208–211		Septimius Severus arrives in Britain to personally deal with northern tribes
		208	Publius Septimius Geta (Viceroy)	
		211		Septimius Severus dies at York
		212		Geta murdered by Caracalla
		*c.*212		Division of Britain into two provinces either by Caracalla or previously by Severus

In this context, one particular event in Gaul could have been especially influential – the martyrdoms at Lyon. In the summer of 177 near Colonia Copia Claudia Augusta Lugdunum (Lyon), an annual meeting of Gallic tribal leaders and delegates took place on the island of Condate (Croix Rousse), at the confluence of the rivers Rhodanus (Rhône) and Arar (Sâone). During the 'Festival of the Altar of the Three Gauls', beginning on 1 August, gladiatorial entertainment was offered. The 'three Gauls' were Lugdunensis, Aquitania and Belgica, which under Augustus were grouped together into a common *concilium* bonded by the then new state-cult. This *concilium* had built a temple on the small island, whence Strabo mentioned an altar inscribed with the names of the 60 tribes surrounded by statues of each of the several states.[1]

The first day of August was the commemoration of Drusus' assembly of Gallic Kings at Lugdunum in 12 BC against imminent attack from the Sugambri, on which day the altar was consecrated to Rome and Augustus.[2] The annual assembly of provincial *flamines* of the *concilia*, at temples of the deified Augustus, became a universal event, for instance other *concilia* were held at Camulodunum (Colchester), and that of Lusitania met at Emerita Augusta (Mérida).[3] From this latter place we have additional evidence that the wife of the provincial priest shared his title: 'flaminica prov. Lusitaniae'.[4]

The elected head of the *concilium* was expected to carry the full financial burden of the celebratory games. Therefore since only men of very great wealth could undertake the office it tended 'to make the post, if not hereditary, at least re-occur frequently in the same families'.[5] While these provincial assemblies and the elected post of head priest were of great importance, 'they had no necessary or essential place in the machinery of the imperial government'[6] and, analogous to the *collegia*, their legal position was left undefined. Indeed they and the provincial governor may have had no relations.[7]

By 177, Marcus Aurelius had passed the new legislation *Senatus consultum de pretiis gladiatorum minuendis* ('The *senatus consultum* for the reduction of the cost of gladiators') granting a special concession to the *Tres Galliae* and likely to other provincial councils to purchase criminals condemned to death at a discount for use as gladiators or sacrifices in the celebratory games.[8] At Lugdunum that year the prisoners included a number of Christians from Vienne and Lugdunum along with their local bishop, the 90-year-old Pothinus and a woman, possibly a tribal convert, named Blandina. With the approval of the *concilium*,[9] they were tortured to death in the amphitheatre. Whether or not Lucius could have been present, tribal representatives, *legati*, relations, or friends from Britannia may well have been eyewitnesses. Also, communications from the Gallic *concilium* to those across the Channel could be relayed fairly swiftly.

Irenaeus wrote to Eleutherius about the martyrdoms, and within a few months the Church from West to East knew of the atrocities at Lugdunum. Its infamy could well have been one of the catalysts of Lucius' resolve to join the Christian religion. At any rate, as a preparing catechumen he surely would have heard of this treatment of Christians.

In the first year of his papacy and perhaps shortly following the events at Lugdunum, Eleutherius responded to Lucius with a mission to Britannia led by at least two bishops; there they baptised him with water and perhaps even christened his kingship. The administrative powers in Britannia would know him by the Roman *praenomen* Lucius, from 'lux' ('light'), but Lucius was also to be remembered as 'Lleufer Mawr' or 'great light'. While this was his name in the Brythonic language, the question remains: can we identify the tribe(s) of which Lucius was king?

SILURIAN ROOTS?

In 1836, Rice Rees published his pioneering work *An Essay on Welsh Saints*. On dating the *Welsh Triads*, he argued that 'as they relate principally to circumstances which took place in the sixth century, most of them must have been formed after that time' but also noted that:

> … [they] belong to different dates, being a method of arranging ancient traditions together, as they occurred to the mind of the inventor; and as they are insulated compositions, the incorrectness of some of them does not necessarily affect the authenticity of the rest.[10]

With due caution Rees addressed the *Triads* as a primary source for Lucius (Lleurwg or Lleufer Mawr). Triad 35 indicates he founded the church at Llandaff, 'the first in the Isle of Britain'[11] and Triad 62 on the three ancient archbishoprics in the land has it that 'the earliest was Llandaff, of the foundation of Lleurwg ab Coel ab Cyllin, who gave lands and civil privileges to such as first embraced the faith of Christ'[12] (Rees noted that the term 'Archbishop' was unknown before the Council of Nice in 325[13]). Rees also provided a further Welsh testimony to Lucius: the *Silurian Catalogues of Saints* related that Lleurwg 'applied to Rome for spiritual instruction; upon which, four persons, named Dyfan, Ffagan, Medwy, and Elfan, were sent him by Eleutherius, Bishop of the See'.[14]

Rees then somewhat critically acknowledged a variant interpretation of Lucius:

> [Writers such as Cressy] must needs add, that after he had Christianized the whole of his dominions, he laid aside his crown; and, in company with his sister, St. Emerita, he toiled his weary way, as a missionary, through Bavaria, Rhaetia, and Vindelicia, until at last he suffered martyrdom near Curia in Germany. *After this extravagance of fiction*, it can be no wonder that some modern writers have denied altogether the existence of Lucius; and it must be admitted that his history ... is, with its most confined limitations, involved in uncertainty. The Welsh accounts authorize no further supposition than that he was the chieftain of that part of Siluria, which was afterwards known by the joint names of Gwent and Morganwg.[15] (my italics)

On noting variance as to whether the two emissaries were Roman and that all four came to be remembered with Brythonic names – underlining why some think it best to 'reject the idea of a mission to Rome as a monkish fabrication', Rees cautions:

> ... There are, however, local indications in the neighbourhood of Llandaff which support the belief of the existence of these persons. Four churches have been called after the names of Lleurwg, Dyfan, Ffagan, and Medwy; and their locality ... determines the situation of the patrimony of Lucius.[16]

Rees, and several scholars after him, reveal that the tradition of Lucius in Wales cannot be ignored, notwithstanding uncertainties about the extent of the ancient king's activities. What is agreed is that southern Wales, London, Gloucester, York, perhaps Northumbria, and possibly even Furness and Edinburgh had localised traditions respecting Lucius.

Rees supported the implications of ancient Welsh sources and the identification of the Silures tribe of south-east Wales, explaining the references in the Welsh Triads. Tribal holdings of the Silures continued into the fifth and even seventh centuries as the kingdoms of Gwent and Glywysing,[17] giving continuity and context in support of our claim that cultural memory remains an important source. Yet, there is in Wales no recorded memory of where Lucius is buried, which is extremely odd if, as Rees supposed, he remained a very localised chieftain with great fame among his own kin. People of other tribes evidently did make claims for his resting-place.

Supposing now that Lucius, starting as a tribal king of the Silures and ended up at Glevum (Gloucester), this would at least include the Dobunni as his subjects. Their tribal capital was at Corinium Dobunnorum (Cirencester). It is near Gloucester, but were Lucius a native of the Dobunni one would expect him to be buried in the tribal capital rather than the Roman military *colonia*. Again, had Lucius been instrumental in rededicating the *curia* of the basilica of Londinium to the Christ, thus founding St Peter-upon-Cornhill, his subjects might have included the Catevellaunian/Trinovantian confederacy, the Catevellaunian tribal centre being at Verilamion/Verulamium (St Alban's) and the Trinovantian capital at Camulodunum (Colchester).

Yet again, another possibility exists for the extent of Lucius' realm or tribal connection, not considered in previous literature. Directly relating to details given in the *Vita Lucii* and somewhat corroborating the Raetian traditon that translates Lucius of Briton to Luzius von Chur, a direct parallel in the movement of people exists in history. A tribe of Britannia, the Brigantes were sent by the Romans to Raetia in the second century.

With the above-instanced bias of considering the Raetian tradition an 'extravagance of fiction',[18] dispassionately pursuing its implications as informed by archaeological knowledge of the British presence in Raetia has not received serious attention. We, however, shall see where it leads us.

BRITTONES IN RAETIA

As discussed in Chapter 5, the tradition of Luzius von Chur in old Raetia has connections with that of Lucius. His Christian kingship in Britannia is a shared detail not satisfactorily explained by treating it as a story in manuscript form, transplanted from Rome or Britain to distant Chur. It is, therefore, worth considering how Lucius, a British king of the second century, could have made contact with Raetia.

There were important contacts made between the provinces of Britannia and Raetia in the late second and third centuries: geographic and military connections between distanced tribes both bearing the name Brigantes. In Britain the Brigantes may have been a confederacy of several tribes including the Carvetii, centred possibly at Luguvalium (Carlisle), and the Parisi perhaps at Petvaria (Brough on Humber). However, while Brigantia was the largest *civitas* in Roman Britain, it had a dispersed rural population with no apparent *oppidum*.[19] Their *civitas* capital was at Isurium Brigantum (Aldborough), a legionary fortress and veteran's *colonia*. Yet Lucius' base may also have been associated with Coria (Corbridge) with a tribal centre at Stanwick in North Yorkshire, formerly the court of the Brigantian Queen Cartimandua.

Judging from the anti-Roman revolts and wars instigated by the Brigantes in the late second century it is not surprising that there are no Roman inscriptions from the north that mention Britons involved in commerce[20] but while they seem not to have produced their own coinage, some may have supported the Roman cause even to the point of adopting Roman names and using imperial coinage. Plausibly at least, a level of diplomatic cooperation might have existed between Brigantians and Romans to facilitate commerce.

From 139 to 142 Antoninus Pius promoted Quintus Lollius Urbicus as governor of Britannia with the role of quelling violent uprisings in the north. Urbicus did overcome a long series of skirmishes by the Brigantes and deported many of them to the Raetian *limes*, the military border between the Empire and the Germanic peoples east of the Rhine (*colour plate 15*).

Shortly following the defeat of the Brigantes in 142, a new wall 75 miles north of Hadrian's Wall was built. This, the Antonine Wall, ran for about 37 miles and was built of turf on a 16ft-wide stone foundation. The Brigantes renewed their hostilities in northern Britannia in *c.*154 and the Romans sent detachments south from the Antonine Wall leaving it exposed. It was possibly at this time that the Blatobulgium (Birrens) fort in Dumfriesshire was destroyed and rebuilt.[21] Antoninus responded by 'evicting some or most of the population from between the two walls'[22] and transplanting them to Upper Germany, settling them 'on either side of the River Nicer (Neckar)'.[23]

The Brigantian deportees were established into military units, the *dediticii Brittones* eventually being organised into *numeri*.[24] Known as Brittones (Britons), they were commissioned to garrison the many forts and stone towers along the length of the *limes*, with the notable presence of their families in adjoining small villages. By 145 we find the Brittones Triputienses on the Odenwald-Neckar *limes* at Eulbach and Schlossau[25] and the Brittones Elantienses[26] south at Neckarburken-Ost some time after 158.[27]

The different *numeri* comprising Britons that we know of are listed in Table 7.2. They were the Brittones Triputienses, Elantienses, Gurvedenses, Murrenses and the Antoninianorus. Some of these *numeri* were later transformed into *exploratores* such as the Triputienses and Nemaning.

Soon after AD 155 the entire central section of the Raetian *limes* was advanced beyond the Neckar, and from Miltenberg-Altstadt on the Main to Lorch this section ran in one single straight line for some 50 miles, fortified with large stone forts, a wall and a wooden palisade. There was no further change in the line of the whole Germano-Raetian *limes*, which was nearly 250 miles long.[28] However, 'the Brittones were kept on the old inner line, where they were entrusted with the building of forts'.[29]

Perhaps as early as AD 145 the Brittones Triputienses stationed on the Odewald may have been moved to Miltenberg and transformed into the exploratores Triputienses[30] but the earliest securely dated *exploratores*, the Nemaningenses, are attested on an inscription near Obernburg, which was set up on 13 August AD 178 and reads:

n. Brit. et expl. Nemaning. c. agent T. Aurel. Firminus centurio Leg XXII Pr.[31]

Table 7.2: Chronology of the known *numeri Brittones* on the Raetian *limes*

Date	*numeri Brittonum*	General location	Archaeological site
Between 115 and 130			Hesselbach
*c.*145	Brittones Triputienses	Odenwald-Neckar *limes*	Eulbach
			Schlossau
			Odenwald
145	exploratores Triputienses		Miltenberg
After 158	Brittones Elantienses		Neckarburken-Ost
By 180-192			Osterburken
	Brittones Gurvedenses		
	Brittones Murrenses		
	Brittones Antoninianorus		
178	exploratores Nemaningenses		Obernburg

In the opposite direction and representing a sort of people-swapping, from Raetia itself we know the Raeti Gaesati were stationed in Britannia by the early third century at Habitancum (Risingham),[32] Mamucium (Manchester),[33] Jedburgh or Cappuck[34] and Aesica (Great Chesters).[35] From Blatobulgium, a fort at Birrens, an altar reads:

MARTI ET VICTORIAE AVG C RAETI MILIT IN COH II TVNGR CVI PRAEEST SILVIVS AVSPEX PRAEF VSLM

To Mars and the Victory of the Emperors, The Raetian tribesmen serving in the Second Cohort of Tungrians commanded by the Prefect Silvius Auspex willingly and deservedly fulfilled their vow.[36]

It is generally agreed that one of the consequences of Quintus Lollius Urbicus' campaigns in northern Britain from AD 138 to 145 was the removal of Britons to the Odenwald-Neckar *limes* in Upper Germania, and that those Britons were of the Brigantian confederacy. Epigraphic evidence supports this, for in AD 145 there were Brittones Triputiensis and Brittones Elantiensis at Odenwald and Neckarburken-Ost[37] respectively. Early on the three Odenwald forts of Hesselbach, Vielbrunn and Würzberg were surrounded by *fossae punicae*, more common in Britain than in Germany, and in the mid 1980s excavations at Hesselbach revealed a British dolphin-type fibula brooch dating to the Flavian-Trajanic period (AD 69-117) and of a kind more common to the Midlands and South Wales.[38] It may have belonged to an *officialis* recruited to the unit from South Wales or the Midlands.[39] This would indicate that tribal Britons from the south of Britannia were being emplaced as superiors over the soldiery of the Brittones who consisted of members from the old Brigantian confederacy of northern Britannia.[40]

Indeed there has been some debate as to whether the centurions of British *numeri* were Britons or Romans, some individuals seem to have retained their tribal names. For example, there was a Cassius Troianus, centurion of the Brittones Murrenses, and a G. Iulius Marinus of the Brittones Gurvedenses. At Niederbieber (near Neuwied), even as late as AD 246, soldiers are recorded with the names Sattara, Dagovassus, Aturo,[41] and at Mainz there is Togius Statutus.[42]

Shortly after 158 it appears the Brittones Elantiensis were moved from their station at Neckarburken-Ost and had, by the reign of Commodus (180-192), joined the garrison at Osterburken where an annexe of 1.35ha had been added to the auxiliary fort.[43] Units of Brittones are also known to have garrisoned forts at Welzheim-Ost, Walldürn, Niederbieber, Öhringen and Benningen. Conversely, in Britannia, the numerus Hnaudifridi and the cives Tuihanti, undoubtedly men from Upper Germany, were stationed at Housesteads. This exchange of peoples from one volatile area of the Empire to another is not unique, but of interest here is that whole families accompanied the Brittones sent to Raetia, people comprised of the Brigantes, Carvetii and Parisi tribal confederacy, and they lived in small settlements adjoining the garrisoned forts.

These unbroken family ties afforded continuation of tribal memory and culture, allowing for such practices as chieftains and allegiance to remain in place, albeit within the confines of ex-patriot enclaves in a new land and in the strictures of forced military service. We shall see below such an example of cultural continuation in the Votadini in Britannia. Our present corpus of archaeological information is still too negligible to answer the question that naturally springs to mind: did the Brittones in Raetia continue to have a royal figurehead?

THE MARCOMANNIC WARS

In *c.*167 the Raetian *limes* proved inadequate against an immense invasion of Germanic tribes including the Quadi and Marcomanni. To meet the emergency Marcus Aurelius immediately recruited new troops, even mobilising slaves as *voluntarii* and 'brigands' from Dalmatia and Dardania.[44] An expanded *Legio VII Claudia* was sent to strengthen the defenses of Raetia and Noricum.

Concerning the military relocation of tribal peoples such as the Brigantes and early Christian foundations in Raetia, Jerris suggested 'the nascent stage of

Christianization in this region should therefore be understood as one aspect of the broader process of Romanization [where] the intimate connection of Christianity with Roman troops may explain the geographic distribution of the earliest churches in the region'.[45] Several early churches in the vicinity of Chur do point to a largely 'private initiative'.[46]

Luzius has lately been recast as a 'local figure from the Prattigau who lived during the fifth or sixth century and worked as a missionary first in an area to the north of Chur known as the Luziensteig, and later in Chur itself'.[47] Though that may be, for the sake of argument it is worth resuming our exploration into linkages for a more traditional version of Lucius of Britain.

As mentioned earlier, part of the Brigantian confederation included the Parisi. The tribal legates of the Parisi in the Gallic province of Gallia Lugdunensis would have been present at Condate in 177, and therein lies another link between the martyrdoms at Lugdunum and Lucius' communications to Pope Eleutherius in the same year. Even if Lucius was not physically present at Condate he could have received an eyewitness account of the Christian community of Lugdunum and their subsequent martyrdoms from Parisi subjects.

GOVERNOR LUCIUS OF BRITANNIA?

It is instructive to entertain other possible identifications for Lucius. He could, over 77 years, have won the allegiance of several British tribes, perhaps instrumental in confederating some like the Parisi under the banner of the Brigantes, or, upon conversion he might have been peace loving (a 'good king'[48]) and useful for the Romans in diplomatic relations with more aggressive tribes like the Silures and Brigantes. It may be no exaggeration that having ruled so long, his influence and regard stretched throughout all Britannia.

There are other, less likely possibilities for the identification of Lucius. For example, from 205 to 208, just after the time of Lucius, the name of the last governor of all Britain was Lucius Alfenus Senecio. This was immediately prior to the division of Britannia in 211 into two provinces, Britannia Superior and Britannia Inferior. Let us suppose for a moment that Lucius the *rex* of Britannia was Lucius the *proconsul* of all Britannia. King Lucius apparently died without an heir, producing a possibly leaderless half-century – which might have been an interpretation of Lucius Senecio completing his post as governor – and for an unstable period of time Britannia was in the throws of administrative change. Eventually London and York became the respective capitals of the two provinces and the first mentioned consular governor of Britannia Inferior is Tiberius Iulius Pollienus Auspex (223-226), resident at London. In Britannia Superior and based at York was a praetorian governor. This division lasted until 296 when Diocletion further divided the island into Britannia Prima (Caerleon and Chester), Secunda (York), Flavia Caesariensis (Lincoln) and Maxima Caesariensis (London).

However, direct identification of personages does not work, as Lucius Alfenus Senecio cannot be the identity of King Lucius since he was born in Curculum/ Cuicul (Djemila) in Numidia, Africa and served as consul and as legate of Syria Coele in *c*.200.[49]

Nevertheless, he is the only governor of all Britain with the name Lucius and the added context of his being the last person to hold his particular post in Britannia before the significant division of the administration reflects remarkably well on the final phase and immediate aftermath of King Lucius' reign.

Should one want to try to pursue alternatives, taking Lucius as a story that weaves an amalgam or composite of other historic figures, it proves possible but strained. From the popular name 'Lucius' alone, two candidates would be worthy of note, but even these are unsatisfactory:

I: Lucius Ceionius Commodus (Lucius Verus) co-emperor, in the East, with Marcus Aurelius from 163 to 166 and died in 169. Lleufer could conceivably be a corruption of Lucius Verus, but the accolade 'Great Light' applied to the former are for opposite reasons to the beliefs of the latter. His dates do agree with Bede's *Ecclesiastical History* scheme (AD 167), but place him before the pontificate of Eleutherius and instead in that of Pope Anicetus (157-168) and Soter (168-177).

II: Lucius Artorius Castus. He was military commander of the Sarmatian cavalry posted in northern Britain in the second century and has been popularly associated with a far more shadowy figure from the sixth century, King Arthur.

However, there are problems with entertaining the idea that Lucius can be identified simply as an amalgam of other historically known figures bearing that name, especially since the name itself was extremely popular in the second century. Any number of acrobatic attempts to find tenuous coincidences between the British king and any other Lucius falls into the arena of speculation on untenable alternatives creating more embroidery (of which Geoffrey of Monmouth was the greatest exponent). A danger remains in reconstructing the context and person of Lucius by straying too far from the evidence.

In pushing too hard for a created amalgam, we discredit the veracity of any other part, including the reality, of a man who wrote to Eleutherius and was called a king of Britannia according to the information held by whomever put him in the *Liber Pontificalis*. It has not been the aim of this work to add to the legend of Lucius but to discover the reality before it was wrongfully deemed legend or the slip of a scribe's quill. Therefore, it is important to return to what is known of the relationship between second-century Brythonic kingship and Roman administration.

Client kingships in Britannia such as Verica[50] and Tiberius Claudius Togidubnus (or Cogidubnus) of the Regnenses (or Regni, formerly the Atrebates) do not seem to have extended much beyond the Flavian period (69-96) but the severe lack of evidence may be ascribed to a variety of reasons. For one, the continuation of

British family and tribal tradition was not the focus of Roman accounts concerning Britannia. History is indeed written by the victors, but it is too much to assume that tribal memory and the lineage of kings and queens ended in a vacuum. Traditional status among the Britons might simply not have been officially recognised by the Roman provincial administration and therefore went unrecorded.

Other material evidence has likely been destroyed in the many tumultuous events in British history, and archaeology and historical studies are continually-evolving disciplines. From these circumstances of a poor material record, together with the truism that *absence of evidence is not evidence of absence*, the limited traces of a king of Britons communicating with the Bishop of Rome may be all that survives of much broader processes of transformation among the tribes of Britannia. However, this does not mean that a renewed search for clues of Lucius being a long-reigning king is moot.

There is only one reported instance of a British client kingship extending beyond this period, that of the Votadini in the north-east. When the Romans abandoned the Antonine and retreated to Hadrian's Wall in 164 they left the Votadini in place as a client kingdom, enjoying the rewards of alliance with Rome without being under its direct rule, while creating a safe buffer between hostile tribes and Britannia. This relationship continued until the Roman withdrawal from Britannia in *c*.410. By *c*.470 a new kingdom of the Guotodin, later known as the Gododdin, encompassed most of the original Votadini lands while in the southern area between the Rivers Tweed and Tyne a separate kingdom was formed called Brynaich (Bryneich). The Gododdin were finally defeated by the Angles who had already invaded Brynaich, subsequently known as Bernicia, in *c*.572[51] at the Battle of Catraeth (Catterick in North Yorkshire).

In the Roman period, the Votadini tribal centre might have been at Traprain Law, though by the sixth century the royal seat was at Din Eidyn (Edinburgh),[52] and they became the subject of the seventh-century poem-cycle by Aneirin known as *Y Gododdin*.[53] Later, Cunedda of the Votadini is the traditional founder of the kingdom of Venedotia (Gwynedd) in North Wales. Therefore, in a very real sense a part of the Brigantian confederation was able to maintain its autonomy right into the age of Bede and in the same geographic area. This naturally raises the question of whether local oral tradition would fortify the discoveries Benedict Biscop or Nothelm would present to Bede from Rome: was Lucius locally remembered in northern Britain, or northern Wales?

King Edwin (reigned *c*.616-632/3) eventually unified Bernicia and Deira into the kingdom of Northumbria. There was a brief division of the kingdom following Edwin's death whereby Deira was ruled by Osric and Bernicia by Eanfrith from *c*.632 to 634. Oswald was able to reunite Northumbria in 634, and by the eighth century the kingdom was prosperous. Two regents spanned the years when Bede was compiling his *Chronica maiora* in 725 and *Ecclesiastical History* in 731, firstly King Osric (reigned 718-729) but all that is known of him is from the mention by Bede that a foreboding comet was seen at the king's death. The second king, Ceolwulf, who reigned from 729 to 737, is far more significant to the context of Bede's writings, as Bede calls him the most glorious king and dedicated his *History* to him.[54]

Bishop Acca is of particular interest because he had gathered together a well-stocked library, partly gained through his earlier travels with Benedict Biscop (Biscop Baducing, *c*.628-690) and Wilfrid (*c*.634-709) to Rome in *c*.687. As mentioned in Chapter 6, Benedict had previously founded Monkwearmouth-Jarrow Abbey in 674, and upon their return from Rome Jarrow's library was enriched with so many important documents it was acclaimed as the cradle of English art and writing. This is where Bede lived and wrote. In addition, Acca lent Bede many materials from his own library at Hexham, so it is supportable to think that Benedict Biscop and Acca in *c*.687, rather than Nothelm in *c*.725, returned to Britain with notes from the *Liber Pontificalis* with mention of Lucius.

There was also another simultaneous route of feasible transmission. The traditions of the local Votadini, once confederates of the Brigantes, continuing through the *Gododdin* and being preserved by the Angles of Bernicia, tenuously survived into eighth-century Northumbria and came to the notice of centres of learning such as Acca's Hexham and Benedict's Jarrow. Indeed both lineages could have operated, with local Northumbrian tradition receiving verification from the ancient *Book of Pontiffs*.

Even if Lucius wasn't especially remembered in northern Britain, if we return to his possible connections to the Brigantes at large, several more possibilities present themselves.

KING LUCIUS OF BRITAIN

One feasible and not altogether fanciful reconstruction of King Lucius of Britain might be formulated. A Brigantian boy of royal stock born in AD 124 succeeds to his tribal throne and thereafter leads the uprisings in northern Britannia in 139 and again in *c*.154, when he was 15 and 30 years old respectively. On both occasions many of his kin are captured by the Roman forces and evicted from their homeland to a completely different quarter of the Empire, the Raetian *limes* in Upper Germania. He and his family members also come in contact with military and/or other prisoner recruits who are devotees to the Christian religion and hear through tribal communications from Lugdunum of the martyrdoms there in 177. Opportunities can even have existed for him to travel between Raetia and Britannia but, whether by fame or in person, he is known and acknowledged among the Brittones as a King of Britannia.

For reasons now lost, not least his being in a state of subjugation, he was the last of his royal line. His personal situation must have been complicated, a King of the Brigantes of Britannia resident either in the Nicer Valley on the Raetian *limes* or remaining in Britannia with a much depleted tribal population and displaced family ties. He is a royal convert to Christianity having sent to the chief official of the Church in the west, Eleutherius the Bishop of Rome. He had pondered how a person of his stature and in his situation might govern as a Christian while under the Roman yoke. Near the end of his life he transfered his rule to another and journeyed on a pilgrimage south, crossing the Channel and moving through Gaul, perhaps with a female accomplice named Emerita, also Christian. They eventually passed through Augusta Vindelica, along the road through Brigantia and down into the valley on the route to Italia. They stopped or were stopped and at Trimmis and Curia Raetorum they met the end of their days in the year AD 201, the location of Lucius' resting place remaining unknown in his home country for centuries. King Lucius of Britain, a strange but compelling story (*colour plate 16 & 17*).

A feasible variant of Lucius reconstructed may run as follows: a tribal Briton of royal lineage, Lleufer, learns of Christianity. Before he decides to submit his royal person to the faith, he rules his subjects with a policy that wins favour from Rome, as it is noticed his people are no longer to be feared. He is invited to take client rule over other tribes, who welcome a fellow Briton overlordship, at least as a buffer who seems to understand diplomacy and Roman administration. In this manner his long rule subsumes tribes around London, Gloucester and even York. In 177 he decides to be baptised, having been a believer for some time, and sends to Rome. In the meantime he has been making overtures to the Brigantian confederacy to cease their rebellions. He had suggested a workable solution to Rome that a group of their ringleaders be exiled to the Raetian *limes* where they could be put to good use. He makes further overtures but they are resistant and suspicious of his apparent pro-Roman, albeit Christian, agenda. Their further rebellions invite more drastic measures, but Lucius again intervenes and advises, transporting a large number together with their families to the *limes*, where their building skills can be put to good use. The advice is timely; recruits are sorely needed in Upper Germania and Raetia. As a Christian, Lucius is for a long time bothered by the recalcitrance of these robust people, and perhaps feels guilty for their absence from cherished homelands, and resolves before the end of his days to go to them as a missionary king of some renown. The rest plays out as we have seen.[55]

Both of these variants posit the Raetian tradition in some factual sense. Yet does the Raetian tradition hang solely upon the tendril that some early missionary presented himself (or was later confused) as king of Britannia – the one shared detail with the Lucius tradition in Britain – *sine qua non* the story of him at Chur crumbles? An answer may only be possible through further excavation and research in the Graubunden region, or through material evidence of his burial in Britain. However, we must return to what can be verified at present, chiefly what the *Liber Pontificalis*, Bede and elements of British oral tradition state: a king of Britannia in the year 177 requested of the Bishop of Rome, Eleutherius, instruction in the Christian religion. Bishops were sent to Britannia and the king was baptised Lucius, the 'Great Light'. His involvement in establishing Christian churches in various locations throughout the island was extensive. He lived and ruled long. He died and was presumed buried in Britain.

CONCLUSIONS

Adolph von Harnack, in an immensely important article of 1904 which was wholly accepted at the time, claimed that King Lucius of Britannia was actually King Abgar of Britio, Edessa, and that the long-debated entry in the *Liber Pontificalis* was the product of a scribal error. Archaeology was in its infancy in 1904 and much subsequent scholarly historical work on the sources discussed had not yet taken place. In particular, the study of Edessa only began to receive serious attention with the redoubtable work of J.B. Segal in the 1950s and 60s. By then the name Lucius *rex* had become straight-jacketed within the world of myth and anachronistic medieval legend. Naturally, historical scholarship and archaeological interpretation shies from what has been deemed legendary, and without much more archeological and historical study there can be no satisfactory conclusions regarding King Lucius of Britain except that he is unlikely to be mere legend. We have come to a position where opinions about the entire Lucius story being 'cock-and-bull'[56] stand roundly challenged.

Lucius does not occupy the British landscape as Joseph of Arimethea or St Alban do and we have seen that only two representations of Lucius are extant in the stained glass windows of York Minster and Gloucester Cathedral. Still, in Britain there remain isolated pockets and echoes of Lucius. Indeed, in *c*.1845 a Lancashire family by the name of King had a boy and they christened him Lucius. By the census of 1881 Lucius King was the curate in charge of Buttershaw, North Bierley in the West Riding of Yorkshire. In 1891, still at Buttershaw, he was listed as a Clerk in Holy Orders. Lucius King represents the tenuous nineteenth-century memory of an ancient king, for at Farnley Tyas (three miles south-east of Huddersfield) exists a small Victorian church dedicated to St Lucius. These, and possibly the handful of churches near Llandaff,[57] are the only British remnants of a remembered King.

Our purpose has been to hold Lucius up to the flickering candle and follow the prismatic refracted strains. That he proves interesting in the light of historical and archaeological scrutiny offers, I hope, an intriguing and promising portent for future study.

APPENDIX A

THE EPISTLE FROM POPE ELEUTHERIUS TO KING LUCIUS

The following is an English translation[1] and discussion of the letter in *Cotton Claudius DII* already mentioned in Chapter 4. The Latin transcription of *Cotton Claudius DII* is from Riley:[2]

Anno centesimo sexagesimo-nono a Passione Christi, scripsit Dominus Euletherius, Papa, Lucio Regi Britanniae, ad correctionem Regis et procerum regni Britanniae:

In the 169th year since the Passion of Christ, wrote Lord Euletherius, Pope, to Lucius King of Britannia, for the improvement of the King and of the nobles of the kingdom of Britannia:

Petistis a nobis leges Romanas et Caesaris vobis transmitti, quibus in regno Britanniae uti voluistis. Leges Romanas et Caesaris semper reprobare possumus, legem Dei nequaquam.

You desired from us the Roman and Caesar's laws to be sent to you, which you wished to make use of in the kingdom of Britannia. The Roman and Caesar's laws we can always reject, the law of God we cannot.

Suscepistis enim nuper, miseratione summa, in regno Britanniae legem et fidem Christi. Habetis penes vos in regno utramque paginam ex illis, Dei gratia.

Indeed you received recently, through the greatest compassion, the law and faith of Christ in the kingdom of Britannia. You have in your power, by the grace of God, in your kingdom either of the scriptures.

Per consilium regni vestri sume legem, et per illam de patientia vestrum rege Britanniae regnum. Vicarius vero Dei estis in regno, juxta Psalmigraphum Regem,

You accept the law through the counsel of your kingdom, and through that law, with sufferance, you rule your kingdom of Britain. For you are the Vicar of God in your kingdom, according to the King who is the Psalm-writer [prophet]

[Psalm, xxiv.1.] *'Domini est terra, et plenitudo ejus orbis terrarum, et universi qui habitant in eo;' et rursum, juxta Psalmigraphum Regem,*

'The earth is the Lord's, and the abundance of the world, and all who live in it,' and again, according to the King, the Psalm-writer,

[Psalm, xlv.7.] *'Dilexisti 'justitam, et o[disti] I[mprobitatem]; propterea 'u[nxit] te Deus, Deus tuus o[leo] l[aetitiae] p[rae] 'co[mitantibus] te;' et rursum, juxta Psalmigraphum Regem*

'You have loved justice, and hated dishonesty, therefore God, your God, has anointed you with the oil of gladness above your fellows;' and again, according to the King, the Psalm-writer [prophet]

[Psalm, lxxii.1.] *'Deus, judicium tuum, etc.'*

'God, your justice, etc.' [God, give the king your justice; your righteousness to the royal son]

Non enim dixit 'judicium' neque 'justitiam Caesaris'. Filii enim Regis gentes Christianae et populi regni sunt, qui sub nostra protectione et pace in regno degunt et consistunt, juxta Evangelium,

Indeed he did not say 'judgement' and neither 'justice of the Caesar'. In fact the King's sons and the people of the kingdom are the Christian people, who under your protection and in peace live and remain in your kingdom, according to the Gospel, just as

[Matt. Xxiii.37.] *'Quemadmodum 'gallina congregat pullos sub alis.'*

'a hen gathers chickens under her wings'

Gentes vero regni Britanniae et populi vestri sunt; quos divisos debetis in unum ad concordiam et pacem, et ad fidem et legem Christi, et ad Sanctam Ecclesiam, congregare, revocare, fovere, manutenere, protegere, regere, et ab injuriosis et malitiosis, et ab inimicis semper defendere.

Indeed the people of the kingdom of Britannia are your people; whom if divided you ought to gather as one and in concord and peace, and recall to the faith and law of Christ, and to the Holy Church, to cherish, maintain, protect, and rule, and to always defend them from injury, wickedness and from enemies.

De regno -[Eccles. X.16.] cujus Rex puer est, et cujus 'principes mane comedunt', non voco Regem propter parvam et nimian aetatem, sed propter stultitiam, et iniquitatem, et insanitatem, juxta Psalmigraphum Regem,

Concerning the kingdom, whose King is a boy, and whose 'princes eat in the morning', I do not call King because he has a small and insignificant[?] lifetime, but because of folly, and iniquity, and insanity, according to the Psalm-writer who is King,

[Psalm, lv.23] '*Viri sanguinum et dolosi non dimidicabunt dies suos, etc.*'

'Men of blood and the deceitful will not live half their days, etc.'

Per commestionem intelligimus gulam, per gulam luxuriam, per luxuriam omnia turpia, et perversa, et mala, juxta Salomonem Regem

We understand appetite through mingling/carousing [intercourse], through appetite luxury, through luxury all shame, and corruption, and evil, according to King Solomon

[Wisdom, i.4.] '*In malevolam animam non introibit sapientia, nec habitabit in corpore subdito peccatis.*'

'Wisdom will not enter the malevolent soul, neither live in a body smited by sins.'

Rex dicitur a regendo, non a regno. Rex eris dum bene regis; quod nisi feceris, nomen Regis non in te constabit, et nomen Regis perdes, quod absit.

He is called king by ruling, not by the kingdom. You shall be king while you rule well; but if you do not do this, the title of King shall not remain with you, and you will lose the title of King, God forbid.

Det vobis omnipotens Deus regnum Britanniae sic regere, ut possitis cum eo regnare in aeternum, cujus vicarius estis in regno praedicto. Qui cum Patre, etc.

Omnipotent God grant to you the kingdom of Britannia so to rule, so that you may with him reign in eternity, whose vicar you are in the aforesaid kingdom. Who with the Father, etc …

The two copies of the letter in *Cotton Claudius DII* begin:

(1) Dominus Euletherius papa … anno [sast] (Centesimo) sexagesimo septimo post passionem xpt [Christ] qui primo [deftinaun] [toro] nam benedic*tiam* Britanne … deo inspirante Lucio Regi Breton. Sebet etiam Rex omnia … facere in Regno.

(2) Anno centesimo sexagesimo nono a passionem xpi … Euletheri papa a Lucio Regi Britannie ad correctionem Regis procerum regni Britann. Petistis …

In red ink in the right margin appears:

Epistola ad Eulethery Lucio Regi Britanni.

Table A.1: List of Biblical quotations used in the purported Epistle of Eleutherius to King Lucius

	Source (Greek Numbering)	Hebrew Numbering	Epistle
I	Psalm 23:1	Psalm 24:1	*Psalmographum Regem*
II	Hebrews 1:9 and Psalm 44:8	Psalm 45:7	*Psalmographum Regem*
III	Psalm 71:2	Psalm 72:1	*Psalmographum Regem*
IV	Matthew 23:37 and Luke 13:34		*Evangelium*
V	Ecclesiastes 10:16		quoted without reference
VI	Psalm 54:24	Psalm 55:23	*Psalmographum Regem*
VII	Wisdom 1:4		*Salomonem Regem* [Solomon, Song of Songs]

The script is written in two columns divided by an illuminated blue floral vine.

Table A.1, above, lists the Biblical quotations used in the Epistle.

I: Psalm 23:1 (Hebrew numbering: Psalm 24:1) The Epistle has:

Domini est terra, et plenitudo ejus orbis terrarum, et universi qui habitant in eo

The Lord's is the earth, and the fullness of the world and all that dwell in it

The full Biblical quote is:

David canticum Domini est terra et plenitudo eius orbis et habitatores eius.

On the first day of the week, a psalm for David: the earth is the Lord's and the fullness thereof: the world, and all they that dwell therein.

II: Hebrews 1:9 and Psalm 44:8 (Hebrew numbering: Psalm 45:7) The Epistle has:

Dilexisti ʼjustitam, et o[disti] *I*[mprobitatem]; *propterea ʻu*[nxit] *te Deus, Deus tuus o*[leo] *l*[aetitiae] *p*[rae] *ʻco*[mitantibus] *teʼ*[3]

Francis Godwin's 1601 translation:

Thou hast loved righteousness, and hated iniquity, therefore God hath anointed thee with the oil of gladness above thy fellows.

However, the Latin may better be rendered using the Biblical quotation:

Dilexisti justitiam et odisti iniquitatem propterea unxit te Deus Deus tuus oleo exultationis prae participibus tuis.

Thou hast loved justice and hated iniquity: therefore God, thy God, hath anointed thee with the oil of gladness above thy fellows.

III: Psalm 71:2 (Hebrew numbering: 72:1) The Epistle has:

Deus iudicium regi da et iustitiam tuam filio Regis iudicabit populum tuum in iustitia et pauperes tuos in iudicio.

(And according to the saying of the Psalm) O God, give thy judgment to the king, and thy righteousness to the king's son, &c'.

Give to the king thy judgement, O God, and to the king's son thy justice: To judge thy people with justice, and thy poor with judgment.

IV: Matthew 23:37 and Luke 13:34. The Epistle has:

gallina congregat pullos sub alis

Like as the hen gathereth her chickens under her wings, 'so doth the king his people'.[4]

The full Latin passage from Jerome's vulgate reads:

Hierusalem Hierusalem quae occidis prophetas et lapidas eos qui ad te missi sunt quotiens volui congregare filios tuos quemadmodum gallina congregat pullos suos sub alas et noluisti.

V: Ecclesiastes 10:16. The Epistle has:

De regno cujus Rex puer est, et cujus 'principes mane comedunt', non voco Regem propter parvam et nimian aetatem, sed propter stultitiam, et iniquitatem, et insanitatem

Woe to thee, O land, when thy king is a child, and when the princes eat in the morning.

The Biblical quote:

Vae tibi terra cuius rex est puer et cuius principes mane comedunt.[5]

VI: Psalm 54:24 (Hebrew numbering: Psalm 55:23). The Epistle has:

Viri sanguinum et dolosi non dimidicabunt dies suos, etc.

The Biblical quote:

Tu autem Deus deduces eos in puteum interitus viri sanguinum et dolosi non dimidicabunt dies suos ego autem fiduciam habeo tui.

But thou, O God, shalt bring them down into the pit of destruction. Bloody and deceitful men shall not live out half their days; but I will trust in thee, O Lord.

VII: Wisdom 1:4: (Solomon, Song of Songs). The Epistle has:

In malevolam animam non introibit sapientia, nec habitabit in corpore subdito peccatis.

The Biblical quote:

Quoniam in malivolam animam non intrabit sapienta nec habitabit in corpore subdito peccatis.

For wisdom will not enter into a malicious soul, nor dwell in a body subject to sins.

Raphael Holinshed, in Book I, Chapter 19 of his 1586 *Chronicle*, quotes John Jewell:

The revered father Iohn Iewell, sometime bishop of Salisburie, writeth in his replie unto Hardings answer (Fol. 119), that the said Eleutherius, for generall order to be taken in the realme and churches before here, wrote his advice to Lucius in maner and forme following, "You have received in the kingdome of Britaine, by Gods maercie, both the law and faith of Christ; ye have both the new and the old testament, out of the same through Gods grace, you your kingdome of Britaine, for in that kingdome you are Gods vicar".[6]

Holinshed's quotation of one of the versions of the letter appears in his Book I, Chapter 9:

You require of vs the Romane ordinances, and thereto the statutes of the emperours to be sent ouer vnto you, and which you desire to practise and put in vre within your realme and kingdome. The Romane laws and those of emperours we may eftsoones reprooue, but those of God can neuer be found fault withall. You haue receiued of late through Gods mercie in the realme of Britaine the law and faith of Christ, you haue with you both volumes of the scriptures: out of them therefore by Gods grace, and the councell of your realm take you a law, and by that law through Gods sufferance rule your kingdome, for you are Gods vicar in your owne realme, as the roiall prophet saith; The earth is the Lords and all that is therein, the compasse of the world, and they that dwell therein. Againe, Thou hast loued truth and hated iniquitie, wherefore God, euen thy God hath anointed thee with oile of gladnesse aboue thy fellows. And againe, according to the saieing of the same prophet; Oh God giue thy iudgement vnto the king, & thy iustice vnto the kings sonne. The kings sons are the Christian people & flocke of the realme, which are vnder your gouernance, and lieu & continue in peace within your kingdome. ★(Note in margin: ★Here wanteth) The gospel saith; As the hen gathereth hir chickens vnder hir wings, so dooth the king his people. Such as dwell in the kingdome of Britaine are yours, whom if the be diuided, you ought to gather into concord and vnitie, to call them to the faith and law of Christ, and to his sacred church: to chearish and mainteine, to rule also and gouerne them, defending each of them from such as would doo them wrong, and keeping them from the malice of such as be their enemies. ★ Wo vnto the nation whose king is a child, and whose princes rise vp earlie to banket and feed, which is spoken not of a prince that is within age, but of a prince that is become a child, through follie, sinne & vnstedfastnesse, of whom the prophet saith; The bloudthirstie and deceitfull men shall not lieu foorth halfe their daies. ★ (Note in margin: Psal. 55) By feeding I vnderstand gluttonie; by gluttonie, lust; & by lust all wickednesse & sinne, according to the saieng of Salomon the king; Wisedome entreth not into a wicked mind, nor dwelleth with a man that is subiect vnto sinne. A king hath his name of ruling, and not of the possession of his realme. You shalbe a king whilest you rule well, but if you doo otherwise, the name of a king shall not remaine with you, but you shall vtterlie forgo it, which God forbid. The almightie God grant you so to rule the kingdome of Britaine, that you may reigne with him for euer, whose vicar (or vicegerent) you are within your aforesaid kingdome. Who with the Sonne and the Holie-ghost, &c.[7]

The English translations by James Pilkington (1563) and Francis Godwin (1601), whom Heal combines,[8] is only partial and does not, for example, include the 'warning about the rule of a child', defining 'a child as one who is foolish and imbecilic'.[9] The passages below appearing in bold, as Heal has, 'were omitted by Godwin and Fuller … added in what is probably James Pilkington's translation'.[10]

You require of us the Roman laws and the emperor's to be sent over to you, which you would [**may**] practice and put in ure within your realm. The Roman laws and the emperor's we may ever reprove, but the law of God we may not. Ye have received of late, through God's mercy, in the kingdom [**realm**] of Britain, the law and faith of Christ; ye have with you within the realm, both parts of the scriptures. Out of them, by God's grace, with the council of your realm, take ye a law and by that law, through God's sufferance, rule your kingdom of Britain. For you be God's vicar in your kingdom. *The Lord's is the earth, and the fullness of the world and all that dwell in it.* And again, according to the Prophet that was a king, *Thou hast loved righteousness, and hated iniquity, therefore God hath anointed thee with the oil of gladness above thy fellows.* And again according to the saying of the Psalm, *O God, give thy judgement to the king, and thy righteousness to the king's son etc.* He said not, the judgement and righteousness of the emperor, but thy judgement and justice; **that is to say, of God.** The king's sons be the Christian people and folk of the realm, which be under your government and live, and continue in peace within your kingdom. As the gospel saith, *Like as the hen gathereth her chickens under her wings*, so doth the king his people. The people and folk of the realm of Britain be yours, whom, if they be divided, ye ought to gather in concord and peace, to call them to the faith and law of Christ, to cherish and maintain them, to rule them, and govern them, **and to defend them always from such as would do them wrong, from malicious men and enemies. A king hath his name of ruling, and not of having a realm. You shall be king, while you rule well; but if you do otherwise, the name of king shall not remain with you, and you shall lose it, which God forbid. The Almighty God, grant you so to rule the realm of Britain,** as you may reign everlastingly with him whose vicar you are [**be in the realm**].

It remains for future research to substantiate the existence of other copies of the Epistle.

APPENDIX B

The translated main points in the *Vita* appear below; the English in quotation marks is a direct translation of the Latin quoted in full at the end of this appendix:[11]

> St Paul the apostle, after the resurrection of Christ, was in Rome preaching for two years, debating with Jews and Greeks. He asked his disciple Timothy to go to Gaul, to proclaim the good news of the kingdom of God.

> St Timothy went to Gaul, and to Burdigalensis [Bordeaux], where he converted the people to the faith of Christ.

> The people suggested to Timothy that he should go to Britannia, in which wild people lived, who served idols, ignorant of Christ, 'where king Lucius seems to reign' (*ubi rex Lucius regnare videtur*).

> Timothy, full of great joy, went to Britannia and evangelised there. The people, who were stunned by the novelty of his doctrine, told all these things to Lucius, who ordered Timothy to be brought into his presence so that he could hear for himself what his teaching was. The king asked him where he was from, and Timothy replied that he was the servant of the Lord, and that he was sent by the apostles to proclaim the word of truth, so that, rejecting idols, Lucius might know the true God. When the eager king heard all that was being said, he said 'I will summon you tomorrow, with a view to hearing something more certain' (*Die crastina superveniente advocabo te, cercius aliquid auditurus*).

> Yet that night, Lucius, while he was asleep, had a revelation in which he saw the heavens open, and an angel of God sitting at his head. After waking at the break of dawn, he summoned Timothy and told him that because of this nocturnal revelation, he knew 'that whatever you instruct is to be done' (*quod quicquid praeciperis, faciendum mihi est*).

> Timothy then explained to Lucius the doctrine of the Father, Son and Holy Spirit, and that by being baptised he would have forgiveness for his sins and be made co-heir of the saints

to resurrection and eternal glory. 'And when with great reverence he heard what was being said, believing, he was baptised, and all near him and related to him and the whole province of his kingdom was converted to the faith' (*Cumque cum magna reverencia audiret quae dicebantur, credens baptizatus est, omnesque propinqui et adfines eius et omnis provincia regiminis illius ad fidem conversa est*).

The temples of idols were destroyed, and churches were built. Lucius was burning with faith and devotion, and he moved to the region of Gaul (*migravit in regionem Galliarum*) and fed the flock with the nourishment of heaven.

Lucius went to Augusta Vindalica [Augsburg], where people had previously worshipped idols, and through his preaching a noble called *Campester* [=of a field] was baptised and was converted to the faith of Christ. He then went to the province of Raetia, and converted the little dwelling of Chur.

(Still apparently in Raetia) he went to a place called *silva Martis* [=Wood of Mars]. He warned the people that they should pray to the Lord, to give up false idols, and to love the true God who is in heaven. He compared them to mute and unthinking animals. Some of the people became angry, and threw him in a well, wanting to bury him with stones. Others disagreed with them. However Lucius rose up out of the well unharmed, and told them not to disturb the peace of Christ with tumult and insurrection.

He then continued to preach the good news of the Lord.

This *Vita* does not mention martyrdom and it provides no dates. These details, including mention of Lucius' sister Emerita, appear later in Notker Balbulus' *Martyrology* of 896.

THE LATIN *VITA*:

Incipit Conversio Vel Vita Beatissimi Lucii Confessoris[12]

(1) Diem festum celebrantes beatissimi Lucii, fratres karissimi, ad memoriam revocemus, qualiter locus iste de tenebrarum caligine liberatus, lumen rerum perciperit. Hinc ergo psalmi resonent, inde concrepent lectiones, hinc tota simul in voce confessionis erumpat ecclesia, que talem ac tantum meruit habere patronum, cuius meritis ac suplicationibus omnibus malis exuta, pleps universa exultat. Omnes ergo congratulemur in Domino et ad edificationem populi, qualiter nobis beati viri adventus inluxerit, perscrutemur, quia sancti viri relegio non peregrinis assertionibus, sed apostolicis surrexit dogmatibus, et de illo vivo fonte, quem Dominus vas electionis esse praedixit, vite poculum ministravit.

(2) Tempore enim illo, quo erat beatissimus Paulus apostolus post resurrectionem domini nostri Iesu Christi in urbe Roma et per biennium, nemine prohibente, disputaret cum Iudaeis atque Grecis, videns cecatum cor eorum et salutaribus monitis nolle adquiescere, et quia

Moyses velamen est positus super cor eorum, cum videlicet sequantur occidentem litteram et non vivificantem spiritum, relictis Iudaeis, ad gentium se praedicationem convertit. Convocans itaque praedictus apostolus Timotheum discipulum suum, dixit ei: 'Surge et vade in regionem Galiarum, et quocumque perveneris, praedica euangelium regni Dei, sicut scriptum est: *Adnunciate inter gentes magnalia et mirabilia Dei*'.

(3) Tunc Timotheus gaudens de praecepto Domini, simul eciam et de doctrina magistri sui, pervenit in partibus Galiarum, praedicans baptismum et penitentiam in remissionem peccatorum. Cumque pervenisset in portum qui dicitur Bordoelem civitatem, praedicans euangelium regni Dei, beatitudinem credentibus, non credentibus autem supplicium denuncians, convertebatque omnes ad fidem Christi, *quodquod erant praeordinati ad vitam eternam*: baptizatis ergo universis qui crediderant, et traditis mandatis, quomodo ad simulacrorum contaminatione mundarentur, et quomodo fidei regulam incorruptam servarent, et quomodo renovari per gratiam baptismatis permanerent, monebat, dicens: '*Omnes qui in Christo baptizati estis, Christum induistis.* Expoliantes ergo vos veterem hominem, id est diabulum cum criminibus suis, induite novum, hoc est Christum cum virtutibus sanctis, ut in novitate vite ambulantes, *liberati a peccato, servi autem facti Deo, habeatis fructum vestrum in sanctificatione, finem vero vitam aeternam*'. Cumque per singulos dies fidelium numerus cresceret, et signis atque virtutibus ostensis, multiplicarentur ad fidem, ordinatis sacerdotibus ac ministris, qui eis divina mysteria celebrarent, distruentes templa idolorum, aedificabant ecclesias.

(4) Peracto ergo ibi non modico tempore et confirmatis in fide Christi discipolis, cepit inquirere, sicubi essent adhuc idolis dediti populi. Tunc unus ex principibus ait ad eum: 'Innotiscimus tibi regionem longinquam qui dicitur Brittania, gentem ferocem, idolis servientem, Christum nescientem, ubi rex Lucius regnare videtur; perge ergo et ibi praedica, ut convertantur et vivant'. Haec audiens beatus Timotheus, magno repletus est gaudio, pergensque festinanter, pervenit in provinciam, ubi rex Lucius regnabat, et secundum praeceptum magistri sui non cessabat euangelizare verba vite. Stupefacti vero populi propter novitatem doctrinae illius, quam audiebant, nunciant hec omnia Lucio regi, qui continuo iubet eum sibimet praesentari, et quae esset eius doctrina, per semet ipsum audire. Cumque coram eo fuisset adductus, rex dixit ad eum: 'Que es tu aut ex qua regione vel de qua civitate?' Beatus Timotheus respondit: 'Ego sum servus domini mei Iesu Christi et discipulus apostolorum: et missus sum ab eis praedicare vobis verbum veritatis, ut recedentes ab idolis, Deum verum, qui est in celis, cognuscatis, per quem omnia facta sunt in caelestibus creaturis, et que in terris in prospectu habentur; adnunciare tibi et omnibus, in quibus est spiritus vitae, euangelium regni et gloriam sempiternam, resurrectionem post mortem et vitam inmortalem, quia regnum huius mundi et divitie eius sicut fumus pertranseunt, Christi vero regnum permanet sine fine et vita sempiterna'. Cumque omnia que dicebantur intentus audiret rex, ait ad eum: 'Die crastina superveniente advocabo te, cercius aliquid auditurus'.

(5) Eadem autem nocte in somnis vidit caelum apertum et claritatem illius, angelum quoque Dei sedentem ad caput suum, ex cuius revelatione cognovit divino nutu hominem Dei ad se missum. Expergefactus autem primo diluculo, iussit beatum Timotheum sibimet praesentari, cui et dixit: 'Ex nocturna revelatione cognovi, quod quicquid praeciperis, faciendum mihi est. Ecce paratus sum ad implendum!' Cui beatus Timotheus dixit: 'Que externa die locutus

sum, hec iterum loquor, ut, relicto errore simulacrorum, unum colatis invisibilem Deum, *quem vidit hominum nemo, neque videri potest, qui solus habet inmortalitatem et lucem habitat inaccessibilem*, et unum unigenitum eius filium Iesum Christum dominum nostrum, ante tempora aeterna ex Patre generatum, et unum paraclytum Spiritum sanctum, ex Patre procedentem et Filio, inluminatorem et doctorem animarum nostrarum, ut baptizati in nomine sanctae Trinitatis, accipiatis remissionem peccatorum vestrorum et efficiamini filii Dei per aquam baptismatis et unctionem Spiritus sancti, coheredes effecti sanctorum in resurrectionem vitae et gloriam permansuram'. Cumque cum magna reverencia audiret quae dicebantur, credens baptizatus est, omnesque propinqui et adfines eius et omnis provincia regiminis illius ad fidem conversa est.

(6) Peracto ergo baptismatis ministerio et fidei gracia confirmata, electis sacerdotibus ac deputatis ministris, distruebantur templa idolorum, et ecclesiae aedificabantur. Coepit autem beatissimus Lucius virtutum successibus pollere, terrena respuere, caelestia desiderare, saeculi huius fallaces divitias contempnere, animarum lucra desiderare, invisibilium amore, ac si videret, flagrare. Revelante sibi Spiritu sancto, quia *nemo potest duobus dominis servire*, quae mundi erant mundo relinquens, fervens fide et devocione, euangelium Christi occulte gestabat in pectore. Relicto regno rebusque paternis, migravit in regionem Galliarum, et quocumque loco oportunitas exigisset, euangelicam disputationem ingressus, oves Domini caelesti pabulo pascere non cessabat. Verbi domini non surdos auditor, illius sermonis recordabatur: *Si diligis me, pasce oves meas*.

(7) Cumque hoc indesinenter ageret, denunciatum est ei, quod esset quedam civitas, que Agusta Vindalica dicebatur, que adhuc gentili errore implicita, idolis immolaret, ubi patricius eiusdem civitatis Campester dicebatur, ibique paucis diebus requievit. Praedicante autem beato Lucio baptismum penitentiae in remissione peccatorum, credidit Campester patricius et baptizatus est, civitatem quoque suam ad Christi fidem perduxit.

(8) Cumque beatissimus Lucius in praedicta civitate moraretur, pervenit ad aures eius, quod in provincia Retiarum adhuc idolis immolarent. Confirmata ergo in Christo ecclesia et, quicquid ad relegionem et fidei graciam pertinebat, peractis *de spe ac resurrectione*, nec non et caritatis iura qualiter invicta servarent, ostensis, vale faciens eis, profectus est. Veniens autem beatissimus Lucius in Curiensi pagello, ad consueta concurrit praesidia. Celiciis tegitur, cinere conspergitur, biduanis ac triduanis ieiuniis maceratur, die noctuque sacris insistens vigiliis, Domini misericordiam precabatur, ut divinitus, luce veritatis eis ostensa, ignorantie tenebre fugarentur.

(9) Cumque ebdomada continua id ageretur, evolutis septem deibus, Spiritu sancto revelante, sermo factus est ad eum, dicens: 'Famule meus, noli timere, *viriliter age, et confortetur cor tuum*; multus enim mihi est populus in hac civitate. Confortare ergo et esto robustus, ne timeas a facie eorum, quia tecum ego sum et non te derelinquo'. Cumque mane facto, de divina revelatione roboratus, letaretur in Domino, cepit publice vanis superstitionibus derogare et fidei gratiam praedicare. Clamabat ergo, dicens: [']*Unus Deus, una fides, unum baptisma! Nam etsi sunt qui dicantur dii sive in caelo sive in terra, sicut sunt dii multi et domini multi, sed nobis unus Deus pater, ex quo omnia et nos in ipsum, et unus dominus Iesus Christus, per quem omnia et nos per ipsum*'.

(10) Cumque hec et his similia proclamaret in auribus eorum, respondentes dixerunt: 'Numquid sol et luna et stellarum globi ac relucentia fulgora divinis numinibus non admiscentur, cum videamus haec omnia suis temporibus dominari et vitae commodum mortalibus ministrare?'

Quibus vir Dei dicebat: 'Credite unum Deum esse, per quem facta sunt omnia, qui fecit caelum et terram et effudit maria, qui caelum quidem luminaribus, terram vero herbis replevit et arboribus, qui caelum obumbrat nubibus et solis calorem temperat, terram vero pluviis fecundat et roribus. Ipse est Deus deorum et Dominus dominorum, *in quo vivimus, movemur et sumus, qui appendit tribus digitis molem terrae* et ambulat super fluctus maris, *qui praecipit soli, et non oritur, et stellas claudit quasi sub signaculo, qui numerat multitudinem stellarum et omnibus eis nomina vocat, cuius spiritus ornavit caelos,* cuius sapiencia fundata est terra'.

(11) Cumque hec et his similia loqueretur, omnes crediderunt in Domino, clamantes et dicentes: 'Unus et verus Deus christianorum, qui tales probatur habere famulos'. Catecizans ergo, his verbis ortabatur, apostolica eis monita proponens, *ut abstinerent ab immolatis simulacrorum et sanguinem et suffocato et fornicacionem.* Praecurrente ergo ieiunio et fidei regula tradita, baptizati sunt universi et magnificabant Deum, qui dederat eis doctorem iustitiae et eruerat de potestate tenebrarum et transtullerat in regnum caritatis sue, quia sedentibus in tenebris et umbra mortis lux orta est eis, et quia perpetuae lucis sacramenta percipere meruerunt.

(12) Cumque cottidianis incrementis fidei cognitio cresceret, et in circuitu positis fidei sacramenta panderentur, denunciatum est ei ab eis, qui iam per eius fuerant admonitione conversi, quod in loco quodam qui dicitur silva Martis insanorum more bubalorum vituli pro diis colerentur. Quod cum audisset beatissimus Lucius, adhuc gentili errore pollutam esse provinciam, adgregata secum non modica turba populi, ad distruendum errorem festinus perrexit. Cumque ad praedictum locum pervenisset, orationi ac precibus admonet esse Domino suplicandum, ut pestem illam, sicut sciret, Dominus auferret. Quo audito, loci illius commanentes subito stupore mirantes, obviam currunt. Quos beatissimus Lucius blando sermone cepit admonere, ut a falsorum deorum veneratione recederent et verum Deum qui est in caelis adorarent. Quibus eciam adiciens dicebat: … *Dii, qui caelum et terram non fecerunt, pereant de terra et de his que sub caelo sunt'.* Cumque hec audirent, more biluino ceperunt insanire et fremere dentibus, quos iterum vir Dei admonens, dicebat: 'Surda et muta animalia colentes, similes illis efficiamini, *sicut equus et mulus, in quibus non est intellectus'.*

(13) Qui continuo ira permoti, videntes iuxta situm loci putei foveam, proiecerunt eum in eam, proiectum autem volebant lapidibus obprimere. Quod cum viderent, qui simul cum sancto viro convenerant, in furorem versi, concursu facto, volebant interficere eos, qui hec facere praesumserunt, eratque inter utrumque populum non minima concertatio. Surgens vero beatissimus Lucius de puteo nihil lesus, fortius praedicabat, conversusque ad eos quos iam in Christo filios vocabat, dixit: 'Quiescite, filii karissimi, et pacientiam domini nostri Iesu Christi nolite in tumultum et sedicionem convertere, quia ipse, *cum malediceretur, non maledicebat, cum pateretur iniurias, non comminabatur, sed tradebat iudicanti se iniuste.* Discat ergo scola domini nostri Iesu Christi exemplo ipsius lesionis vicem non rependere, sed magis maledicentes se benedicere et pro persequentibus exorare'.

(14) Sedato ergo populo, pace percepta, divina providentia disponente, apparuerunt agrestia illa animalia, quae offendiculum in populo faciebant. Quod cum vir Domini conspexisset, magno repletus est gaudio, et fixis genibus in terram, oculis ac manibus in caelum porrectis, ut id eciam qui iam baptizati erant facerent, admonebat. Tunc clara voce, audientibus cunctis, hanc fudit orationem a Domino: 'Omnipotens, adorande, colende, tremende, benedico te, quia per Filium tuum unigenitum evasi minas hominum impiorum, et salvam fecisti a persequentibus

animam meam *nec conclusisti me in manus inimici*; insuper et ostendisti mihi offendiculum, quod per machinationem demonum erat in populo tuo. Ecce enim nunc tempus acceptabile esse, nunc dies salutis, in quo electi tui de tenebris producantur ad lucem, in quo, ostensis signis et virtutibus, cognuscant filii tui, quia *tu es absconditus Deus, qui facis mirabilia solus*, qui non dispicis contritos corde et afflictos miseriis! Qui et oves et boves et universa iumenta camporum hominum usibus deputasti et populo tuo de mundis et inmundis animalibus per Moysen famulum tuum praeceptum dedisti, ut munda ederent, inmunda reprobarent, tu hec bruta animalia ad laudem et gloriam nominis tui, deposita ferocitate, fac mansuescere et usibus servorum tuorum tibi famulantium deservire'.

(15) Cumque conpleta fuisset oratio, surgentibus eis ab humo, adpropinquare ceperunt bubali illi, qui a longe stare videbantur. Et stupentibus cunctis atque mirantibus, usque ad vestigia beati viri pervenerunt, pedes eius lambentes. Videntes autem turbae tam inopinatum miraculum, timuerunt valde et glorificabant Deum, dicentes: 'Vere magnus est Deus christianorum'. Acceptis ergo vincolis et iugo vir beatissimus et alligans in capitibus eorum, addito eciam vehiculo, honus ligni ipse suis manibus superponens, constricto vehiculo, via qua venerant revertebantur.

(16) Mirantibus autem cunctis atque stupentibus, alii prae gaudio flere ceperunt, alii, elevata voce, clamabant, dicentes: 'Magnus es, Domine, et praeclarus, laudabilis in virtute et invisibilis, qui eciam agrestia et muta animalia manibus subdis servorum tuorum'. Alii dicebant: 'Magnus dominus noster Iesus Christus et magna virtus eius et sapientiae eius non est numerus, qui cecis visum, surdis auditum, claudicantibus gressum et mutis dignatur conferre sermonem, qui nos per beatissimum Lucium famulum suum a mortis tenebris liberatos perduxit ad lucem'. Alii in ymnis et confessionibus benedicebant Deum, cantantes et psallentes in cordibus suis, quia fecisset cum illis misericordiam.

(17) Cumque hec et his similia proclamarent, auditis signis et virtutibus, hii qui in civitate remanserant, acceptis lampadibus et turribulis, procedentes in occursum illis, has voces dabant ad caelum: 'Via iustorum recta facta est, sanctorum iter praeparatum est', et adicientes dicebant: 'Confitemini Domino et invocate nomen eius, laudamini in nomine sancto eius, qui congregat dispersos Israel'. Ingredientibus autem civitate et congaudentibus ad invicem de signis atque mirabilibus demonstratis, more cervorum desiderabant pervenire ad fontem aquarum.

(18) Cumque paucis diebus qui noviter venerant fidei regulam doceret et monitis salutaribus animaret, tradens eis apostolica praecepta, baptizavit universos, et plenius eos de divinis scripturis instruens, ad propria remeare permisit. Confirmatis itaque in Christo discipolis, qualiter fidei firmitas teneretur *de spe ac de resurrectione*, simulque permanente cum angelis gloria, virtutum successibus letabatur in Domino, eo quod in diebus illius pax et dilectio eclesie populum conservaret.

(19) De virtutibus vero et miraculis, quibus in hoc loco vir sanctissimus claruit, non est nostrae facultatis evolvere, quanti caeci inluminati, leprosi mundati et ab inmundis spiritibus diversis temporibus sunt curati, quantique a febribus et diversis passionibus sunt liberati, et cetera virtutum insignia, quae litteris conprehendere nostra nequivit signitia.

(20) Libet, fratres karissimi, in largitorem munerum oculos mentis adtollere et sancti huius gloriam nostraeque restaurationis gratiam praedicare, quomodo memor nostri Dominus

infra cacumina montium velut in tenebris resedentibus ex regibus gentium nobis apostolum suscitaverit et ex principibus terre euangelistam direxerit: *qui aliquando non populus, nunc autem populus Dei, et qui non consequuti misericordiam, nunc autem misericordiam consecuti*; et ut populus adquesitionis et sancta gens vocaremur; ut recte nobis illud propheticum conveniret, quo ait: *Tunc saliet clodus sicut cervus, et aperta erit lingua mutorum*, ut convenienter, quasi expediti conpedibus et calciatis pedibus, in praeparatione euangelii per singula annorum curricula quasi in occursum pio praesuli properantes, cum propheta dicere valeamus: *Quam pulchri supra montes pedes adnunciantes et predicantes pacem, adnunciantes bonum, praedicantes salutem* in Christo Iesu domino nostro, cui honor et gloria per infinita saecula saeculorem amen.

APPENDIX C

The following chronological list (Table C.1) of authors and works referring to King Lucius is intended to be as comprehensive as possible, including those writings that directly mention Lucius. Also included in this catalogue are objects associated with the king, namely the plaque of St Peter-upon-Cornhill and the purported coins provided by Sir Robert Bruce Cotton. Doubtless, further sources may be identified in the future and added to this sequence.[13]

for Table C.1 see over

	Date	Author	Title	Country of Origin
1	c.498-c.530		Liber Pontificalis: Catalogus Felicianus	It. (Rome)
2	725	The Venerable Bede (c.672/3-735)	Chronica Maiora	Br.
3	731	The Venerable Bede (c.672/3-735)	Historia Ecclesiastica gentis Anglorum	Br.
4	8th c.		Vita Lucii confessoris Curiensis (Codex Sangallensis 567)	Sw.
5	c.796	Nennius	Historia Brittonum	Br.
6	821	Bishop Victor III of Chur (820-833)	Petition to Emperor Louis the Pious	Sw. (Chur)
7	After c.850		Bern Codex 178	Fr.
8	896	Notker Balbulus (c.840-912)	Martyrology	Sw.
9	c.988	Aethelweard (flourished 973-998)	Chronicle	Br.
10	c.1082	Marianus Scotus (1028-1082/3)	Chronicle (printed in 1559, Basel)	Sw. (Basel)
11	c.1125		The Book of Llandaff (De Primo Statu Landauensis Ecclesiae)	Br.
12	c.1125	Community of St David's, Wales	Letter from St Davids to Pope Honorius II 1124-1130	Br.
13	c.1135, 1148, 1154	Henry of Huntingdon (?-after 1154)	Historiae Anglorum	Br.
14	Completed c.1135	Ordericus Vitalis (1075-c.1142)	The Ecclesiastical History of England and Normandy	Fr.
15	Completed 1134-1138	Geoffrey of Monmouth (c.1100-c.1155)	Historia Regum Britanniae (The History of the Kings of Britain)	Br.
16	Between 1129 and c.1143	William of Malmesbury (c.1096-c.1143)	De Antiquitate Glastoniensis Ecclesiae	Br.
17	c.1143	Alredus (Alfred) of Beverley (?-1154/7)	Annales sive Historia de gestis regum Britanniae	Br.
18	1122-1154		The Anglo-Saxon Chronicle (Laud MS)	Br.

	Date	Author	Title	Country of Origin
19	*c.*1155	Wace (*c.*1115–*c.*1183)	*Roman de Brut*	Fr.
20	*c.*1177	Joceline/Jocelyn of Furness (flourished mid 12th c.)	*The Life of St Kentigern*	Br.
21	Mid 12th c.	Joceline/Jocelyn of Furness (flourished mid 12th c.)	*De Britonum Episcopum* (Only in Stow's 1598 Survey of London)	Br.
22	Mid 12th c.	Joceline/Jocelyn of Furness (flourished mid 12th c.)	*Vita Helena*	Br.
23	12th c.	Walter Mape	*De Nugis Curialium*	Br.
24	1188	Gerald of Wales (*c.*1146–*c.*1223)	*The Journey Through Wales*	Br.
25	1193	Gerald of Wales (*c.*1146–*c.*1223)	*The Description of Wales*	Br.
26	*c.*1202	Ralph de Diceto (?–*c.*1202)	*Chronicle*	Br.
27	1213	Radulphus Niger (*c.*1140–1217)	*Chronicon succinctum de Vitis Imperatorum et tam Franciae quam Angliae Regum, a Christo ad Anno 1213*	Br.
28	*c.*1214	John of Wallingford (John de Cella) (1195–1214)	*Chronica Joannis Wallingford*	Br.
29	*c.*1217	Prince Alexander Neccham/Neckam (1157–1217)	*De sapientia diuina*	Br.
30	?*c.*1166–1216		Letter from Eleutherius to Lucius (included among the Leges Edwardi bonis Regis)	Br.
31	*c.*1236	Roger of Wendover (?–1236)	*Flores Historiarum*	Br.
32	1240–53	Matthew Paris (1200–1259)	*Chronica Maiora*	Br.
33	*c.*1250–75		*The Welsh Triads*	Br.
34	*c.*1268	Martinus Polonus/Martin of Troppau or Oppaviensis (?–1278)	*Chronicon Pontificum et Imperitorum*	Cz.

	Date	Author	Title	Country of Origin
35	?c.1224		*Annals of the Church of Rochester* (cited by Jeremy Collier)	Br.
36	Mid to late 13th c.	Robert of Gloucester (mid to late 13th c.)	*Chronicle*	Br.
37	Before 1311	John Fiberius/Bever (John of London) (died c.1311)	Cites inscription of Lucius at Gloucester (referred to by Fuller)	Br.
38	Before 1313	Ralph de Baldoc/Baudake (flourished 1294–1313)		Br.
39	Between 1231 and 1513		Brass Plaque in St Peter-upon-Cornhill, London	Br.
40	c.1333		*Le Brut (Brut d'Engleterre)*	Fr.
41	c.1338	Robert Mannyng (Robert de Brunne) (c.1275–c.1338)	*Chronicle*	Br.
42	c.1350	Richard of Cirencester (c.1335–c.1401)	*Chronicle*	Br.
43	c.1351	(Claudius) Henricus de Erfordia (flourished c.1351)		Ger.
44	c.1399		The '*Short Chronicle*' of Kirkstall Abbey	Br.
45	Before 1400/6	Petrus de Natalibus (?–1400/6)	*Legends of the Saints*	It. (Venice)
46	c.1440s	Reginald Pecock (c.1395–1460)	*Repressor of Overmuch Blaming the Clergy*	Br.
47	1443	John Flete (c.1398–1466)	*The History of Westminster Abbey*	Br.
48	1454	Thomas Rudborne jnr (flourished 1447–1457)	*Historia major … ecclesiae Wintoniensis*	Br.
49	c.1460	John Capgrave (1393–1464)	*Chronicle of England*	Br.
50	c.1465	John Hardyng (1378–c.1465)	*Chronicle* (printed by Richard Grafton in 1543)	Br.

	Date	Author	Title	Country of Origin
51	1492	Hermannus Schedelius: (flourished c.1492)	*Nuremburg Chronicle*	Ger.
52	1499	Francesco Colonna (1433-1527)	*Hypnerotomachia Poliphili (Poliphilo's Strife of Love in a Dream)*	It. (Venice)
53	1490s (printed in 1521)	Henry Bradshaw (c.1450-1513)	*Life of St Werburgh*	Br.
54	Before 1510 (published in 1516)	Johannes Nauclerus (Naukler) (c.1425-1510)	*Memorabilium omnis aetatis et omnium gentium chronici commentarii*	Ger.
55	1513	Henry Bradshaw (c.1450-1513)	*De Antiquitate et Magnificentia Urbis Cestriae* (lost)	Br.
56	1513	Robert Fabyan (?-1513)	*The Concordance of Histories*	Br.
57	c.1521	Polydore Vergil (PV Castellensis) (c.1470-1555)	*Historiae Angliae*	Br.
58	1523, 1531	Christopher St German (c.1460-1540/1)	*Dialogus de fundamentis legum et cansientia (Doctor and Student)*	Br.
59	1527	Hector Boethius/Boece/Boyce (c.1465-1536)	*Historia Gentis Scotorum*	Br.
60	1528	Giles Tschudi (1505-1572)	*De prisca ac vera Alpina Rhaetia* (printed in 1538)	Sw.
61	1536	Edward Foxe (c.1496-1538)	One of the compilers of the *Collectanea Satis Copiosa* (unpublished portions)	Br.
62	?1540s	Paul Jovius/Paolo Giovio (1483-1552)	*Descrip. Brit.*	It. (Nocera)
63	1543		*John Hardyng's Chronicle* (printed by Richard Grafton)	Br.
64	1544	Sebastian Munster (1488-1552)	*Cosmographia Universalis*	Ger.
65	1545	Thomas Dempster (1579-1625)	*Anglicae descriptionis et historiae Compendium*	Fr. (Paris)
66	?1530s	Jean Bouchet (1476-c.1550)	*Annales d'Aquitaine*	Fr.
67	(printed in 1770/4)	John Leland (1506-1552)	*De Rebus Britannicus Collectanae*	Br.

	Date	Author	Title	Country of Origin
68	1550s	William Paradine (?-?)	*Ang. Desrip. Comp.* (quoted by Usher and referred to by Fuller)	Fr
69	1555	Robert Barnes (1495-1540)	*Vitae Romanorum Pontificum*	Sw. (Basel)
70	1555	William Turner (?-1568)	*A newe booke of spirituall Physik for dyverse diseases of the nobilitie and gentlemen of Englande*	Ger. (Emden)
71	1557-1559	John Bale (1495-1563)	*Scriptorum illustrium majoris Britanniae ... Catalogus*	Sw. (Basel)
72	1559		*Marianus Scotus's Chronicle*	Sw. (Basel)
73	1559	John Feckenham (c.1515-1584), Last Abbot of Westminster	Speech in the House of Lords	Br.
74	1561	John Morwen (1519/20-c.1583)		Br.
75	1563	John Foxe (1516-1587)	*Actes and Monuments (Book of Martyrs)*	Br.
76	1563	Thomas Harding (1516-1572)	*A Confutation*	Br.
77	1563	James Pilkington (1520-1576)	*Confutation of an Addition*	Br.
78	1563	Richard Grafton (?-1572)	*Abridgement of the Chronicles of England*	Br.
79	1565	John Stow (1525-1605)	*A Summarie of Englyshe Chronicles*	Br.
80	1566	Hans Heinrich Bandlin (1522-1595)	*Prosopographiae heroum atque illustrium virorum totius Germaniae*	Ger.
81	1566	John Martiall (1534-1597)	*A replie to M. Calfhill's blasphemous Answer made against the Treatise of the Cross*	Fr. (Louvain)
82	1566	Robert Horne (1564/5-1640)	*An answere made by Robert bishoppe of Winchester to a booke...touchinge the othe of supremacy*	Br.
83	1567	Nicholas Sander (1530-1581)	*The rocke of the Churche*	Fr. (Louvain)
84	1567	Thomas Stapleton (1535-1598)	*A Counterblast to M. Horne's vayne blast against M. Fekenham*	Fr. (Louvain)

	Date	Author	Title	Country of Origin
85	1567	John Jewel (1522–1571)	*Defence of the Apology*	Br.
86	1568	Richard Grafton (?–1572)	*A Chronicle at Large*	Br.
87	1568	William Lambarde (1536–1601)	*Letter from Eleutherius to Lucius translated into English*	Br.
88	c.1570	James Calfhill (1529/30–1570)	*An answer to John Martiall's Treatise of the Cross*	Br.
89	1570 edition	John Foxe (1516–1587)	*Acts and Monuments*	Br.
90	1571	Sir Christopher Wray (c.1522–1592), Speaker of the House	Opening address to the House of Commons	Br.
91	1572	Matthew Parker (1504–1575), (Archbishop of Canterbury 1559–1575)	*De antiquitate Britannicae Ecclesiae*	Br.
92	c.1572	Richard Davies (c.1505–1581) Bishop of St Asaph and St Davids	Correspondence with Matthew Parker regarding Lucius	Br.
93	c.1573	John Caius (1510–1573)	*Hist. Cantab.*	Br.
94	c.1575	Nicholas Harpsfield (1519–1575)	*Historia Anglicana ecclesiastica*	Br.
95	1575	Thomas Cartwright (c.1535–1603)	*The Second Replie against Maister Doctor Whitgift's second answer*	Br.
96	1576	Richard Bristow (1538–1581)	*Demands to be Proponed of Catholiques to the Heretikes*	Fr./Belg. (Antwerp)
97	c.1577	Achilles Pirmin Gasser (1505–1577)	*Augustanae urbis descriptione*	Ger. (Augsburg)
98	1580	William Fulke (1538–1589)	*A retentive to stay good Christians in true faith*	Br.
99	Completed 1586	Raphael Holinshed (died c.1580)	*Chronicle*	Br.
100	1586	William Camden (1551–1623)	*Britannia*	Br.
101	1586	Caesar Baronius (1538–1607)	*New edition of the Roman martyrology*	It. (Rome)
102	1587	John Bridges	*A Defence of the Government Established in the Church of England for Ecclesiastical Matters*	Br.

	Date	Author	Title	Country of Origin
103	1588	Anthony Marten (c.1542–1597)	An Exhortation to stirre up the mindes of all her Maiesties faithfull Subiects	Br.
104	1589	Timothy Bright (1549/50–1615)	An Abridgement of the Booke of Acts and Monumentes	Br.
105	1590s	Marcus Velserus (1558–1614)	Rer. Vindel.	Ger. (Augsburg)
106	1592	Robert Dallington (1561–1636/8)	Hypnerotomachia: The Strife of Love in a Dreame	Br.
107	1596	Caesar Baronius (1538–1607)	Annales Ecclesiasticae	Fr./Belg. (Antwerp)
108	1598	John Stow (1525–1605)	Survey of London	Br.
109	1601	Francis Godwin (1562–1633)	A Catalogue of the Bishops of England	Br.
110	1603	Robert Parsons (1546–1610)	Treatise of Three Conversions	Br.
111	1607	William Camden (1551–1623)	Britannia	Br.
112	1588–1607	Caesar Baronius (1538–1607)	Annales Ecclesiastici a Christi nato ad annum 1198	It. (Rome)
113	1602	Thomas Fitzherbert (1552–1640)	A Defence of the Catholyke Cause	Fr./Belg. (Antwerp)
114	c.1604	John Whitgift (c.1530–1604) Archbishop of Canterbury	The Defence of the Answer to the Admonition	Br.
115	1604	William Hakewill (1574–1655)	Society of Antiquaries debate: Origins of Christianity in the island of Britain	Br.
116	1606	Matthew Sutcliffe (1549/50–1629)	The subversion of Robert Parsons...a Treatise of Three Conversions	Br.
117	1607	John Ross	Britannica, sive de Regibus Veteris Britanniae	Ger. (Frankfurt)
118	1613	Francis Mason (1565/6–1621)	Of the Consecration of the Bishops in the Church of England	Br.
119	1616	Francis Godwin (1562–1633)	De Praesulibus Angl.	Br.
120	1611, 1618, 1632	John Speed (1552–1629)	History of Britain	Br.

	Date	Author	Title	Country of Origin
121	Before 1626	Philippus Ferrarius (?–1626)	*Novum Lexicon Geographicum* (1657 edition by William Dillingham, London)	Fr.
122	*c.*1631	Sir Robert Bruce Cotton (1570/1–1631)	*The Cotton Collection*	Br.
123	1631	John Weever (1576–1632)	*Ancient Funerall Monuments*	Br.
124	1639	Archbishop James Usher/Ussher (1581–1656)	*Ecclesiastical Antiquities of Britain*	Br.
125	1641	Peter Heylin (1600–1662)	*Help to History*	Br.
126	1643	Heribert Rosweyde (1569–1629), Jean Bolland (1596–1665)	*Acta Sanctorum*	Fr./Belg. (Antwerp)
127	1655	Thomas Fuller (1608–1661)	*The Church History of Britain*	Br.
128	1658	Sir William Dugdale (1605–1686)	*The History of St Paul's Cathedral*	Br.
129	1661	Thomas Fuller (1608–1661)	*The Church History of Britain*	Br.
130	1668, 1856	Hugo Paulinus de Cressy (1605–1674)	*The Church History of Brittanny or England, from the beginning of Christianity to the Norman Conquest*	Br./Fr.
131	*c.*1633–*c.*1670	Richard Smith/Smyth (1590–1675)	*Collected Papers*	Br.
132	1670	John Milton (1608–1674)	*History of Britain*	Br.
133	1672	Sir Robert Bruce Cotton (1570/1–1631)	*A Brief Abstract of the Question of Precedence between England and Spain*	Br.
134	1674	Sir Richard Baker (1568–1645)	*A Chronicle of the Kings of England*	Br.
135	1676	Aylett Sammes (*c.*1636–*c.*1679)	*Britannia Antiqua Illustrata*	Br.
136	1685	Edward Stillingfleet (1635–1699)	*Origines Britannicae*	Br.
137	1697	James Tyrrell (1642–1718)	*The General History of England*	Br.
138	1698	Johann Jacob Hofmann (1635–1706)	*1698: Lexicon Universale*	Sw. (Basel)

	Date	Author	Title	Country of Origin
139	1701	Jeremy Collier (1650–1725)	*Historical Dictionary*	Br.
140	1708	Jeremy Collier (1650–1725)	*Ecclesiastical History of Great Britain*	Br.
141	1712	Sir Robert Atkyns (1647–1711)	*The Ancient and Present State of Glostershire*	Br.
142	1714 edition	Jeremy Collier (1650–1725)	*Ecclesiastical History of Great Britain*	Br.
143	1716	John Le Neve (1679–c.1741)	*Fasti Ecclesiae Anglicanae*	Br.
144	1717	Mary Delarivier Manley (c.1670–1724)	*Lucius, the First Christian King of Britain* (a Play)	Br.
145	1720	John Strype (1643–1737)	*An Acurate Edition of Stow's Survey of London*	Br.
146	1732	John Horsley (c.1685–1732)	*Britannia Romana*	Br.
147	1737	Hugh Tootell (1671–1743) (pseudonym: Charles Dodd)	*The Church History of England*	Belg. (Brussels)
148	1748	John Smith (flourished c.1748)	*The Britons and saxons not converted to Popery*	Br.
149	1756-9	Alban Butler (1710–1773)	*The Lives of the Fathers, Martyrs and Other Principal Saints*	Br.
150	1806	Richard Gough (1735–1809)	*Edition of William Camden's Britannia*	Br.
151	?1830s	Henry Dugdale (1769–1840)	*Citing from an MSS*	Br.
152	1836	Rice Rees (1804–1839)	*An Essay on the Welsh Saints*	Br.
153	1848		*Monumenta Historica Britannica* (published by Command of Her Majesty Queen Victoria)	Br.
154	1849/50	Henry Hallam (1777–1859)	*Observations on the Story of Lucius, the first Christian King of Britain*	Br.
155	1863	William Makepeace Thackeray (1811–1863)	*On A Lazy Idle Boy* (Roundabout Papers; *Cornhill Magazine*)	Br.

	Date	Author	Title	Country of Origin
156	1879		*1700th Anniversary of St Peter Cornhill (Sermon preached by Dr Tait, Archbishop of Canterbury)*	Br.
157	1883–5	Louis Marie Olivier Duchesne (1843–1922)	*Eleuthere et le roi Breton Lucius*	Fr.
158	1888, 1890	William Henry Anderdon (1816–1890)	*Britain's Early Faith*	Br.
159	1889	William Lindsay Alexander (1808–1884)	*The Ancient British Church*	Br.
160	1892	Mary Helen Agnes Allies (1852–1927)	*History of the Church in England; From the Beginning of the Christian Era to the Accession of Henry VIII*	Br.
161	1892	Sir William Mitchell Ramsay (1851–1939)	*The Church in the Roman Empire before 170 AD*	Br.
162	1894	William Cathcart (1825–1910)	*The Papal System; Ancient British and Irish Churches*	Br.
163	1894	Christian Matthias Theodor Mommsen (1817–1903)	*Die Historia Brittonum und Konig Lucius von Britannien*	Ger.
164	1895, 1897	Rev. Canon George Forrest Browne (1833–1930)	*The Church in These Islands Before Augustine*	Br.
165	1896	Francis John Haverfield (1860–1919)	*Early British Christianity*	Br.
166	1898	William Edward Collins (1867–1911), Bishop of Gibraltar	*The Beginnings of English Christianity*	Br.
167	1904	Adolph von Harnack (1851–1930)	*Der Brief des britischen Konigs Lucius an den Papst Eleutherius*	Ger.

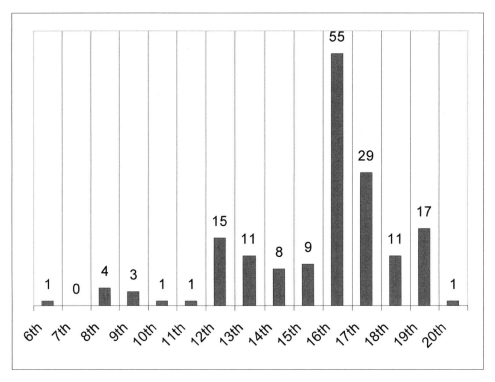

Chart C.2: Frequency of occasions King Lucius has been mentioned from the sixth to the twentieth century, acknowledging there may be several more references not yet discovered

Quoting the entries from each of these works is beyond the scope of this book, however a few are worth citing in full. Below are the relevant sections from Matthew Paris, Ralph de Diceto and Edward Stillingfleet.

MATTHEW PARIS (*THE GREAT CHRONICLE*: 1200-1259)

Matthew Paris (1200-1259) compiled *Chronica Maiora* (*The Great Chronicle*)[14] though it was published much later by Bishop Parker in 1571, and at Zurich in 1589 and 1606. The following are the relevant passages from Book I (discussed in Chapter 3):

> Britannia primo fidem Christi suscepit. Papa xvus.
> Anno gratiae CLXXXV. Eleutherius Papa sedit in cathedra Romana annis xv., mensibus sex, et diebus quinque, et [cessavit] sedes diebus sex. Eodem tempore Lucius, Britannorum rex, ad eundem Papam epistolas direxit, petens ab eo ut Christianus efficeretur. Beatus vero pontifex, comperta Regis devotione, misit ad illum doctores religiosos, Fagaunum et Duvianum, qui regem ad Christum converterent et lavacro abluerent salutari. Quod cum factum fuisset, concurrerunt ab baptismum nations diversae, exemplum Regis sequentes, ita ut in brevi nullus inveniretur infidelis. Beati igitur

doctores, cum per totam Britanniam paganismum delevissent, templa, quae in honore plurimorum deorum fundata fuerant, uni Deo ejusdemque sanctis dedicaverunt, diversisque ordinatorum coetibus expleverunt. Constituerunt etiam in diversis civitatibus regni xx. et viii. episcopos, qui tribus archiepiscopis et sedibus metropolitanis submittebantur. Prima sedes Londoniis erat, cui submissa est Loegria et Cornubia, quas provincias Sabrina a Kambria sejungit. Secunda apud Eboracum, cui submissa est Deira et Albania, quas magnum flumen Humbri, a Loegria secernit. Tertia in urbe Legionum, cui subjacuit Kambria, id est, Wallia, quam Sabrina a Loegria secernit. Hanc urbem super Oscam fluvium in Glammorgantia olim fuisse sitam, veteres muri et aedificia protestantur.

Fides Christi in Britannia confirmatur.
Anno gratiae CLXXXVI. Beati antistites Fagaunus et Duvianus Romam reversi, cuncta quae fecerant, impetraverunt a Papa beatissimo confirmari. Quibus peractis, redierunt in Britanniam praefati doctores, cum aliis quampluribus, quorum doctrina gens Britonum [in fide Christi in brevi fundata refulsit. Istorum autem] nomina et actus in libro reperiuntur, quem Gildas historicus de Victoria Aurelii Ambrosii conscripsit.

Lucius rex ecclesias Britanniae libertatibus munivit.
Anno gratiae CLXXXVII. Gloriosus Britonum rex Lucius, cum infra regnum suum verae fidei cultum magnificatum esse vidisset, possessions et territoria ecclesiis et viris ecclesiasticis abundanter conferens, chartis et monimentis omnia communivit. Ecclesias vero cum suis coemiteriis [ita] constituit esse [libera ut] quicunque malefactor ad illa confugeret, illaesus ab omnibus remaneret. Deinde in dilectione Dei et proximi feliciter vivens, regnum suum in tranquillitate maxima moderavit.

The addition regarding King Lucius' grants to churches across Britain can also be found in Roger of Wendover's *Flores Historiarum* (*c.*1236), under the year 184. As further evidence that Matthew Paris was closely following the *Flores*, under the year 188 he reproduced a blunder in Wendover, substituting *esca* for the word *ecclesia*.[15]

Eleutherii constitutum.
Anno gratiae CLXXXVIII. Eleutherius, Romanae urbis episcopus, constituit ut nulla esca a Christianis repudiaretur, quae tamen rationalis et humana esset.

De Lucio imperatore.
Anno gratiae CXC. Lucius [Commodus] imperator, cunctis incommodus, in domo Vestali strangulates interiit.

Lucius rex Britannorum obiit.
Anno gratiae CCI. Inclitus Britannorum rex Lucius, in bonis actibus assumptus, Claudiocestriae ab hac vita migravit ad Christum, et in ecclesia primae sedis honorifice sepultus est. Quo defuncto, discidium inter Britones surrexit, quia absque haerede decessit, et Romana potestas infirmata est. Mansit itaque Britannia in discidio usque ad adventum Severi, qui eam postea Romanae restituit dignitati.

RALPH DE DICETO [*CHRONICLE*: WRITTEN C.1202]

Master Ralph de Diceto was the Dean of London in the early thirteenth century and wrote a *Chronicle* in *c*.1202, following Bede's *Ecclesiastical History* but also including details from Geoffrey of Monmouth (discussed in Chapter 3):

> Beda, Libro I, Capitulo iiii Eleuther papa, ad quem Lucius rex Britanniae missa epistola se fieri Christianum impetrat. Eleuther ergo misit Faganum et Duvianum, qui regem Lucium baptizaverunt, templa etiam, quae in honore plurimorum deorum fundata erant, uni Deo dedicaverunt. Erant tunc in Britannia xxviii flammines, et tres archi-flammines, et ubi erant flammines episcopos, ubi autem archiflammines archiepiscopos posuerunt. Lundoniensi archiepiscopo subjacuit Loegria et Cornubia, Eboracensi Deira et Albania; urbi autem Legionum Kambria.

> Beda, Libro I, Capitulo Vicesimo Sexto. Post dies hos constructa est extra Cantuariam ecclesia sancti Martini.

An intriguing note appears in the margin beside this entry:

> Nota de primatu Christianitatis in Anglia: – 'Lucius rex Britanniae primus fuit in Angliabaptizatus, sed tota Christianitas ipsius tempore adepta cito periit omnino deleta. Primus autem martir in Anglia, quae adhuc Britannia diceb atur, fuit beatus Albanus, qui, baptizante beato Amphibalo, decollatus, et beatus Amphibalus est evisceratus. Postea vero Christianitas in Anglia fuit destructa et deleta. Deinde anno gratiae DC misso Sancto Augustino a beato Gregorio, baptizatus est AEdelbertus rex Cantiae, et nunquam postea penitus deleta est Christianitas; unde Lucius primus tempore, Albanus primus martirio, Augustinus primus fuit apostolatu. Albanus tamen, quia martir primus, id est, praecipuus omnium Christianorum Angliae, titulo Christianitatis insignitur, et merito signifer appellatur'.[16]

Edward Stillingfleet (1635–1699) wrote critically, in 1685, concerning the references of the Raetian tradition of Lucius (discussed in Chapter 6):

> For (l) [(l) Pet. De Natal. L. I. c. 24.] Petrus Equilinus saith, That he was baptized by Timothy, a Disciple of St. Paul; and he had it from a much better Authour, for (m) [(m) Notker. Martyrol. 8 lend. Junii.] Notkerus Balbulus saith, That King Lucius was baptized by Timothy; not the Timothy to whom Saint Paul wrote his Epistles; But the Brother of Novatus, whose Names are extant in the old Martyrology published by Rosweyd, 12 Cal. Julii; who were both, saith (n) [(n) Baron. A.D. 166. n. 2.] Baronius, Sons to Pudens a Roman Senatour; the same who is supposed to have been marryed to Claudia Rufina the Britain; and therefore his Son might not improbably be employ'd in his work of converting a British King. (o) [(o) Naucler. Chron. Vol. 2. Gen. 6.] Nauclerus takes notice, That this Relation agrees best with the Tradition of the Church of Curia, a noted City of Rhaetia. And (p) [(p) Pantal. De Viris illustrib. Germ. P. I.] Pantaleon calls Lucius the Disciple of Timothy; out of the Annals of the Church. From whence (q) [(q) M. Velser. Rer.

Vindel. L. 6.] Marcus Velserus shews, that he did not die here in Britain, but went over into those parts of Rhaetia to preach the Gospel, and there suffer'd Martyrdom: or, at least, ended his days; For they are not agreed about the manner of his death. (r) [(r) Tschud. Descript. Rhet. C. 18.] Aegidius Tschudus saith the former, who adds, that there is a place near Curia called Clivus S. Lucii still; and (s) [(s) Munster. Cosmograph. L. 3. p.518] Munster saith, near the Episcopal palace, there is Monasterium Sancti Lucii. And (t) [(t) Ferrar. Nova Topograph. p. 44.] Ferrarius in his new Topography to the Martyrologium Romanum, reckons King Lucius of Britain one of the Martyrs of Curia, which the Germans call Chur, and the Italians Choira. And the (u) [(u) Rom. Martyr. 3 Non. Dec.] Roman Martyrology saith, That there his memory is still observed. (w) [(w) Notker. Balbul. 8 Calend. Junii] Notkerus Balbulus saith, that he converted all Rhaetia, and part of Bavaria. If so, they had great reason to preserve his Memory, and the British Church, on the account of King Lucius his converting their countrey, hath as much right to challenge Superiority over Bavaria and Rhaetia, as the Church of Rome hath over the British Church on the account of the conversion of Lucius by Eleutherius. If this tradition hold good, the other cannot; which differs as to time, Persons, and the remainder of his life, which our writers say, was spent here; and (x) [(x) Galfr. Monu. L. 2. c. 2.] Geffrey, from the British History saith, That he died at Gloucester, and left no heir to succeed him. Wherein he is follow'd by (y) [(y) Fordon. Scotichron. L.3. c. 36.] John Fordon, who saith, that after the death or disappearance of King Lucius the Royal stock failed, and then the Romans appointed Governours instead of Kings. But, by that expression, vel non comparente, Fordon seems to doubt, whether he did not withdraw in his old age, according to the German tradition.[17]

NOTES

INTRODUCTION

1: Ashe 1982:74.
2: Heal (2005) has focused on the story's usefulness to Reformation polemicists, but not especially the veracity of its content.
3: Harnack, A. 1904. *Der Brief des britischen Konigs Lucius an den Papst Eleutherus,* Sitzungsberichte der koniglich preussischen Akademie der Wissenschaften, pp. 909 - 916.

CHAPTER I

1: Fuller 1661. *The Church History of Britain.*
2: Mommsen 1894 *Die Historia Brittonum und Konig Lucius von Britannien.*
3: From the MSS of Brussells, Vienna and Amiens.
4: The 1892 editor dates the consulships of Verus and Herenianus to AD 171 and that of Paternus and Bradua to AD 185. Online at www.tertullian.org/fathers/chronography_of_354_13_bishops_of_rome.htm
5: Duchesne 1883-5. *Eleuthere et le roi Breton Lucius.*
6: Translation by Louise Ropes Loomis, 1965.
7: New Advent Library: www.newadvent.org
8: The consuls in 185: Triarius Maternus and Ti. Claudius M. Appius Atilius Bradua Regillus Atticus. In 191: Popilius Pedo Apronianus and M. Valerius Bradua Mauricus. The only Paternus in the consulships was Cn. Cornelius Paternus in 233. Paternus on the other hand *might* be identified as Tarrutienus Paternus, promoted to the senate with consular rank and the prefect of the Praetorian Guard of 179 who was involved in the attempted assassination of the Emperor Commodus in 182. Through the instigation of Sextus Tigidius Perennis, Commodus removed Paternus from the prefecture, but he then murdered Saoterus, Commodus' male concubine. Paternus, along with Julianus, son of the lawyer Publius Salvius Julianus, and Vitruvius Secundus who had charge of the imperial correspondence, were all summarily executed in *c.*189 (Grant 1996:73, 184; Garzetti 1974:533; Birley 1966:284).
9: Harnack, A. 1904. *Der Brief des britischen Konigs Lucius an den Papst Eleutherus,* Sitzungsberichte der koniglich preussischen Akademie der Wissenschaften, pp. 909-916.
10: Harnack 1902:835 *Die Mission und Ausbreitung des Christentums in den ersten drei*

Jahrhunderten (1902; English translation, *The Mission and Expansion of Christianity in the First Three Centuries*, in two volumes, 1904-1905). My Italics.

11: Fuller 1661. *The Church History of Britain*.

12: Reviewed by Mathew in 1907.

13: Mathew 1907:767-770.

14: In Volume Three of Zahn's *Forschungen zur Geschichte des neutestamentlichen Kanons und der altkirchlichen Litteratur* (eight volumes, 1881-1908) relating to the tombs of the Apostles as derived from the *Hypotyposis* of Clement of Alexandria, he notes: '*Thaddeus et Iudas in Britio Edessenorum*' (Zahn 1884:70). In his first volume, Zahn notes that *Britio* equates with *Beruto*. This was also the opinion of Justus Lipsius (Joost Lips) in 1884 and Tixeront.

15: Bishop Brooke Foss Wescott (1825-1901) was Bishop of Durham from 1890 to 1901 and assisted Fenton John Anthony Hort (1828-1892) in editing a critical edition of The New Testament in the Original Greek.

16: Palmer (1991) following Devos (1967) who had shown that the confessor-bishop of Edessa must be Eulogius (377-387) and that there is only one date in that period which fits Egeria's journey to Edessa. She left Jerusalem on 25 March 384 and reached Edessa on 19 April. Her three-day stay was followed by a visit to Harran on 23 April (1991:8).

17: Although Palmer (1991:5) prefers to date the translation of St Thomas to Edessa in the second century. [Palmer, A. 1991. King Abgar of Edessa, Eusebius and Constantine. In, Bakker, H. (ed.) *Sacred Center* ... pp. 3-29].

18: As Harnack, cited above, noted 'The Christianizing of Edessa was a spontaneous result' (Harnack 1902:835).

19: Millar 1993:576.

20: Olmstead, A.T. 1942. The Mid-Third Century of the Christian Era. II. In, *Classical Philology*, Volume 37, Number 4 (October 1942), pp. 398-420. Birtha: Olmstead 1942:404.

21: Poidebard, A. 1934. La trace de Rome dans le désert de Syrie. Le limes de Trajan à la conquête arabe. *Bibliothèque Archéologique et Historique* 18; 87 f. Pl. 86-87.

22: Justus Lipsius (Joost Lips) 1884, also Tixeront quoted the *Acta Thaddaei* that Thaddaeus died in 'Berythe en Phenicia', but of course Harnack preferred Edessa to Beirut (Scavone 1999:331).

23: Segal 1970:5.

24: Segal 1970:23.

25: Segal 1970. *Edessa The Blessed City*, p. 70. Segal was not persuaded that Abgar was necessarily *ever* a Christian. Drijvers (Drijvers, H.J.W. 1980. *Cults and Beliefs at Edessa*. Leiden, p. 14) took up Segal's challenge of Abgar VIII's conversion to Christianity and considered the story apocryphal. More recently Ball has considered the claim 'controversial' (Ball 2001:95, 465, *f*.275).

CHAPTER II

1: Geoffrey Book vii., I-IV (Thorpe 1966:170-185).

2: Anderdon 1888 (1890 reprint), Alexander 1889, Allies 1892.

3: Watts 1991:9. Petts, D. 2003. *Christianity in Roman Britain*. Stroud: Tempus.

4: Thomas 1981:43 (Watts 1991:9).

5: *Adversus Iudaeus vii* (Fuller 1661:43). A better English translation may be '... locales in Britain beyond the reach of Rome accepted the true Christ'.

6: *Homil. iv in Ezekiel interp., i*

7: Orig. in Lucae c. I. Hom. 6. III. 939. ed. Huet. Fuller (1661:43) had 'divided' for *dividuntur*, divided presumably by the Channel, although 'apart from our world' may be a better rendering.

8: Niblett 2001:33. Socrates' and Stephen's Feast Day is 17 September, Aaron and Julius 1 July, Augulius 7 February (Fuller 1661:55).

9: Romans 16:10.

10: Tract XIV, Ps 8.

11: *Kata Ioudaion = Adversus Judaeos* in Latin.

12: The section beginning with the words *Dioti kai ai brettanikai*

13: Greek and translation kindly provided by Gianna Giannakopoulou, 2007 (Chrysostomou Orations. 1970. *Library of Greeks; Everything by Saint Fathers,* Volume 3. Greek Publishing Organisation. p. 40).

14: Anderdon 1888 (1890) made the point 'the short work of Gildas, *which we have in print* ... is more in the nature of a sermon' and 'though [Lucius] is not found in the [extant copies of the work in print] it certainly occurred in more ancient manuscripts of it ... in chapter vii by Rudborne, *Hist Mag Wint* 1 I, c.i ... [besides] in another work of Gildas, cited by Matthew of Westminster, *ad ann.* 186' (ibid 228).

15: Paying homage to Sellar & Yeatman's 1930 *1066 and All That.*

16: Further research is required into the claims of antiquity for four churches in southern Wales, in the region of Llandaf: Llan-Lleirwg (now St Mellon's) near Cardiff; St Medwy, Llanfedwy; Merthyr Dyfan (Diruvianus the Martyr); St Ffagan, Gwent (Anderdon 1888 (1890):229-230, Appendix C; Lingard Volume I, p. 2; Rees, *Welsh Saints,* p. 84; Williams, *Ecclesiastical Antiquities of the Cymry,* p. 73).

17: Panel 16 of the Great East Window (S11); King Lucius is above a shield of St Wilfrid and Pope Eleutherius is above a shield of St Peter. Thanks to Vicky Harrison and Amanda Daw at York Minster.

18: The mason's grafitto of the name Lucius in the Lady Chapel of Gloucester Cathedral implies a statue of the king prior to the Dissolution. Also at Gloucester, in the ancient church of St Mary de Lode is a supposed effigy of Lucius but this seems highly unlikely.

19: *The Peterborough Chronicle*: Number XLIV of the Records of Civilization, Sources and Studies; Austin P. Evans, Editor; Translated with an introduction by Harry A. Rositze, Columbia University Press, New York, 1951

20: *Augustan History* p. 115.

21: *Augustan History* ibid.

22: *Augustan History* p. 117.

23: Eusebius 4:15.

24: Eusebius 4:26.

25: *Liber Pontificalis (Catalogus Felicianus).*

26: Eusebius 4:21, 4:26.

27: Dumville 1985:3.

28: *Hist. Brit.* 10.

29: Campbell 1962:xiii *f* 2.

30: Campbell 1962:xxi.

31: Preface: p. 84 of *Monumenta Historica Britannica*; Published by command of Her Majesty, MDCCCXLVIII (1848).

32: Known as MS 17110 E, held at the National Library of Wales in Aberystwyth.

33: The Iolo MSS, article 4 and 6, as cited by Anderdon 1888 (1890) is an ancient Welsh poem that contains mention of Lleirwg, Ffagan, Medwy, Elvan and the martyr (Merthyr) Diruvuanus (Dyvan).

34: Greenway 1996:lxviii-lxix.

35: Greenway 1996:lxxxv.

36: Greenway 1996:lxxxix.

37: Huntingdon i. 37 at n. 176.

38: Tatlock 1950:34 (footnote 166). For another example of Geoffrey's borrowing from Henry, see the description of the four roads in i. 7 at n. 35, echoed in HRB, c. 39. (Greenway 1996:civ-cv).

39: Greenway 1996:48-49.

40: Greenway 1996:48-51.

41: Greenway 1996:532-533.

42: Greenway 1996:534-535.

43: Greenway 1996:ibid.

44: Greenway 1996:ibid.

45: Greenway 1996:534.

46: Greenway 1996:ibid.

CHAPTER III

1: Flint 1979:448. For example Alfred of Beverley 'thought it worthy of at least some serious attention by historians' while William of Newburgh accused Geoffrey of 'attempting to give historical falsehood the colour of truth by turning it into Latin' (ibid 447).

2: Flint 1979:447-467.

3: As, for example, the case with Bede's *Ecclesiastical History*, where he has confused the sense of his earlier statement in the *Chronica maiora* (see above in Chapter 1).

4: Thorpe 1978:117.

5: Stillingfleet 1685:64.

6: Adaptation of Sir Winston Churchill's 1939 radio broadcast: 'I cannot forecast to you the action of Russia. It is a riddle, wrapped in a mystery, inside an enigma; but perhaps there is a key. That key is Russian national interest.' www.phrases.org.uk/meanings/31000.html

7: Thorpe, L. (transl.) 1966. *Geoffrey of Monmouth; The History of the Kings of Britain.* Harmondsworth: Penguin Books.

8: Contemplate for a moment the accidental loss of other primary sources; for instance on the immense embarrassment and sorrow felt by the great Theodor Mommsen (1817-1903) when his library study was consumed by flames in the early hours of 7 July, 1880, destroying several rare manuscripts including Jordanes.

9: Hammer 1936:127.

10: Footnote by John Sheridan Brewer in his 1845 edition of Fuller (Fuller 1661:35).

11: Bromwich 2006.

12: Quoted by Hugh Williams, 1912.

13: Anderdon 1888 (1890 reprint), *Iolo* MSS, article 4 and 6.

14: Gerald of Wales; *Description of Wales*, Book I, Ch. 18 (Dimock 1868). Translation by Thorpe in 1978.

15: Recently published by Antonina Harbus in 2002.

16: Llanerch facsimile reprint 1989:55.

17: Llanerch facsimile reprint 1989:83.

18: The *Collectanea de rebus eccle. Ruffensis* or *Textus Roffensis*.

19: Thorpe 1966:53.

20: Flint 1979:449.

21: *The Brut or The Chronicles of England*; Edited from MS. Rawl. B 171, Bodleian Library, & c., By Friedrich W. D. Brie, Ph.D., London 1906.

22: Hingeston 1858:67.

CHAPTER IV

1: Manley 1717:7 *Lucius* (line spoken by the page, Silvius, in Act 1, Scene 1).

2: Ferguson 1993:92.

3: Also Alan Smith's 1979 Lucius of Britain: Alleged King and Church Founder. *Folklore*, Volume 90, Number 1, pp. 29-36. Rachel Bromwich's 2006 *The Triads of the Island of Britain*. Cardiff: University of Wales Press, by necessity deals with Lleirwg.

4: Heal 2005:593.

5: Heal 2005:597.

6: Heal 2005:ibid.

7: Heal 2005:598 (F. Liebermann 1913, *A Contemporary MS. of the Leges Anglorum Londinis collectae*).

8: Heal 2005:599.

9: Printed in London, 1568, folio 130v. Heal 2005:598.

10: Brewer 1845 (Fuller 1661:30).

11: Camden 1607:I. XCVII.

12: Rankov 1990:171 (Rankov, N.B. 1990. Singulares Legati Legionis: A Problem in the Interpretation of the Ti. Claudius Maximus Inscription from Philippi. *Zeitschrift für Papyrologie und Epigraphik* 80. pp. 165-175.)

13: Birley 1966:269.

14: Birley 1966:282. The next year, 180, the consuls were *Bruttius Praesens* and *Iulius Verus* (ibid).

15: See Chapter 3 above for the *Annals of Rochester*.

16: A *Marcus Herennius* had shared the consulship with *Gaius Valerius Flaccus* in 93 BC, the name 'Herennius may derive from the Palmyrene *Hairan*, which appears in variant forms on other inscriptions from El Kantara' (Southern 1989:102).

17: Riley 1860:632-633.

18: Heal 2005:600.

19: Cott. MS Cleo. E VI, folios 180-182 (Heal 2005:600).

20: Heal 2005:600.

21: Heal 2005:ibid.

22: Guy 1982:196.

23: Guy 1982:496.

24: Heal 2005:599.

25: J. Guy, in A. Fox and J. Guy, *Reassessing the Henrician Age* (Oxford, 1986), pp. 162-3 (Heal 2005:599-600).

26: Stillingfleet 1685:65.

27: Thanks to Nick Ford for bringing this document to my attention.

28: Where the king, David, is first and foremost Godly, indeed Jesus is 'Son of David', and this would not have been lost on Lucius or Eleutherius.

29: One of these historiographers was, as we shall see, most likely Jocelyn of Furness, whose twelfth-century work may have been loaned to Holinshed by John Stowe.

30: Ross 1607:35 (Hardin 1992:240).

31: Morgan 1981:42.

32: Armistead & Davis, 1989. Baker wrote *A Chronicle of the Kings of England* in 1674, Aylett Sammes *Britannia Antiqua Illustrata* in 1676 and Tyrrell *The General History of England* in 1697.

33: An example of Holinshed's *Chronicle* (Leir) being quarried by Shakespear (Lear).

34: Hallam, H. 1849. Observations on the Story of Lucius, the first Christian King of Britain. *Archaeologia*. Volume 33. London: Society of Antiquaries of London, pp. 308-335.

35: Hallam 1849:308.

36: Hallam simply calls them 'Whitaker and Henry' (Hallam 1849:ibid).

37: Hallam 1849:308.

38: Hallam 1849:309.

39: Hallam 1849:310.

40: Hallam 1849:308.

41: Hallam 1849:312-313.

42: Hallam 1849:313.

43: Hallam 1849:ibid. One wonders why the Society published this rather than the more accurate LVC.

44: John Horsley had attempted this as early as 1732 but archaeological methods really began to mature as of the mid nineteenth century.

45: Duchesne 1883-5 *Lib. Pontif.* I. 136, p. ciii; Mommsen 1894 *Hist. Britt.* p. 115 (Haverfield 1896:419).

46: Haverfield 1896:419. Duchesne was ordained a Catholic priest in 1867 and became a central figure in the revival of learning, while Mommsen was possibly the greatest Classicist of the nineteenth century, amongst many achievements he pioneered the study of epigraphy and received the Nobel Prize for Literature in 1902.

CHAPTER V

1: From the monastery of Saints Peter and Paul, Gloucester, also in John Fiberius/Bever (*c.*1311) and the *Abbreviation of the Brit. Chron.*, quoted by Usher, *Brit. Eccl. Antiq.* 73 (Fuller 1661:41). The first two lines were cited by Fuller. The entire stanza appears on the 1860s Hardman window in Gloucester Cathedral.

2: Haverfield 1896:419.

3: The inscription was reported in the *British Epigraphist Society Newsletter* of Autumn 2002 by Simon Corcoran, Benet Salway, and Peter Salway.

4: The Archbishop of Canterbury Rowan Williams made this observation at the 1400 anniversary of the reorganization of the Diocese of London at St Paul's Cathedral on 22 May 2004.

5: Notable contributions to the study are by Charles Thomas and Dorothy Watts.

6: Bell, T. 2005. The Religious Reuse of Roman Structures in Early Medieval England. *British Archaeological Reports*, British Series 390. Oxford: Archaeopress.

7: English rhyme known as *Oranges and Lemons* dating to the seventeenth or eighteenth century. The street selling of 'frippery', old clothes, and food outside St Peter's may indicate why the bells bespeak these trades.

8: Stillingfleet 1685.

9: Stillingfleet 1685:66-67.

10: Smith, A. 1979. Lucius of Britain: Alleged King and Church Founder. *Folklore*, Volume 90, Number 1 (1979), pp. 29-36.

11: Rees 1836:84.

12: Lyon 1787:11-12 (Smith 1979:33).

13: Darrell 1797:10 (Smith 1979:33).

14: Benham 1902:2.

15: Merrifield 1969:202.

16: Wheeler 1934:295.

17: Thanks to Martin Fitzsimons at St Helen's House, Bishopsgate for permission to photograph the plaque (I believe the first time it has ever been photographed) and to Dr Charlotte Tupman for her assistance with the photography and transcription, 2007.

18: Ellis 1811:40.

19: 1807:512.

20: Except that the original steeple was destroyed and was not re-erected before the Great Fire.

21: Sparrow Simpson 1880:225.

22: Gairdner 1880:6-7.

23: Gairdner 1880:7. Gairdner notes that the margin is mutilated, 'the edge of the paper having been cut by the binder, so that it is uncertain what the date assigned to the conversion of Lucius was. But it was probably 163 (clxiii), the L being now lost' (ibid).

24: Thorpe 1976:126. In Thorpe's index under Lucius he states 'he is buried in London in the year A.D. 156' (Thorpe 1976:344).

25: Thorpe 1976:344.

26: *Scriptorum illustrium majoris Britanniae … Catalogus.*

27: A 1648 Notarial Record of Gloucestershire also begins with the words *Bee it knowne*.

28: *Le Brut* (the first part, to 1333) has Lucius reigning for 13 years and buried at Gloucester.

29: Fuller 1661:41.

30: Dancey's statement that Hardman was commissioned in 1867 to '… to restore, re-lead the old, produce and fix new glass in places from where the old was lost. This they did, the new work being a good and faithful match of the old, both as to color, style of figures and dress, as well as the make of the glass' (Dancey 1911:97) is misleading as the Lucius window is slightly earlier (1862 or 1865) in date and is a wholly new design. In other words it does not derive from a scene of Lucius in older glass as Dancey suggests (Thanks to Robin Lunn of Gloucester Cathedral from clearing up this point). As for the difference of opinion in the dating of the window see Nikolaus Pevsner 1970 and Brooks, A. 2002. Gloucestershire: The Vale & Forest of Dean. *Buildings of England* series), and Welander (1993).

31: Smiles 1994: 98-99, figures 49-51.

32: Smiles 1994:105-6, figures 57 and 58.

33: Thanks to Richard Cann of Gloucester Cathedral for these details and further investigation into the identity of the Earl. It is interesting that the first three figures either died in prison or were murdered, leaving the title Duke of Gloucester forfeit; echoing Lucius' representing the last of his line. As such the 1860s commissioners at Gloucester Cathedral and Powell created a well-thought design for the window.

34: Dancey 1911:106.

35: Short, H.H.D. 1946-8. Graffiti on the reredos of the Lady Chapel of Gloucester Cathedral. *Bristol and Gloucester Archaeological Transactions.* Volume lxvii, 1946-8, pp. 21-36. Also, Welander 1991:563-4.

36: Bryant, R. and Heighway, C.M. 2003. Excavations at St Mary de Lode Church, Gloucester, 1978-9. *Transactions of the Bristol and Gloucestershire Archaeological Society.* Volume 121 (2003), pp. 179-200.

37: Bell 2005:216.

38: Heighway 1984:38.

39: Heighway 1984:47.

40: It is interesting to note that Richard (Dick) Whittington (*c.*1350-1423) bequeathed monies for the Grey Friars library at Newgate and that there hangs a memorial to him in St Peter-upon-Cornhill.

41: Usher: 1639 *Britannicarum ecclesiarum antiquitates*; p. 36 and in his *De Brittanicarum Ecclesiarum Primordiis*; pp. 49-50. Godwin and Fasti of Le Neve (John Le Neve: *Fasti Ecclesiae Anglicanae*, published in 1716) also cite this list.

42: Facsimile reprinted in 1989 from the series *Historians of Scotland* by Llanerch Enterprises (ISBN 0947992294).

43: Jocelyn's *Life of Kentigern*; Chapter XI and XXVII (Llanerch 1989:55, 83).

44: Stow 1598 (Wheatley 1956:422-423).

45: Stow 1598 (Wheatley 1956:174).

46: Francis Godwin (1562-1633), Bishop of Llandaff and Hereford. In 1601 he published his *Catalogue of Bishops of England since the first planting of the Christian Religion in this island*.

47: Hugh Paulinus de Cressy (*c.*1605-1674) wrote *The Church History of Brittanny or England, from the beginning of Christianity to the Norman Conquest.* Volume I was published at Rouen in 1668. Volume II was not discovered until 1856 at Douai and is yet to be published.

48: *Eborius episcopus de civitate Eboracensi provincia Britannia.*
Restitutus episcopus de civitate Londinensi provincia suprascripta.
Adelfius episcopus de civitate colonia Londinensium.
Mansi, *Concil.* ii, coll. 476-7 from the oldest, Corbie Codex, list of signatories (Miller 1927:79).

49: As in Geoffrey of Monmouth; VI, 2 (Thorpe 1976:145).

50: Cited by Leland, 1770; Volume II, p. 38.

51: The theological character of the pre-Augustine Church in Britain may have been affected by Pelagianism, as seems to be the case with *Fastidius Priscus* by 431, and the Roman mission's renowned Synods and dialogues with the 'Celtic Church' were a concerted effort to bring the British Church back into alignment with Roman practice and thought.

52: Marsden 1987:4.

53: Wheeler 1934:296, footnote 7. The question did not go unnoticed by J.N.L. Myers in his response, Some Thoughts on the Topography of Saxon London (*Antiquity*, Volume 8 (1934) pp. 437-442) and later, in his 1936 review of Wheeler's London and the Saxons (*Journal of Roman Studies*, Volume 26, Part 1, pp. 87-92). His tone is one of incredulity at Wheeler's 'toying' with the legend of King Lucius.

54: Merrifield 1969:82.

55: Marsden 1987:69, figure 57.

56: Brigham 1990:65.

57: Brigham 1990:67.

58: Marsden 1987:43.

59: Brigham 1990:67.

60: Brigham 1990:92.

61: Marsden here notes the example of Silchester (G. Boon, *Silchester, the Roman city of Calleva*, Newton Abbot, 1974, p. 109; J. Wacher, *The Towns of Roman Britain*, London, 1976, p. 45).

62: Marsden 1987:68.

63: Thanks to Martin Fitzsimons of St Helen's House for informing me of these stories.

64: Thomas, C. 1981. *Christianity in Roman Britain to AD 500*. Berkeley: University of California Press.

65: Struck 1997:496-498.

66: Wheatley 1956:174-175.

67: George Billam. Unfortunately this Bible does not appear to be within the present inventory of the churches possessions.

68: Thackeray made his visit to Chur in the Autumn of 1863.

69: Thackeray 1863:124.

CHAPTER VI

1: Alban Butler (1710-1773) included St Lucius of Chur in his 1756-9 *The Lives of the Fathers, Martyrs and Other Principal Saints*.

2: Thackeray 1863:124. Butler, A. 1756-1759. *The Lives of the Fathers, Martyrs and Other Principal Saints*. London. John Murray's travel handbooks of the nineteenth century.

3: Please refer to Appendix C for a list of sources for the tradition of St Luzius von Chur.

4: Harbus 2001.

5: Uri, Schwyz, Unterwalden, Lucerne, Zug and Fribourg remained Roman Catholic.

6: He died in 1551 and was buried in the university church. In 1557, his body was dug up and burnt, and his tomb demolished, by Mary's commissioners; it was subsequently reconstructed by order of Elizabeth. Pollard, A.F. 1910. *Encyclopedia Britannica*, 11th Ed. Volume XIII. Cambridge: Cambridge University Press, p. 676.

7: Especially Zwingli's *De vera et falsa religione* of 1525.

8: Vermigli died in 1562 at Zürich.

9: Others like Edmund Grindal (*c.*1519-1583) went to Strasburg and then Frankfurt.

10: Monssen, L.H. 1981. Rex gloriose martyrium: A Contribution to Jesuit Iconography. *Art Bulletin*, lxiii, pp. 130-137 (Heal 2005:603). The College's address is: www.englishcollegerome.org/pages/welcome.htm

11: The engraving is in Giovanni Battista Cavalieri's *Ecclesiae Anglicanae trophae* (Rome, 1584) (Heal 2005:604, figure 1; Noreen 1998:699).

12: Fuller 1661 Book I, p. 40.

13: Bonjour, Offler and Potter 1952:175.

14: Stillingfleet 1685:58.

15: Stillingfleet 1685:ibid.

16: Balle 1993:341.

17: Jerris 2002:102.

18: Jerris 2002:87.

19: Jerris 2002:102. Simonett, C. *Geschichte der Stadt Chur* 22.

20: Jerris 2002:ibid. Büttner, H. 1961. *Frühmittelalterliches Christentum und fränkischer Staat zwischen Hochrhein und Alpen*. Darmstadt: Wissenschaftliche Buchgesellschaft, p. 112.

21: Jerris 2002:88.

22: Jerris 2002:102. Müller, I. 1956. Zur Karolingischen Hagiographie. *Schweizer Beiträge zur allgemeinen Gescichte* 14, pp. 12-14.

23: Tanner 1979:155.

24: Jacobsen 1997:fig. 18

25: Th.Von Mohr (ed.). *Codex diplomaticus: Sammlung der Urkunden zur Geschichte Cur-Ratiens und der Republik Graubunden*, 2 vols. (Chur, 1848-1852), 1, no. 15 (Jacobsen 1997:1134).

26: Bonjour, Offler and Potter 1952:34.

27: Jerris 2002:87.

28: Both Biscop and Wilfrid set out for Rome before 664 (Wormald 1976:150).

29: Whitelock 1976:26.

30: Known as Waldo of Reichenau since he became Abbot of that establishment immediately after his time at St Gallen in 786 until 806.

31: St Gall, Reichenau, Fleury, St Emeram, Fulda and Mainz all possessed copies of Bede's works, 'and there were doubtless others at an early date at Corbie, Echternach, Würzburg, Reichenau, and Lorsch'. (Beeson 1947:74).

32: Lewis 1976:490.

33: Lewis 1976:ibid.

34: Wallace-Hadrill 1954:622.

35: Lewis 1976:406-7.

36: Lewis 1976:407.

37: Whitelock 1976:29.

38: Meyvaert 1976:56.

39: Krush (ed.) 1896. Passiones Vitaesque Sanctorum aevi Merovingici et Antiquiorum Aliquot. *Monumenta Germaniae Historica; Scriptorum rerum Merovingicarum*. Volume III, pp. 1-7.

40: Krush 1896:3.

41: Caesar Baronius *Annales Ecclesiastici a Christi nato ad annum 1198*. Written by order of St Philip Neri and produced in 12 volumes between 1588 and 1607. The four children of Pudens and Claudia are believed to be two sons: Novatus and Timotheus, and two daughters: Praxedes and Pudentiana, apparently the figures behind the ancient churches in Rome Santa Prassede and Santa Pudenziana.

42: This is in a collection of papers and letters of Richard Smith/Smyth, in Series 4, Part 3, sold at Sotheby's in 1970.

43: Book I was published in 1668 at Rouen. The second book was not discovered until 1856, at Douai. This Timotheus should not be confused with the Bishop and friend of St Paul. The mother of that earlier Timotheus was Eunice (2 Timothy 1:5). He died in *c*.80 and it might be that *Galatia*, where Paul's disciple preached, was later confused with *Gaul*, giving rise to a similar concept as would fuel the fable that St Paul himself travelled to Britannia.

44: Krush 1896: 4.

45: Holinshed 1586 (1807 edition):45.

46: Book I, Chapter V. Incidentally, Holinshed also mentioned a hymn entitled *Gaude Lucionum* which seems to have been sung at Chur but of which hardly a trace remains.

47: Drayton's *Poly-Olbion; A chorographicall description of all the tracts, rivers, mountains, forests, and other Parts of this Renowned Isle of Great Britain* (completed in 1619 and published in 1622), xxiv.

48: There are several examples of the masculine form of the name as in C. Severius Emeritus, a *centurio regionarius* who restored the *locus religiosus* at *Aquae Sulis* (Bath); *RIB* 152 (Mattingly 2006:303).

49: Schedel's *World History* is also known as *Die Schedelsche Weltchronik*, the *Liber Chronicarum* and the *Nuremburg Chronicle*, printed in 1493.

50: *Silva Martis* was identified in 1603 as *Martinswald* by Johannes V, Bishop of Chur. It was later identified as Maienfeld (Krush 1896:5-6, Lütolf, A. 1871. *Die Glaubensboten der Schweiz vor St. Gallus, Luzern*.

CHAPTER VII

1: Strabo iv. 3. Hardy 1890:229. Hardy, E.G. 1890. The Provincial Concilia from Augustus to Diocletian. *The English Historical Review*, Volume 5, Number 18, pp. 221-254.

2: The first annual *sacerdos* or *flamen* (priest) of the altar of Augustus had been an *Aeduan* tribesman *C. Iulius Vercundaridubnus*.

3: Hardy 1890:231.

4: *C.I.L.* ii. 35, 160, 4198, 4233. Hardy 1890:239.

5: Hardy 1890:237.

6: Hardy 1890:241.

7: Hardy 1890:ibid.

8: Birley 1966:275, 329. Thanks to Dr Charlotte Tupman for her assistance in the Latin translation.

9: Grant 1994:45,180.

10: Rees 1836:Section 4, p. 79. The earlier published *Triads of the Isle of Britain* by Iolo Morganwg (Iolo MSS) complement *The Welsh Triads* from a number of thirteenth-century sources, subject to the same caution. Iolo's repute, similar to Geoffrey of Monmouth, may explain Rees' use of '*inventor*' over '*compiler*'. Anderdon (1888) successfully criticized Rees' excesses in his claims about Catholic positions, and Bromwich (2006) demonstrated the Triads were not written before the thirteenth century.

11: Triad 35, Third Series (Rees 1836:Section 4, p. 82). See also a translation by W. Probert (1977): 'Lleirwg, son of Coel, son of St. Cyllin, and called Lleuver the Great , who built the first church in Llandav, which was the first in the Isle of Britain, and who gave the privilege of the country and tribe, with civil and ecclesiastical rights, to those who professed faith in Christ.' The latter phrase then appears in Triad 62.

12: Rees 1836:Section 4, p. 82. Rees dates this Triad 62 as not older than the seventh century (ibid:83). A fuller translation is given in Probert, W. (Transl.) 1977. *The Triads of Britain*; compiled by Iolo Morganwg (Edward Williams). London: Wildwood House.

13: Rees 1836:Section 4, p. 82. This is of course an anachronistic doubt, as Rees dates the Triads in question to the seventh century, by which time the main sees will be recorded as archbishoprics.

14: Rees 1836:Section 4, pp. 82-83. Rees dates Triad 62 as not older than seventh century (p. 83). Probert (1977) has 'First, Llandav, through the favor of Lleirwg, son of Coel and grandson of Cyllin, who first gave lands [etc.]. Second York, through the favor of Constantine … The third was London, through the favor of the Emperor Maximus. Afterwards there were Caerleon-upon-Usk, Celliwig in Cornwall, and Edinburgh in the North; and now there are St. David's, York; and Canterbury'. The latter information dates Triads 62 and 35.

15: Rees 1836:Section 4, p. 83.

16: Rees 1836:Section 4, p. 84. Questioning the antiquity of each of the four churches, on evidence then available Rees could conclude nothing more than that Lleurwg Sant *might* have ancient roots.

17: Snyder 2003:190.

18: Rees 1836:Section 4, p. 83.

19: Snyder 2003:200-201.

20: Snyder 2003:201.

21: Grant 1996:18.

22: Grant 1996:ibid.

23: Grant 1996:19.

24: Garzetti 1974:460; Southern 1989:81-140.

25: Southern 1989:97.

26: Southern 1989:95.

27: Southern 1989:104.

28: Garzetti 1974:460-461.

29: Grant 1996:19.

30: *C.I.L.* xiii 6599.

31: *C.I.L.* xiii 6629.

32: *RIB* 1216; 1217; 1235.

33: *RIB* 576.

34: *RIB* 2117.

35: *RIB* 1737 and 1724. Southern 1989:109.

36: *RIB* 2100

37: *C.I.L.* xiii 6511; 6514; 6517; 6518 and 6490.

38: Southern 1989:95.

39: Frere 1974:495 [Frere, S. S. 1974. Review of Baatz, D. 1973. Kastell Hesselbach und andere Forschungen am Odenwaldlimes. *Britannia,* Volume 5, pp. 494-496.]

40: Also at Walldürn four reliefs of *Epona* may be associated with the *exploratores* stationed there in AD 232 (Southern 1989:96-97; *C.I.L.* xiii 6471 and 7343).

41: *C.I.L.* xiii 7754.

42: *C.I.L.* xiii 7054.

43: Southern 1989:104.

44: Grant 1996:36.

45: Jerris 2002:87.

46: These churches include St Peter at Schaan (Lichtenstein), Zillis, Berschis, Castelmur and Schiedberg (near Sagogn) (Jerris 2002:87-88).

47: Jerris 2002:102, note 14.

48: Sellar, W.C. and Yeatman, R.J. 1930. *1066 and All That: A Memorable History of England, comprising all the parts you can remember, including 103 Good Things, 5 Bad Kings and 2 Genuine Dates.* Methuen & Co. Ltd.

49: Graham, A.J. 1966.

50: Henig 2002.

51: Snyder 2003:85.

52: Snyder 2003:217.

53: Jocelyn of Furness recorded King *Leudonus* or *Lot*, from which Lothian allegedly took its name, in the *Life of St. Kentigern.*

54: At the same time when that great work was completed, there was an attempted coup within Northumbria, and Ceolwulf was deposed for a short period in the autumn of 731, while Bishop Acca of Hexham may have been driven from his Episcopal see. Not much more is known about this event, but Acca returned to his Hexham and Ceolwulf continued to rule until 737.

55: Thank you to Dr Gary D. Knight, for suggesting the essence of this variant reconstructed Lucius.

56: Williams 1952:184.

57: Noted above by Rees (1836) and Anderdon (1888).

APPENDIX A

1: English translation kindly provided by Tehmina Goskar.
2: Riley 1860:632-633.
3: Editorial additions by Riley, 1860:632-633.
4: Heal 2005:598.
5: Jerome's Latin Vulgate of AD 405.
6: Hooker/Vowell 1807:511-512.
7: Hooker/Vowell 1807:43-44.
8: Heal 2005:598.
9: Heal 2005:599.
10: Heal 2005:599.

APPENDIX B

11: Thanks to Dr Charlotte Tupman for kindly spending time with the Latin text and providing these translated details.
12: Krush (ed.) 1896. Passiones Vitaesque Sanctorum aevi Merovingici et Antiquiorum Aliquot. In, *Monumenta Germaniae Historica; Scriptorum rerum Merovingicarum,* Volume III, pp. 1-7.

APPENDIX C

13: For example, Giovanni Battista Cavalieri's *Ecclesiae Anglicanae trophae* (Rome, 1584).
14: Luard, H.R. (ed.) 1872. *Matthaei Parisiensis, Monachi Sancti Albani, Chronica Majora.* London: Longman & Co.
15: Luard 1872:129-130.
16: Stubbs 1876:66.
17: Stillingfleet 1685:58-59.

BIBLIOGRAPHY

Armistead, J.M. and Davis, D.K. 1989. Delariviere Manley. 1717. Lucius, The First Christian King of Britain. A Tragedy. *The Augustan Reprint Society*. Numbers 253-254. Pasadena: The Castle Press

Ashe, G. 1982. *Avalonian Quest*. London: Methuen

Ashe, G. 1990. *Mythology of the British Isles*. London: Methuen

Balle, G. 1993. Review of Hochuli-Gysel, A. 1986 and 1991. Chur in romischer Zeit. *Britannia*, Volume 24 (1993), pp. 340-341

Ball, W. 2000. *Rome in the East; The Transformation of an Empire*. London: Routledge

Beeson, C.H. 1947. The Manuscripts of Bede. *Classical Philology*, Volume 42, Number 2, pp. 73-87

Bell, T. 2005. The Religious Reuse of Roman Structures in Early Medieval England. *British Archaeological Reports*, British Series 390. Oxford: Archaeopress

Benham, W. 1902. *Old St. Paul's Cathedral*. London: Seeley and Co. Limited

Birley, A. 1966. *Marcus Aurelius*. London: Eyre & Spottiswoode

Birley, A. 1971. *Septimius Severus, the African Emperor*. London: Eyre & Spottiswoode

Bonjour, E., Offler, H.S., and Potter, G.R. 1952. *A Short History of Switzerland*. Oxford: Clarendon Press

Bonner, G. (ed.) 1976. *Famulus Christi; Essays in Commemoration of the Thirteenth Cententary of the Birth of the Venerable Bede*. London: SPCK

Brewer, J.S. 1845. *Thomas Fuller 1661: The Church History of Britain*. Oxford: Oxford University Press

Brigham, T. 1990. A Reassessment of the Second Basilica in London, A.D. 100-400: Excavations at Leadenhall Court, 1984-86. *Britannia*, Volume 21 (1990), pp. 53-97

Bromwich, R. 2006. *The Triads of the Island of Britain*. Cardiff: University of Wales Press

Brooke, C. 1973. The Archbishops of St David's, Llandaff and Caerleon-on-Usk. In Chadwick, N., Hughes, K., Brooke, C., and Jackson, K. (eds.) *Studies in the Early British Church*. Connecticut: Archon Books, pp. 201-242

Campbell, A. (ed.). 1962. *The Chronicle of Aethelweard*. London: Thomas Nelson and Sons Ltd

Chibnall, M. (ed.). 1980. *The Ecclesiastical History of Orderic Vitalis*. Oxford: Clarendon Press

Colgrave, B. and Mynors, R.A.B. (eds.). 1969. *The Venerable Bede; The Ecclesiastical History of the English People*. Oxford: Clarendon Press

Cookson, N. 1987. The Christian Church in Roman Britain; A Synthesis of Archaeology. *World Archaeology*, February, pp. 426-433

Crook, J. 2000. The Architectural Setting of the Cult of Saints in the early Christian West *c.*300-*c.*1200. *Oxford Historical Monographs*. Oxford: Clarendon Press

Crummy, N., Crummy, P. and Crossan, C. 1993. *Colchester Archaeological Report 9: Excavations of Roman and later cemeteries, churches and monastic sites in Colchester, 1971-88*. Colchester: Colchester Archaeological Trust Ltd

Cruse, C.F. (Transl.). 1979 (Popular Edition, tenth printing). *Eusebius Pamphilus; The Ecclesiastical History*. Grand Rapids: Baker Book House

Dancey, C.H. 1911. Ancient Painted Glass in Gloucester Cathedral. *Transactions of the Bristol and Gloucestershire Archaeological Society*. Volume 34, pp. 97-109

Davies, J. 1965. *The Early Christian Church*. London: Weidenfeld and Nicolson

Dimock, J.F. (ed.). 1868. Giraldi Cambrensis. Opera. Volume 6. Description Kambriae. In, *Rerum Britannicarum Medii Aevi Scriptores; Chronicles and Memorials of Great Britain and Ireland during the Middle Ages*. London: Longmans, Green, Reader and Dyer

Duchesne, L. 1955. *Le Liber Pontificalis*. Volume I. Paris: E. De Boccard

Dumville, D.N. (ed.). 1985. *The* Historia Brittonum; *The Vatican Recension*. Cambridge: D.S. Brewer

Ferguson, A.B. 1993. *Utter Antiquity; Perceptions of Prehistory in Renaissance England*. Durham: Duke University Press

Frere, S. 1967 (1987 reprint). *Britannia; A History of Roman Britain*. London: Pimlico

Flint, V.I.J. 1979. The Historia Regum Britanniae of Geoffrey of Monmouth: Parody and Its Purpose. A Suggestion. *Speculum*, Volume 54, Number 3 (July 1979), pp. 447-468

Forester, T. (transl.). 1853 (AMS edition reprint 1968). *Orderic Vitalis; The Eccliastical History of England and Normandy*. London: Henry G. Bohn

Gairdner, J. (ed.). 1880. A Short English Chronicle. *Three Fifteenth-Century Chronicles*, pp. 1-80. London: printed for the Camden Society

Gallagher, C. 1990. Political Crimes and Fictional Alibis; The Case of Delarivier Manley. *Eighteenth-Century Studies*, Summer, pp. 502-521

Garzetti, A. (transl. Foster, J.R.) 1974. *From Tiberius to the Antonines; A History of the Roman Empire AD 14-192*. London: Methuen & Co. Ltd

Giles, J.A. (Transl.). 1845. *The Biographical Writings and Letters of Venerable Bede; A Chronicle of the Six Ages of the World compiled by Bede*. London

Graham, A.J. 1966. The Division of Britain. *The Journal of Roman Studies*, Volume 56, Parts 1 and 2, pp. 92-107

Grant, M. 1994. (1996 reprint). *The Antonines; The Roman Empire in Transition*. London: Routledge

Greenway, D. (ed. and transl.). 1996. *Henry of Huntingdon; Historia Anglorum, The History of the English People*. Oxford Medieval Texts. Oxford: Clarendon Press

Guy, J.A. 1982. Henry VIII and the Praemunire Manoeuvres of 1530-1531. *The English Historical Review*, Volume 97, Number 384 (July 1982), pp. 481-503

Hallam, H. 1849. Observations on the Story of Lucius, the first Christian King of Britain. *Archaeologia*. Volume 33. London: Society of Antiquaries of London, pp. 308-335

Hammer, J. 1936. The Poetry of Johannes Beverus with Extracts from his 'Tractatus de Bruto Abbreviato'. *Modern Philology*, Volume 34, Number 2 (November, 1936), pp. 119-132

Harbus, A. 2002. *Helena of Britain in Medieval Legend*. Cambridge: D.S. Brewer

Hardin, R.F. 1992. Geoffrey among the Lawyers: Britannica (1607) by John Ross of the Inner Temple. In, *Sixteenth Century Journal*, Volume 23, Number 2, pp. 235-249

Haverfield, F. 1896. Early British Christianity. *The English Historical Review*, Volume 11, Number 43, pp. 417-430

Heal, F. 2005. What can King Lucius do for you? The Reformation and the Early British Church. *English Historical Review*,Volume 120, Number 487, pp. 593-614

Heighway, C. 1984. Anglo-Saxon Gloucester to A.D. 1000. In, Faull, M. (ed.) *Studies in Late Anglo-Saxon Settlement*. Oxford: Oxford University Department of External Studies, pp. 35-53

Henig, M. 2002. *The Heirs of King Verica; Culture & Politics in Roman Britain*. Stroud:Tempus

Higham, N.J. 2002. *King Arthur; Myth-making and History*. London: Routledge

Hungeston, F.C. (ed.) 1858. John Capgrave; *Rerum Britannicarum Medii Aevi Scriptores*. London: Her Majesty's Stationery Office

Jacobsen, W. 1997. Saint's Tombs in Frankish Church Architecture. *Speculum*, Volume 72, Number 4 (October 1997), pp. 1107-1143

Lewis, A.R. 1976. The Dukes in the Regnum Francorum, A.D. 550-751. *Speculum*, Volume 51, Number 3 (July 1976), pp. 381-410

Llanerch Enterprises, 1989 (facsimile reprint). *Two Celtic Saint; The lives of Ninian and Kentigern*. Llanerch Enterprises (ISBN: 0947992294)

Longworth, I., and Cherry, J. (eds.) 1986. *Archaeology in Britain since 1945*. Trustees of the British Museum. London: British Museum Publications

Loomis, L.R. (transl.) 1916 (1965 reprint). *Liber Pontificalis*. New York: Octagon Books, Inc

Luard, H.R. (ed.). 1872. *Chronica Majora, Rerum Britannicarum Medii Aevi Scriptores, Matthaei Parisiensis, Monachi Sancti Albani; Chronicles and Memorials of Great Britain and Ireland during The Middle Ages*.Volume I. London: Her Majesty's Stationery Office

Magie, D. (transl.). 1980-1991. *Scriptores Historiae Augustae*. The Loeb Classical Library

Marsden, P. 1980. *Roman London*. London:Thames and Hudson

Marsden, P. 1987. *The Roman Forum Site in London*. London:The Museum of London

Mattingly, D. 2006. *An Imperial Possession; Britain in the Roman Empire, 54 BC – AD 409*. London: Allen Lane

McClure, J., and Collins, R. (ed.). 1999. The Venerable Bede; The Greater Chronicle. In McClure, J. and Collins, R. (eds.) *Bede; The Ecclesiastical History of the English People*. Oxford World's Classics. Oxford: Oxford University Press, pp. 305-340

Merrifield, R. 1965. *The Roman City of London*. London: Ernest Benn Limited

Merrifield, R. 1969. *Roman London*. London: Cassell

Meyvaert, P. 1976. Bede the Scholar. In, Bonner, G. (ed.) *Famulus Christi; Essays in Commemoration of the Thirteenth Centenary of the Birth of the Venerable Bede*, pp. 40-69. London: SPCK

Millar, F. 1993. *The Roman Near East; 31 BC – AD 337*. Cambridge: Harvard University Press

Miller, S.N. 1927. The British Bishops at the Council of Arles (314). *The English Historical Review*,Volume 42, Number 165 (January 1927), pp. 79-80

Millett, M. 1990 (1996 reprint). *The Romanization of Britain; An Essay in Archaeological Interpretation*. Cambridge: Cambridge University Press

Millett, M. 1995 (2000 reprint). *Roman Britain*. London: B.T. Batsford/English Heritage

Milne, G. (ed.) 1992. *From Roman Basilica to Medieval Market; Archaeology in Action in the City of London*. London: Her Majesty's Stationary Office

Morgan, F. 1981. *Women Playwrights on the London Stage 1660-1720*. London:Virago

Niblett, R. 2001. *Verulamium; The Roman City of St. Albans*. Stroud:Tempus

Noreen, K. 1998. Ecclesiae militantis triumphi: Jesuit Iconography and the Counter-Reformation. *Sixteenth Century Journal*, Volume 29, Number 3, pp. 689-715

Petts, D. 2003. *Christianity in Roman Britain*. Stroud:Tempus

Potter,T.W., and Johns, C. 1992 (2002 edition). *Roman Britain*. London:The British Museums Press

Rawl, M.S. (ed.) 1906. *The Brut* or *The Chronicles of England*. Bodleian Library & co. London: Friedrich W. D. Brie

Rees, D. (ed.) 1997. *Monks of England; The Benedictines in England from Augustine to the Present Day*. London: Society for Promoting Christian Knowledge

Rees, R. 1836. *An Essay on the Welsh Saints or the Primitive Christians usually considered to have been the Founders of Churches in Wales*. London: Longman, Rees, Orme, Brown, Green, and Longman

Richards, J. 1980. *Consul of God: the Life and Times of Gregory the Great*. London: Routledge

Rodwell, W. 1984. Churches in the Landscape: Aspects of Topography and Planning. In, Faull, M. (ed.) *Studies in Late Anglo-Saxon Settlement*. Oxford: Oxford University Department of External Studies, pp. 1-23

Rositze, H.A. (transl.). 1951. The Peterborough Chronicle. In Evans, A.P. (ed.). *Records of Civilization, Sources and Studies*. Number XLIV. New York: Columbia University Press

Salway, P. 1981. *Roman Britain*. Oxford: Clarendon Press

Scavone, D. 1999. Joseph of Arimathea, the Holy Grail, and the Edessa Icon. *Arthuriana*, Volume 9, Number 4

Scullard, H.H. 1979 (1991 reprint). *Roman Britain; Outpost of the Empire*. London: Thames and Hudson

Segal, J.B. 1970. *Edessa 'The Blessed City'*. Oxford: Clarendon Press

Sherley-Price, L. (transl.) (Revised by Latham, R.E.). 1990. *The Venerable Bede; The Ecclesiastical History of the English People*. Penguin Books

Smiles, S. 1994. *The Image of Antiquity; Ancient Britain and the Romantic Imagination*. New Haven: Yale University Press

Smith, A. 1979. Lucius of Britain: Alleged King and Church Founder. *Folklore*, Volume 90, Number 1 (1979), pp. 29-36

Smith, W. and Wace, H. (eds.). 1967. *A Dictionary of Christian Biography*. New York: AMS Press Inc

Snyder, C.A. 2003. *The Britons*. Oxford: Blackwell Publishing

Southern, P. 1989. The *numeri* of the Roman Imperial Army. *Britannia* 20, pp. 81-140

Sparrow Simpson, W. (ed.). 1880. Chroniculi S. Pauli London ad Annum 1399. Documents Illustrating the History of S. Paul's Cathedral. *Camden Society New Series*, Volume 26, pp. 222-228. Westminster: J.B. Nichols and Sons for the Camden Society

Stephenson, J. (transl.). 1989 (facsimile reprint). William of Malmesbury; *The Kings Before the Norman Conquest*. London: Llanerch Enterprises

Stubbs, W. (ed.). 1876. Master Ralph de Diceto; *Chronical, Rerum Britannicarum Medii Aevi Scriptores, Radulfi De Diceto*. Volume I. London: Her Majesty's Stationery Office

Struck, M. 1997. Review of Crummy, N., Crummy, P., and Crossan, C. 1993. Excavations of Roman and Later Cemeteries, Churches and Monastic Sites in Colchester, 1971-88. *Britannia*, Volume 28, pp. 496-498

Tatlock, J.S.P. 1950. *The Legendary History of Britain*. Berkeley: Berkeley University Press

Thackeray, W.M. 1863. On a Lazy Idle Boy. *Cornhill Magazine* Number 1 (1863), pp. 124-128

Thomas, C. 1971. *The Early Christian Archaeology of North Britain*. Oxford: Oxford University Press

Thomas, C. 1981. *Christianity in Roman Britain to AD 500*. Berkeley: University of California Press

Thomas, C. 2003. *Christian Celts; Messages and Images*. Stroud: Tempus

Thompson, A.H. (ed.) 1969. *Bede; Life, Times and Writings*. Oxford: Clarendon Press

Thorpe, L. (transl.) 1966 (1976 reprint). *Geoffrey of Monmouth; The History of the Kings of Britain*. Harmondsworth: Penguin Classics

Thorpe, L. (transl.) (1978 reprint). Gerald of Wales; *The Journey Through Wales and The Description of Wales*. Harmondsworth: Penguin Books

Turner, R.V. 1994. *King John*. London: Longman

Wacher, J. 1974 (1995 edition). *The Towns of Roman Britain*. London: BCA

Wallace-Hadrill, J.M. 1954. Review of Schieffer, T. Winfrid-Bonifatius und die christliche Grundlegung Europas. *The English Historical Review*, Volume 69, Number 273 (October 1954), pp. 619-622

Wallace-Hadrill, J.M. 1988. *Bede's Ecclesiastical History, A Historical Commentary*. Oxford: Clarendon Press

Waterfield, R.E. 1973. *Christians in Persia; Assyrians, Armenians, Roman Catholics and Protestants*. London: Allen and Unwin

Watts, D.J. 1991. *Christians and Pagans in Roman Britain*. London: Routledge

Watts, D. 1998. *Religion in Late Roman Britain*. London: Routledge

Welander, D. 1991. *The History, Art and Architecture of Gloucester Cathedral*. Wolfeboro Falls: Alan Sutton

Wheatley, H.B. 1912 (1956 reprint). *Stow's Survey of London*. Everyman's Library, Number 589. London: J. M. Dent & Sons Ltd

Wheeler, R.E.M. 1934. The Topography of Saxon London. *Antiquity*, Volume 8, Number 31 (1934), pp. 290-302

Whitelock, D. 1972. *Two of the Saxon Chronicles: Parallel; with supplementary extracts from the others*. Oxford: Clarendon Press

Whitelock, D. 1976. Bede and His Teachers and Friends. In, Bonner, G. (ed.) *Famulus Christi; Essays in Commemoration of the Thirteenth Centenary of the Birth of the Venerable Bede*, pp. 19-39. London: SPCK

Williams, S. 1952. Geoffrey of Monmouth and the Canon Law. In, *Speculum*, Volume 27, Number 2, pp. 184-190

Williamson, G.A. (transl.) 1984. *Eusebius Pamphilus; The Ecclesiastical History*. Penguin Books

Wood, M. 1986. *Domesday: A Search for the Roots of England*. BBC Publications

Wormald, P. 1976. Bede and Benedict Biscop. In, Bonner, G. (ed.) *Famulus Christi; Essays in Commemoration of the Thirteenth Centenary of the Birth of the Venerable Bede*, pp. 141-155. London: SPCK

FURTHER READING

Chronologically after Harnack's 1904 article:

Williams, H. 1912. *Christianity in Early Britain*. Oxford: Clarendon Press

Baker, E.A. 1924. *The History of the English Novel*. New York: Barnes & Noble Inc.

Belloc, H. 1925. *A History of England*. London: Methuen & Co. Ltd

Wall, J.C. 1927. *The First Christians of Britain*. Talbot & Co.

Collingwood, R.G., and Myres, J.N.L. 1934. *Roman Britain and the English Settlements*. Oxford: Clarendon Press

Wand, J.W.C. 1937 (1953 reprint). *A History of the Early Church to AD 500*. London: Methuen & Co. Ltd

Home, G. 1948. *Roman London: A.D. 43 – 457*. London: Eyre and Spottiswoode

Richardson, H.G. 1949. The English Coronation Oath. In, *Speculum*, Volume 24, Number 1, pp. 44-75

Lewis, L.S. 1955. *St. Joseph of Arimathea at Glastonbury*. London: James Clarke & Co.

Jackson, K.H. 1958. The Sources for the Life of St. Kentigern. In Chadwick, N., Hughes, K., Brooke, C. and Jackson, K.H. (eds.) *Studies in the Early British Church*, pp. 273-357. Cambridge: Cambridge University Press

Brooke, C. 1958. The Archbishops of St. David's, Llandaff and Caerleon-on-Usk. In Chadwick, N., Hughes, K., Brooke, C. and Jackson, K.H. (eds.) *Studies in the Early British Church*, pp. 201-242. Cambridge: Cambridge University Press

Perowne, S. 1962. *Caesars and Saints*. London: Hodder and Stoughton

Bonser, W. 1964. Lucius. In Bonser, W. *Romano-British Bibliography 55 BC-AD 449*, p. 106. Oxford: Basil Blackwell

Guide to the Antiquities of Roman Britain. Published by The Trustees of the British Museum. London, 1966

Durant, G.M. 1970. *Britain; Rome's Most Northerly Province: A History of Roman Britain, AD 43-AD 450*. London: G. Bell and Sons, Ltd

Stenton, F. 1971 (third edition). *Anglo-Saxon England*. Oxford: Oxford University Press

Morris, J. 1973. *The Age of Arthur*. New York: Charles Scribner's Sons

Cary, M., and Scullard, H.H. 1975. *A History of Rome: Down to the Reign of Constantine*. Macmillan

Wallace-Hadrill, J.M. 1975. *Early Medieval History*. Oxford: Basil Blackwell

Trimingham, J.S. 1979. *Christianity among the Arabs in Pre-Islamic Times*. London: Longman

Carroll, W.H. 1985. *The Founding of Christendom*. Two volumes. Chicago: Christendom Press

Ashdown, P. 2004. King Lucius and the Evangelisation of Britain. *The Glastonbury Review*, December 2004, Number III. Online at Orthodox Britain: www.uk-christian.net/new_boc

CHRONOLOGICAL BIBLIOGRAPHY OF JUDAH BEN ZION SEGAL (1912-2003)

The Diacritical Point and the Accents in Syriac (1953) Oxford: Oxford University Press

Pagan Syriac Monuments in the Vilayet of Urfa (1953) *Anatolian Studies*, JBIAA 3

Some Syriac Inscriptions of the 2nd-3rd Century A.D. (1954) *Bulletin of the School of Oriental and African Studies*; Volume 16, Number 1, pp. 13-36, University of London

Two Syriac Inscriptions from Harran (1957) *Bulletin of the School of Oriental and African Studies*; Volume 20, Number 1/3, pp. 513-522, University of London

New Syriac Inscriptions from Edessa (1959) *Bulletin of the School of Oriental and African Studies*; Volume 22, Number 1/3, pp. 23-40, University of London

New Mosaics from Edessa (1959) *Archaeology*, XII, 3 (Autumn 1959), pp. 151-157

Edessa and Harran (1963) Inaugural Lecture at the School of Oriental and African Studies, University of London

The Hebrew Passover from the Earliest Times to A.D. 70 (1963) Oxford: Oxford University Press

The Sabian Mysteries: The Planet Cult of Ancient Harran (1963) *Vanished Civilizations of the Ancient World* (ed. Edward Bacon) New York: McGraw-Hill and London: Thames and Hudson

The Hebrew Passover (1965) *Bulletin of the School of Oriental and African Studies*; Volume 85, Number 2, p. 255, University of London

Four Syriac Inscriptions (1967) *Bulletin of the School of Oriental and African Studies*; Volume 30, Number 2, pp. 293-304, University of London

Edessa: The Blessed City (1970) Oxford: Clarendon Press, reprinted by Gorgias Press (2005)

Notes: The Church of Saint George at Urfa (Edessa) (1972) *Bulletin of the School of Oriental and African Studies*; Volume 35, Number 3, pp. 606-609, University of London

Notes: The Church of Saint George at Urfa (Edessa) (1973) *Bulletin of the School of Oriental and African Studies*; Volume 36, Number 1, p. 109, University of London

Notes: Observations on a Recent Article on Syriac Inscriptions (1973) *Bulletin of the School of Oriental and African Studies*; Volume 36, Number 3, pp. 621-622, University of London

(With contributions by H.S. Smith) *Aramaic Texts from North Saqqâra with some fragments in Phoenician* (1983) London: Egypt Explorations Society

A History of the Jews of Cochin (1993) London: Valentine Mitchell & Co. Ltd.

(With a contribution by E.C.D. Hunter) *Aramaic and Mandaic Incantation Bowls in the British Museum* (2000) London: British Museum Press

Whisper Awhile (2000) Minerva Press

INDEX